The Ecole Normale Supérieure and The Third Republic

Robert J. Smith

State University of New York Press
Albany

For my mother and father

Published by State University of New York Press, Albany

Printed in the United States of America

For information, address State University of New York Press, State University Plaza, Albany, N.Y., 12246

Library of Congress Cataloging in Publication Data

Smith, Robert J., 1935–
The Ecole normale supérieure and the Third Republic.

Based on the author's thesis, University of Pennsylvania.
Bibliography: p. 179
1. Ecole normale supérieure (Paris, France)—History—19th century. I. Title
LB2077.P3S65 37039.944 81–8810
ISBN 0–87395–540–4 AACR2
ISBN 0–87395–541–2 (pbk.)

Contents

Illustrations

Acknowledgements

SINCE this book began at the University of Pennsylvania as a dissertation on the *normaliens* of 1890–1904, subsequent versions broader in scope have developed slowly, and I have accumulated many financial, intellectual, and personal debts. The individuals who have helped me so generously, however, bear no responsibility for the errors and limitations of this study.

For his advice and kindness, I am grateful to the late Otakar Odlozilik, who supervised the dissertation completed in 1967. Grants awarded by the Fulbright–Hays Commission, the American Philosophical Society, and the SUNY Research Foundation as well as a sabbatical leave from SUNY College at Brockport made it possible for me to carry out research on the project in Paris. While many librarians and archivists in France and the United States have been marvelously sympathetic and helpful, I would like to thank in particular: Pierre Petitmengin, Louis Bergeron, and Jean–Claude Chamboredon, who facilitated my work in the library and archives of the Ecole Normale; Serge Hurtig, Georgette Latrabe, and Anne–Marie de Thomas, who arranged for me to use the library and archives of the Institut d'Etudes Politiques; and Chantal de Tourtier–Bonazzi of the Archives Nationales, who has been so generous over many years with professional advice and moral support.

Others shared valuable insights about the Ecole Normale and its graduates. Madame Lucien Herr, who died in 1980, permitted me to see letters received by Lucien Herr, and on several occasions shared her own memories of her husband's life. Pierre Jeannin helped me to select a list of Normale's alumni for interviews; I wish to thank those men and women for taking the time to grant interviews or reply to correspondence.

I am much indebted to Antoine Prost, Alice Gérard, C. Rod Day, William B. Cohen, Victor Karady, Terry Shinn, W. Paul Vogt, and

Fritz Ringer for sharing their ideas about French education, for demonstrating by their own work how educational history should be written, and for reading and criticizing portions or all of my work on the Ecole Normale. I wish to thank as well those colleagues and friends in other fields of French or European history—Sabine Jessner, Christopher Johnson, James Friguglietti, Edmund A. Brown, and John Kutolowski—who discussed the subject, read the manuscript, or encouraged the author. I am deeply grateful to Bonnie Kelley, who did all these things for many years.

Student assistants—Barbara Lukens, Susan Wylegala, and Susan Graziano—provided essential help in coding the statistical data and developing tables, and Nancy Oshier of Brockport's computer center ran the series of programs necessary to produce the tables in the text. Many thanks also to Brenda Peake for typing the manuscript.

Finally, I wish to express my deepest gratitude to Marie Louise and Jean Pierre Blum and Françoise and Eugene C. McCreary for sharing their knowledge and friendship; to my children, Patience and Patrick, for their understanding and support; and to my wife and colleague, Sumiko Higashi, for being a thoughtful critic and a sure source of confidence.

Introduction

> La gloire des Cousin, des Fustel, des Pasteur, et de tant d'autres, qui ont régné sur la pensée, est aujourd'hui offusquée par celle des Jaurès, des Painlevé, des Herriot, et des Blum, qui ont gouverné ou qui gouvernent la France.—Hubert Bourgin

FRANCE has long been a society of opposing tendencies in precarious balance, of new and old institutions in conflict. A bewildering array of educational institutions in France continues to reflect the conflicting claims of present and past, necessity and tradition. By the eighteenth century the ancient but lifeless universities taught an outmoded classical curriculum which was the basis of general education on the secondary level but was impractical for most careers in the modern world. The monarchy, instead of reforming the universities, chose instead to establish a number of separate scientific schools to supply the army and other government agencies with competent engineers and technicians.[1] In addition to improving scientific education in France, these first *grandes écoles* served to buttress the social prestige and political power of the nobility and the upper bourgeoisie; on the whole the lower social orders were excluded. A pattern of opposition and competition between the universities which were generally open to the public, and the *grandes écoles,* which were exclusive, has persisted to the present day.[2] Likewise during the nineteenth century and much of the twentieth, secondary education for the bourgeoisie and primary education for the people reflected the persistence of social stratification in an era of political change. The tension between merit and privilege, democracy and aristocracy, found expression in these and other elements of a complicated educational structure.[3]

The history of the Ecole Normale Supérieure touches many issues concerning French education, society, and politics. This was the *grande école* founded during the Revolutionary era to dominate the educational structure itself—to educate the elite of its corps of teachers and administrators. Yet despite such an important task, the Ecole Normale did not, before the Third Republic, have the prestige of the scientific *grandes écoles,* and in particular the Ecole Polytechnique. A teaching career did not appeal to the nobility, the upper bourgeoisie, or even the more ambitious elements of the middle class. The Ecole Normale's students came largely from the cultivated middle class, especially families of school teachers and others who sought secure employment for their sons. Neither middle class origins nor a career in teaching augured well for admission to the ruling class. Although the *normaliens* presided over the nation's famous *culture générale,* which students absorbed at the secondary level, only rarely before the Third Republic did they leave the field of education for high public office. They comprised a marginal elite well contained within their own sphere.

This book studies the partial transformation during the Third Republic of this school for professors into one for national leaders as well. When France at last was forced to live with a democratic republic, the intellectuals from the Ecole Normale, more than any other single group, created the necessary ideological synthesis. They had a recognizable and legitimate identity, a strategic monopoly of power in the field of education, and sufficient breadth of outlook to be creative in new circumstances. For several decades the Ecole Normale Supérieure vied in prestige with the Ecole Polytechnique, and the *normaliens* appeared to be members of the ruling class.

Developing a theme already suggested by Maurice Barrès and expressed explicitly by Julien Benda, Hubert Bourgin (who entered Normale in 1895 with the class or *promotion* of that year) excoriated the *normaliens* for having betrayed their scholarly calling.[4] A former comrade-in-arms of Lucien Herr and other socialists at the Ecole Normale, Bourgin became a Maurrasian anti–Semite between the wars. From this perspective he described the political *normaliens* as a left wing mafia engaged in a sinister quest for power. In reality the *normaliens* both in and out of politics comprised a pluralistic elite; although most of them shared a liberal republican bias, they remained intellectuals who steadfastly expressed their individual views. As a study of the Ecole Normale, Bourgin's book has some value because of its insights into cetain individuals whom he knew well; unfortunately Bourgin's own political agenda made it impossible for him to treat many of his protagonists fairly. It is curious that since the publication of Bourgin's impassioned but flawed work, the Ecole Normale has attracted so little scholarly attention.[5]

Although parts of this study touch upon the thought of the *normaliens,* this is primarily a social and political rather than an intellectual history. The next chapter reviews the period before the Third Republic, when the school became preeminent in the preparation of professors for the *lycées* and the university faculties. The *normaliens* regularly outdistanced any competitors for advanced degrees (the *agrégation* and the doctorate), and they dominated the state's educational bureaucracy. Only a relatively small number pursued careers outside the sphere of education. Subsequent chapters describe the *normaliens'* social origins, education, general ideas, careers, and political affinity with the Third Republic. The modesty of their origins, assiduously exaggerated by officials, became a useful myth and made them symbols of, as well as spokesmen for, the Republic's political ideals. Their republicanism, radicalism, and socialism were broadly compatible with their alma mater's long-standing liberal tradition. Their preeminence in education enhanced their political power as the country became caught up with educational reform in the 1880s and periodically thereafter. And finally their literary and oratorical skills were at a premium under the Republic as newspapers, political parties, and elections assumed greater importance.

Politically the star of the Ecole Normale rose during the Third Republic and declined during the regimes which followed. Although the *normaliens* have continued to occupy important places in scientific research, literature, and the university, there is little doubt that the famous address of the Ecole Normale—45 rue d'Ulm—lost under the Fifth Republic the political lustre that it enjoyed under the Third. The aura of political power and prestige once conferred by Jaurès, Herriot, and their followers has largely vanished, for the school no longer sends a significant minority of its graduates into politics. This study examines the special circumstances surrounding the rise after the Franco–Prussian War of this hitherto marginal elite to the status of a strategic political elite and suggests why such a new role was not sustained after the Second World War.

1
The Evolution of a Republican Institution, 1795–1870

> Cette source de lumière si pure, si abondante, puisqu'elle partira des premiers hommes de la République, en tout genre, épanchée de réservoir en réservoir, se répandra d'espace en espace dans toute la France, sans rien perdre de sa pureté dans son cours. Aux Pyrénées et aux Alpes, l'art d'enseigner sera le même qu'à Paris, et cet art sera celui de la nature et du génie . . . —Joseph Lakanal

THE French Revolutionary Government, the National Convention (1792–95), founded the Ecole Normale Supérieure in 1795 to educate teachers who would carry the ideas of the Enlightenment and the Revolution throughout France. The old elites appeared finally to have yielded to new ones, and the King's subjects had become citizens of a republic. So that France as a whole would learn to think like a republic, the new regime sought to establish a national educational system. This idea was not new, for during the Enlightenment it appeared to some observers that education was too important to be left exclusively to private bodies like the Jesuits or the Oratorians. Several *philosophes* suggested that the state should set up a national system which would provide for the education of teachers.[1] Nevertheless, although the void left after 1762 by the departure of the Jesuits provoked widespread discussion of education, no coherent national system emerged. Later, on the eve of the Revolution, several of the *cahiers de doléances* called for schools to train teachers, and during the

Revolution itself, citizens from virtually all parts of France exerted direct pressure upon their legislators to establish public education to replace schools formerly run by the religious teaching orders.[2] Such public pressure as well as their own social and political theories caused the revolutionaries to introduce a series of comprehensive projects for a national educational system. But in that period of turmoil the demand for public education, like the demand for a democratic republic, was far easier to express than to satisfy. All of the comprehensive projects failed.

To meet the immediate needs of war and revolution, the Convention instead set up a number of specialized schools for which there were precedents earlier in the century. The monarchy had established such *grandes écoles* as the Ecole Royale Militaire (1751), the Ecole Navale (1773), the Ecole des Ponts et Chaussées (1775), and the Ecole des Mines (1778) to train sons of nobles and upper bourgeois for specific careers at state expense. Now similarly the First Republic sought to obtain a loyal and competent elite by setting up its own *grandes écoles*. The purpose of one such school was to train selected citizens in the manufacture of cannon and gunpowder by putting them through a one–month course in Paris. Another, the Ecole de Mars, trained patriotic youth for war. Inaugurated in July 1794, it disbanded four months later after having put its recruits through a regimen so spartan that they fled to their homes. But other new creations survived. The Convention founded medical schools at Paris, Montpellier, and Strasbourg to train military physicians for the war effort by giving them practical experience in addition to the traditional bookish and theoretical medical education. The Ecole Polytechnique, like the medical schools, turned out to be an enduring institution. To obtain badly needed engineers, the Convention voted in September 1794 to set up an Ecole Centrale des Travaux Publics, and three months later 386 students met in Paris to form the first class. The following year the name was changed to the Ecole Polytechnique, and ever since the school has supplied engineers to the military, state agencies, and private business.[3]

The first version of the Ecole Normale Supérieure responded more directly to the popular demand for a comprehensive system of general education. Like the other educational projects set in motion by the Convention, the Ecole Normale was conceived to satisfy an immediate need.[4] However, in this case the need was sweeping as well as urgent: to train a corps of republican teachers who would instruct other teachers in the departments, who in turn would staff the projected public primary schools. Ultimately the *normalien* was to become the intellectual model for the transformation of illiterate and parochial provincials into well–informed citizens loyal to a democratic and republican nation. It followed that the prestige and power of the Ecole Normale and the *normalien* would depend in large part upon the priority that the state placed upon national public education. At the outset in the Year III of the Revolution that priority was high.

Joseph Lakanal (1762–1845), representing the Committee of Public Instruction, presented the proposal for the Ecole Normale to the Convention on 9 Brumaire Year III (30 October 1794), and the Convention passed the measure with only a minor change: instead of only four months, the course would last "at least" four months. The decree read in part as follows:

> The National Convention, wishing to hasten the epoch in which it will have instruction necessary for French citizens uniformly accessible throughout the whole Republic, decrees:
>
> Art. 1. There will be established in Paris an Ecole Normale to which citizens already advanced in the useful sciences will be called from all parts of the Republic in order to learn, under the most skillful professors in all fields, the art of teaching.
>
> Art. 6. The Committee of Public Instruction will designate the citizens which it believes to be the best qualified to fill the positions of professors in the Ecole Normale and will fix their salary in consultation with the Committee of Finance.
>
> Art. 7. These professors will give lessons to the students in the art of teaching morality and of shaping the hearts of young republicans to the practice of public and private virtues.
>
> Art. 8. They will teach them first to apply to the teaching of reading, writing, the first elements of arithmetic, of practical geometry, of history and French grammar, the methods outlined in the elementary books adopted by the National Convention and published by its orders.
>
> Art. 11. The students trained at this republican school will return at the end of the course to their respective districts; in the three major towns of the district designated by the administration, they will open an Ecole Normale, whose object will be to transmit the teaching method which they will have acquired in the Ecole Normale of Paris to the citizens and citizenesses who wish to commit themselves to education.[5]

Republican enthusiasm, so evident in the decree itself, could not save the school from poor planning and the uncertain atmosphere in which it was launched. About fourteen hundred students of various abilities, ages, backgrounds, and interests, many of whom had left jobs and families in the provinces, arrived in Paris during the second week of December 1794. When the inauguration of the Ecole was postponed until January 20, they were forced to fend for themselves in Paris for several weeks without support, and when classes began at the Museum, formerly the Jardin du Roi, but now a scientific academy founded in 1793, the amphitheatre could accomodate only about half of them. Moreover, as the spring wore on inflation made their stipends inadequate, and bread was in short supply. Enthusiasm evaporated, and patience wore thin. Other difficulties were more fundamental. Ostensibly the purpose was to train teachers for *primary* instruction: hence the repeated emphasis in the Convention's charge upon methods, morality, and patriotism. But the professors were the most learned savants in the land. They included Lagrange, Laplace, and Monge in mathematics, Berthollet in chemistry, La Harpe in literature, and Volney in history. Although some of these men did their best from time to time to make suggestions about teaching methods, by experience and inclination they preferred to adhere to the subject matter itself and to conduct their classes on a high plane. Thus the Ecole's curriculum, which was well balanced between the arts and sciences, prepared students more in the subjects themselves than in the methods of teaching them to others.

On 19 May 1795, the Ecole Normale of the Year III came to an end. The Republic had immediate tasks more urgent than education, the Ecole appeared not to be fulfilling its promise, and the Finance Committee was unable and unwilling to find or allocate sufficient funds for it to continue. The critics stressed that the instruction was largely academic rather than practical, oriented toward higher learning rather than the primary level. Moreover, as the finances of the Republic continued to fail, it became clear that only a few of the provincial *écoles normales* which were planned to train primary teachers would materialize. It was doubtful, therefore, that the students of the Ecole Normale of Paris would find jobs when they returned to their homes. It appeared to many, and to the students most of all, that they were wasting their time. Disenchantment on the part of legislators and students alike as well as the financial crisis of the regime led to the Ecole's closing in May 1795 with no promise that it would reopen.

The entire situation changed under the Empire.[6] To organize and control the education of a loyal and competent ruling class, Napoleon created a vast state corporation, the University, to direct secondary and higher education throughout France.[7] The Ecole Normale reemerged in altered form as a part of Napoleon's educational masterplan. Most of Normale's graduates would become professors in the *lycées* and thus at the secondary level guard the gates to higher education; a smaller number would earn doctoral degrees and become professors in the faculties of letters or sciences. So instead of leading a national educational crusade at the primary level, as envisioned in the Year III, the *normaliens* would give instruction to bourgeois youth destined later to find places in the ruling class. The first class, or *promotion,*[8] of the revived Ecole Normale met in 1810. It comprised forty–five students in the Division of Letters and ten in the Division of Science—a total far less than the fourteen hundred which assembled in Paris in 1795. The smaller scale of the institution was an indication that for this regime the purpose of education was to select and train elites.

Napoleon's Ecole Normale resembled a secular version of the Jesuit colleges of the Old Regime. The students' uniforms, their compulsory attendance at chapel, and the rigid daily schedule of a boarding school (an *internat*) reflected the military and authoritarian values of the regime. The Emperor intended that the *normalien* should be schooled rather than educated. Outwardly under the Empire the Ecole Normale resembled its rival institution, the Ecole Polytechnique. In practice, however, Normale enjoyed considerable autonomy within the University, and over the course of the nineteenth century, the *normaliens* gained a reputation for liberalism and independence. Whereas the Ecole Polytechnique retained a military cast and an authoritarian pedagogy, the Ecole Normale became a haven for intellectuals eager to exchange ideas as well as to earn academic degrees. This was due in part to the fact that the Director of the Ecole Normale reported directly to the Minister of Education rather than to the Minister of War, as was the case at the Ecole Polytechnique. Furthermore, although the Director's political reputation played a role in his selection, he was seldom willing and never able to prevent the Ecole Normale's professors and students, despite a curriculum which exaggerated classical studies, from creating an essentially liberal intellectual tradition.

At the core of this tradition was an emphasis upon critical discussion. Despite the stifling and authoritarian atmosphere of the Empire, a government order of 1811 encouraged intellectual freedom at the Ecole Normale:

> Art. 57. In addition to the lessons of the professors of the Faculties, there are seminars *[conférences]* of which the Director of the Ecole determines the number, the duration, the object, and the mode.
>
> Art. 59. In these seminars, the students of the Faculty of Letters explain and analyze the classical authors, and respond to the difficulties which they bring up among themselves. They read their compositions, such as translations, discourses, descriptions, historical accounts, Latin verse, commentaries, questions of philosophy, grammar and history.
>
> Art. 60. In the Division of Sciences, the students discuss the principal difficulties of the preceeding lessons; they compare the diverse methods of solution; they read their compositions or make their reports on the compositions already presented; they repeat the experiments in physics and chemistry.
>
> Art. 61. To develop in the students the art of criticism, the teaching assistant *[répétiteur]* has them, one by one, examine the compositions presented in the seminars. The designated students make a reasoned report in writing and orally. The report is discussed by the Division [Letters or Sciences], which determines the ones worthy of being submitted to the Director of the Ecole.[9]

Whereas instruction at the Ecole Polytechnique stressed memory work and deductive reasoning from unquestioned premises,[10] the educational process at the Ecole Normale was quite different even from the beginning. The *normaliens* often attended some lectures given *ex cathedra* at the Sorbonne, but their real education took place in the small *conférence* and in discussions among themselves at the rue d'Ulm. In this way they developed a critical and independent turn of mind which made some governments wary but which proved to be a political asset during the Third Republic. By their education the *normaliens* learned far better how to invent and think for themselves than to imitate and obey orders.

The Ecole Normale was unique among the *grandes écoles* also because it did not grant its own diploma. Instead *normaliens* competed with students in the Faculties for the basic academic degrees granted by the University, that is, the baccalaureate, the *licence,* the *agrégation,* and the doctorate. Whereas the baccalaureate was the secondary school leaving certificate required for a broad range of government positions, the other three degrees led specifically only to various ranks in the teaching profession. The length of the course at the Ecole Normale and the degree which one prepared each year varied with the political fortunes of the school. Although the *normaliens* finally acquired certain advantages in their competition for the University's degrees, it is important to note that even as students they were never alienated or entirely isolated from the rest of the University, which eventually they would serve. Clearly the elite of the University, the *normaliens* faced competition, nevertheless, from other students.

Under the Empire, when the course of study lasted only two years, the *normalien* took examinations for the baccalaureate at the end of the first and for the *licence* at the end of the second. Then like the student who attended the Sorbonne, he began his teaching career rather humbly as a master *(maître d'étude)* in a *lycée* or a *collège.*[11] Only as a practicing teacher could he advance his candidacy for the *agrégation,* and during this period he appeared to enjoy no special advantage over the non–*normalien* in the competition. However, the Director of the Ecole could select ten second-year students based upon their "success and good conduct" and recommend to the Grand Master of the University that they be retained at the Ecole Normale for a third year, serve as teaching assistants *(répétiteurs),* and receive the title and compensation of an *agrégé.* The degree to which the *normaliens* were able to dominate the competition for the *agrégation* depended both upon changing government statutes and the number of other candidates. Their marked advantage during the nineteenth century gradually diminished in the twentieth following the reorganization and general revival of separate universities within the overarching Napoleonic University.[12]

Political upheavals during the nineteenth century affected the Ecole Normale adversely on several occasions without permanently dislodging it from its privileged niche in the University.[13] Under the Bourbon Restoration, the Napoleonic University remained despite numerous critics, and the Ecole Normale continued to operate essentially under the original statute of 1810. The new regime even introduced several favorable measures during the early years. First, the period of studies was increased from two years to three. Although this meant that the students might deepen their understanding, it did not mean that they could use the third year for the *agrégation.* That degree was still reserved for a minority of the best students, and so the *licence* remained the goal of the final year. A second innovation concerned the character rather than the duration of instruction. According to the 1810 statute, the *normaliens* attended lectures at the Sorbonne along with other students of the Faculties. According to a new statute, the courses at the Faculties were considered secondary; they would merely supplement the more important seminars given at the Ecole Normale by its own professors *(maîtres de conférences)*. Thus the school was able to take on more of its own academic character and partially to emancipate itself from the tutelage of the Sorbonne. A third measure (introduced in 1818) assured that the *normaliens* would be recruited widely by examination in the capital of each of the sixteen educational districts, or Academies. Itinerant school inspectors would no longer be free to select candidates according to their own sometimes haphazard methods. In principle at least, the entrance examination was open to the widest possible number of students, and they all had an equal chance to be admitted on the basis of merit. The stipulation remained, however, that before a candidate was allowed to compete, he should secure from the government official in charge of his Academy (the Rector) a statement that he was of sound moral character. We are not able to tell how often governmental discretion thwarted the claims of merit.

As the Bourbon regime became more reactionary in the 1820s, the Ecole Normale became suspect. The *normaliens* seemed too proud of their learning, too little inclined to be submissive to traditional authorities, and too much attached to the philosophical ideas of the Enlightenment. There was a good deal of truth in all of these charges. Ultra-Catholic suspicions gained force after 1820, and soon after becoming Grand-Master of the University in 1822, the Abbé Frayssinous closed down the Ecole Normale. Already in 1821 the Royal Council had sought to assure the recruitment of more docile *normaliens*. In the provincial Royal Colleges (the Napoleonic *lycées*), it had created special annexes called *écoles normales partielles* which were intended to groom suitable candidates for the Ecole Normale of Paris by stressing "moral character." Specifically their object was: "to dispose the teaching personnel to take an attitude in conformity with the duties imposed upon it, to give youth a religious and monarchical direction in strengthening its attachment at the same time to the institutions which France owes to its King, and to tighten the links uniting the teachers of humane science with the clergy, the repository of divine doctrines."[14] These *écoles normales partielles* were preparatory schools and political and religious screening devices for a more loyal Ecole Normale of Paris.

When Frayssinous suppressed the Ecole Normale itself in 1822, however, the *écoles normales partielles* were left with no real function. They were only secondary schools whose curriculum was identical with that of the *collèges* to which they were attached. They were in no sense equal to the task of training professors of secondary and higher education. Soon the Abbé, who was by 1824 the Minister of both Education and Religion, realized that education would only deteriorate without the Ecole Normale, and he saw this as a danger rather than as an advantage to the state. Given a religious climate which would not permit him simply to resurrect the old Ecole Normale, he resorted to subterfuge. At the major Royal Colleges he planned to set up what he called *écoles préparatoires,* which would receive scholarship students and prepare them for the teaching profession. The *écoles préparatoires* were to be genuine institutions of higher learning similar to the Ecole Normale. In reality Frayssinous created only one *école preparatoire* in 1826, and that was located in Paris at the Royal College of Louis-le-Grand; the Ecole Normale had revived under a different name. The principal of Louis–le–Grand became the Director, and the students took their courses at the Sorbonne. With the coming to power of the moderate Martignac Ministry in 1828, the Ecole Normale returned to its former quarters at the Collège du Plessis, thus escaped the administrative supervision of Louis–le.Grand, and saw its own seminars again take precedence over the lectures at the Sorbonne. But the duration of the course remained at two years instead of three, and the school did not immediately regain its former prestige.

A rise in fortune occurred under the July Monarchy. The original name, Ecole Normale, was restored, and the duration of the course was extended again to three years, which it remained for the rest of the century. The first year of general studies ended with examinations for the *licence;* during the second year, the "year of genius," the students developed their expertise in an academic area; and the third year prepared both for the *agrégation* and for the classroom. In 1838 Director Victor Cousin instituted a two–week teaching apprenticeship in one of the Parisian *lycées* during the spring of the third year. This was a logical (and lasting) culmination of the *normaliens'* efforts to instruct each other in their seminars.

While the institution rose in prestige under the careful management of Victor Cousin, its Director from 1835 to 1840, the students were in fact inmates of an austere and confining institution.

> The students were separated into two study rooms, each one directed by a study master *(maître surveillant);* silence was the rule there absolutely; diverse movements had also to be made in silence, with order and punctuality. No changing places in the study period, no studying together was permitted without the authorization of the Assistant Director upon the advice of the study master. In winter as in summer the rising time was five o'clock. The days and meals began and ended with prayer; during the [meals] a student read; dangerous or futile books were not to enter the Ecole; the reading of newspapers was forbidden as inimical to study. . . .[15]

In minor respects, nevertheless, the student's life was not so harsh as before. With permission, individual students might leave the Ecole more frequently. The rules of 1810 had permitted no leaves, but under the Bourbons a slow relaxing of the boarding school regime took place: the regulation of 1815 permitted a leave once a month, and that of 1826 specified twice a month. Finally in 1836 the students were allowed as many as two leaves per week: all students had permission to leave the school on Sunday between nine in the morning and eight in the evening, and in addition they could request special permission to leave on Thursday afternoons. Another sign of change under the July Monarchy was that the Ecole devoted less time to religious observance. Chapel did not become completely voluntary, however, until 1869.

There was evidence during the July Monarchy that the Ecole Normale's overall reputation was on the rise. To set it apart from other *écoles normales* which trained teachers for the secondary level, it was given in 1845 the august title of "Ecole Normale Supérieure." Another sign of its rising fortune was the government's decision to furnish it new quarters. The present building on the rue d'Ulm replaced the venerable but quite dilapidated Collège du Plessis. On 4 November 1847, Guizot presided over the inauguration of the new edifice with eminent men such as Adolphe Thiers and Victor Hugo in attendance.[16]

Political ideas at the rue d'Ulm came to the surface during the Revolution of 1848 and the Second Empire. Mobilized into the National Guard, the *normaliens* followed their Director in May and June in defending the bourgeois Republic against working class insurgents.

Ecole Normale Supérieure ca. 1850
Courtesy of Musée de l'Education, Paris.

Promotion of 1894, letters
Courtesy of the Bibliotèque, Ecole Normale Supérieure.

Only a few students went over to the workers' side. In the presidential election which followed, most of the *normaliens* supported Lamartine, while their professors preferred Cavaignac. Then as the Napoleonic regime emerged, Francisque Sarcey recalled, three fourths of the *normaliens* were ready to revolt.[17] They were liberals, supportive of civil liberties and a moderate democracy and opposed to socialism, authoritarianism, or plutocracy.[18] The Ecole's political preferences soon attracted the attention of the new Minister of Education, Fortoul.

The Minister sought to lower the level of intellectual sophistication in secondary and higher education as a whole.[19] During the July Monarchy the *agrégations* in letters and sciences had become more specialized by dividing into separate *agrégations* in letters, philosophy, history, grammar, mathematics, physical science, and natural science. Fortoul eliminated these and restored the original *agrégations* of letters and sciences. He believed that specialized and advanced studies made young minds presumptuous, that tender spirits should not be taught to soar but rather to know their limits. To eliminate philosophical and historical discussions of an imaginative or speculative character, Fortoul stressed rote memory work, routine, and a spirit of awe before constituted authorities and Creation. Some wryly observed that astronomy risked becoming once again a branch of theology. The duration of studies at the Ecole Normale was not shortened again to two years, but the first year was wasted in mechanical exercises which had already been done in the *lycées.* Only in the second year did the students study for the *licence,* and the third year was taken up entirely with the perfection of teaching techniques rather than with preparing for the *agrégation* as well. This was a period when serious study and independent work in the library were discouraged: the studious Fustel de Coulanges was suspect.[20] Instead of savants, who might become troublesome, the government preferred to turn out "modest professors." Among the victims of the regime's insistence upon political and religious orthodoxy were Director Paul Dubois, Director of Studies Vacherot, and Professor Jules Simon, all of whom lost their posts at the Ecole. Still, the institution's own traditions managed to survive these attacks upon individuals.

Fortoul himself soon realized that under the diluted academic regimen, the Ecole Normale could no longer develop competent university professors as well as teachers for the *lycées.* Thus he established a two-year post graduate program at the Ecole so that the very best students might prepare for the doctorate. Only a handful of students went through this program, however, for in 1856 Fortoul's successor restored the old rhythm of studies: *licence* at the end of the first year, examinations within the Ecole devoted to fields of specialization in the second, and the *agrégation* at the end of the third. This remained the pattern throughout the Third Republic. Those graduates who intended to become university professors would write their doctoral theses while they held their first teaching posts in the *lycées*. The devaluation of studies in the early years of the Second Empire was temporary, for the men who succeeded Fortoul, including the *normalien* Victory Duruy,[21] appreciated the importance of the Ecole Normale for the advancement of national education.

By the beginning of the Third Republic the Ecole Normale was well entrenched.[22] The *normaliens* had become the aristocracy of a corps of public secondary school teachers which had grown rapidly in the nineteenth century in response to the rising numbers of students. From the beginning of the Second Empire to the early Third Republic, the public secondary school population more than doubled, and the number of teachers increased nearly as much. In 1842 there were 3744 public secondary school teachers, and in 1887 there were 9751.[23] Of these, the *normaliens* were more likely than others to be *agrégés* or doctors, and so they practically monopolized the most coveted posts in the *lycées* and the Faculties. In 1842 there were 361 *normaliens* among all of the secondary teachers, or about ten percent; but in the Royal Colleges they made up over half of the professors and administrators. In 1865 eight percent of all secondary teachers were *normaliens,* but they made up about a quarter of the professors and administrators.[24] Their percentage declined because their own numbers remained small and practically constant, but evidence suggests that their status in the profession rose rather than fell in the nineteenth century.

It remained true, however, that the *normalien* dominated a profession of rather uncertain status. Although the secondary professor had "the education and culture of the bourgeoisie, he had neither its wealth, its influence, nor its connections."[25] Unlike a legal career, a career in education was traditionally a social *cul de sac:* it led so far and no further. But during the Third Republic this rule seemed no longer to apply to the *normalien.* As the "republic of dukes" yielded in the 1880s to an educative republic and after the First World War to a "republic of professors,"[26] the men of the rue d'Ulm gained status and power. They were well placed to explain and interpret the bewildering events which were transforming France. During the Second Empire an expanding network of railroads and highways did much to unify France and bring the French into closer contact with each other. But the cultural and psychological adjustment to this structural change consumed much of the nation's energy for the next half century. Eugen Weber has brilliantly described the evolution between 1870 and 1914 of peasants who barely understood the national language into citizens aware of France and a world beyond their own villages.[27] The school was crucial to the assimilation of new ideas, to the adjustment to a different standard of living, and to the creation of a new national culture. Although the primary schools bore the brunt of this burden, alumni of the Ecole Normale quickly assumed leadership in the articulation of national educational policy. They dominated the pinnacle of an institution which had become more important than it had ever been before. Their rising prestige in education permitted some to lead brilliant careers in journalism, administration, and politics. An aura surrounded the rue d'Ulm as some alumni became "notables" of the Republic. Temporarily, for the situation did not last much beyond the Second World War, the Ecole Normale Supérieure became a fertile source of national leaders as well as scholars and schoolmasters.

The school's fame might be attributed in part to the small numbers of its graduates: the very scarcity of the *normaliens* seemed to proclaim their brilliance. The *promotions* of 1810 to 1869 numbered 1,066 students in Letters and 622 in Science. Each year a total of about thirty new students were admitted. During the Third Republic the numbers crept slowly upwards, averaging about forty per year in the nineteenth century and over fifty in the twentieth. But even with this increase the *promotions* of the Third Republic (1870–1940) numbered only 1,928 students in Letters and 1,310 in Sciences. At the same time the Ecole Polytechnique admitted over two hundred students per year, and annual admissions to the Ecole Libre rose steadily from under one hundred in the 1880s to over six hundred by 1940. By sheer numbers, therefore, the *normaliens* could never dominate government administration or politics. Yet the highly select character of this elite contributed to its mystique and was a source of strength in the social and political climate of the Third Republic. The remainder of our study focuses primarily upon the graduates of the Ecole Normale during this regime.

2

Through the Eye of a Needle: The Concours

Augustin disserta sur une pensée de Pascal, exposa l'historie des Pays-Bas de 1609 à 1715, confronta les jugements de valeur et les jugements de vérité, traduisit en grec une page de Fénelon et en français un passage du *De Officiis,* compara en latin Tite-Live, Salluste et Tacite, et attendit son destin.—J. Malègue

LIKE the appreciation of Latin or Greek, the idea of attending the Ecole Normale could arise only in a special cultural atmosphere produced by both the school and the family. If the student did well in school and merited the praise of his teachers, there was a chance that he could attend one of the *grandes écoles.* If his family was aware of the Ecole Normale they might persuade him to prepare for it. Otherwise he might be discovered and assisted by an official of the University. At some point the candidate required encouragement to prepare for the formidable entrance examination for the rue d'Ulm, the *concours.*

Inspector Nicolas–Félix Deltour (prom. 1842) on one of his visits to the Tarn fell upon some Latin verses written by the young Jean Jaurès (prom. 1878). Delighted by what he saw, he explained to Jean the opportunity which the Ecole could open up for him, convinced his family that he should leave home and the Collège de Castres to prepare in Paris at the Collège Sainte Barbe, and arranged for a scholarship to make it possible.[1] Another alumnus, Inspector Glachant (prom. 1845), discovered the young Edouard Herriot (prom. 1891) whose translation and explanation of a passage from Cicero's *Pro Milone* was so skillful that the Inspector offered him a scholarship to prepare for the Ecole Normale in Paris. But Herriot was confused and went home to discuss the matter with his father, a military officer who had risen from the ranks:

> We both knew nothing about the celebrated school to which I was being attracted. My father led me to the officer's club; we consulted the *Dictionnaire Larousse* (oh yes!); he then encouraged me to try for Normale, which I did. He renounced his plans for a military career for me, thinking that the teaching profession would more easily permit his eldest son to help the family in case his own war wounds shortened his life.[2]

Similarly was Georges Cogniot (prom. 1921) directed to the Ecole Normale. The eldest of seven children in a poor peasant family, Cogniot attended the *lycée* of Vesoul. One day he heard a school inspector pronounce to him, "My boy, you shall be a *normalien*." At first this statement had no meaning for him, but once informed of the Ecole's importance, he left Vesoul with a scholarship to prepare for the *concours* at the *lycée* of Lyons.[3]

Thus the recruitment of candidates was not left entirely to chance or the knowledge of the family. The University actively sought out the best prospects. One advantage of the centralization of the French secondary system was that it afforded opportunities for bright students to rise within it. Each year the officials in the local *lycées* put their best pupils on display in the national competitive examinations in the various subjects—the *concours généraux*. Some bright prospects inevitably went undiscovered, but the likelihood was great that a student who demonstrated extraordinary promise early in his academic career would become the pride of his *lycée*, a successful contestant in the *concours généraux*, the recipient of a scholarship to a great *lycée* of Paris, and ultimately a successful aspirant to one of the *grandes écoles*. However, the young man who did not show early signs of brilliance was far less likely to end up in one of the *grandes écoles* unless his family could afford to subsidize his education in a *lycée* until he matured and began to compete successfully for the national prizes.

Once the student's success in school was established and his teachers and his parents had impressed upon him that he must "prepare for Normale," he faced a most serious national competition. Unless his family lived in Paris or in another large city with an important *lycée*, he left home to become a boarding student at one of the great *lycées,* most typically in Paris. *Lycées* in Paris such as Louis-le-Grand and Henri IV monopolized preparation for the Ecole's Division of Letters, while several of the great provincial *lycées* were also quite successful in preparing students for Normale-Sciences.[4] Science candidates who were residents of Paris, Bordeaux, Toulouse, Lyon, Nancy, or Dijon could live at home while taking classes to prepare for the Ecole Normale's *concours.* Candidates for either Division who did not happen to live near a major *lycée* left home at the age of sixteen or seventeen to endure the spartan life of the boarding school, a wrenching experience in many cases.

At first Raoul Blanchard (prom. 1897) felt homesick at Louis-le-Grand. "The beginning of October 1895, I left my family, to which I was tenderly attached, I abandoned my home town which I loved so much. For the first time, I put on the uniform of the boarding students *(internes),* which had the effect on me of prisoner's garb."[5] To be a boarding student meant not only to be far from home but also to be cut off (until after the First World War) from the daily life of the city. Paul Dimoff (prom. 1899) recalled the atmosphere at Henri IV:

> We felt ourselves separated from the world, locked up in a carefully closed milieu, where noises from outside hardly penetrated. No newspaper, of course, was admitted to the *lycée;* during the week we learned of events only from the accounts of the day students. Only on Sundays, for a few hours, did we regain contact with the outside.[6]

Poor food, forbidding accommodations, and confinement made the *lycée* boarding student's life both a physical and a psychological trial. During the nineteenth century in particular the *lycée* resembled a jail. Until the end of the century conversation during meals was forbidden—silence was the rule except for the recreation period or in response to questions posed by the teacher in class. Jules Isaac recalls peering out between the bars of Lycée Lakanal at the forest and park nearby, "forbidden to the captive youth."[7]

The *lycées* were austere, for education was conceived as training in academic subjects practically to the exclusion of all else: 6:30 reveille and study period; 7:30 breakfast and short recreation; 8–10 classes; 10–12 study; 12–2 dinner, recreation, and study; 2–4 classes; 5–8 study; 8 dinner, after which the students went straight to the dormitory and bed.[8] Although physical confinement became less severe after the First World War, Paul Nizan (prom. 1924)remembered confinement of another sort. Louis–le–Grand in the early twenties was "a sort of great barracks of pale bricks . . . where nineteen year old boys were not able to learn much about the world due to their life among the Greeks, Romans, the idealist philosophers, and the doctrines of the July Monarchy."[9] On the other hand Robert Brasillach (prom. 1928) cast a rosy glow over his experience at Louis–le–Grand in the mid-1920s. "Today I think with pleasure about that Louis–le–Grand of my adolescence, where I led a life so much at variance with all my habits, and where I knew so many joys, the discovery of the world, the discovery of Paris, the discussions, the fever of youth, friendship." Brasillach at a distance of fifteen years could pass over the confining aspects of his experience and refer to Louis–le–Grand as "a large and beautiful house, where the discipline was not too rigorous. We were free all day on Sunday and all afternoon on Thursday."[10]

Having endured life in the *lycée* and completed its six year course of study, the student, now seventeen or eighteen, would take the examination for the baccalaureate. Only after having passed this could he enroll in one of the special *lycée* classes which prepared for the *grandes écoles.* To prepare for Normale–Letters one entered "superior rhetoric," also known as *premieure supérieure,* and dubbed *cagne* in student argot. "Special mathematics," or *taupe,* prepared for both Normale–Sciences and the Ecole Polytechnique. The memoirs are practically unanimous in their judgment that the instruction in these classes was of very high quality. The best *lycée* professors, men such as Alain, Bergson, or Lanson, could be found typically in the *cagnes* of Paris, but also in the great *lycées* of the provinces. A tribute to these classes is the widespread conviction among *normaliens* that their distinctive character or spirit, the famous *esprit normalien,* was in fact the *esprit de cagne* or *esprit de taupe:* the *normalien* was made at the elite classes of the *lycées* more truly than at the rue d'Ulm itself. In this sense the Ecole Normale served to legitimize or confirm rather than to create its elite.

It was understood that it took three years of *cagne* or *taupe* to prepare for the Ecole although exceptional students might succeed after one or two years.[11] Prior to the law of 1904 which limited to three the number of attempts a student might make to pass the examinations, a young man might be a candidate each year between his eighteenth and twenty–fifth birthdays. The normal pattern for a candidate who had just received the baccalaureate in his provincial *lycée* was to attend a Parisian *cagne* or *taupe* the first year without taking the exams for Normale at the end; after a second year he would take the exams for the first time, more or less for practice; he would then make his second assault on the Ecole at the end of his third year, a serious attempt. After 1904 this left open the possibility of a fourth year of *cagne* or *taupe* before the third and final attempt to pass Normale's *concours.* Thus emotion ran high at the end of the year in these classes, for the system was based upon vigorous competition in which far fewer succeeded in their quest than failed. The chance for success was on the order of one in ten.[12]

Until the Reform of 1904 every *normalien,* whether he was destined to the Sciences Division or Letters, had to know his Latin. Despite the liberalization of the baccalaureate in the reform of 1890, which permitted a candidate to substitute modern languages for Latin, the ancient tradition of the priority and value of classical languages remained strong at the rue d'Ulm. It was only in the *concours* of 1904 that the Ecole Normale offered options to its candidates. Instead of a common exam for all candidates in Letters consisting of Latin, Greek, French, Philosophy, and History, from 1904 there were three options—Latin–Greek (A), Latin–Foreign Languages (B), and Latin–Sciences (C) (the last being suppressed in 1928). Thus there was still no way to avoid Latin if one were a candidate for Normale–Letters. This was a possibility, however, for candidates in Sciences, who could substitute Mathematics–Foreign Language for the traditional Mathematics–Latin. But although the modification of the Ecole's *concours* reflected the trend toward "modern studies" in the University as a whole in the twentieth century, the classical tradition was quite persistent.[13] However preferable modern languages were to some of the reformers, Latin remained the mark of the good bourgeois, as it had been since the Renaissance. The great majority of the candidates for the Ecole elected Group A (Latin– Greek) rather than Group B or C. The choices of the 204 who took the written examination in 1928 were: A–148, B–34, and C–22. The *promotion* which was finally admitted that year in the Division of Letters was made up of 21 in A, 3 in B, and 5 in C.[14] It would take several generations, when different teachers were in place in the *lycées,* before "modern studies" would be suggested to students as an equivalent and excellent alternative to the classics. Thus the immense inertia of classicism was felt with particular force at the Ecole Normale despite the fact that some of the most eloquent opponents of classicism were *normaliens.*

The written parts of the examinations were printed each year and have been preserved.[15] A summary of the exams of 1890 and

1901 will give a general idea of their character. For Letters there were six tests which were taken on six successive days: philosophy (six hours), Latin composition (six hours), translation from Latin to French (four hours), translation from French to Greek (four hours), history (six hours), and French composition (six hours). The questions themselves over the course of the whole Third Republic undoubtedly deserve careful analysis for what they might reveal about the University, but we have not undertaken that task here. The classical authors used in 1890 and 1901 for translations were Caesar, Cicero, and Quintillian. In 1890 the philosophy question dealt with an ancient problem: "Can one, otherwise than through skepticism, reconcile these two propositions—all existence is particular, and only the universal is an object of science?" In 1901 the examiners in philosophy asked the candidates to write an essay on "respect for the human person as a principle of social morality." The history questions could be rather broad—"Italy before the expedition of Charles VIII"—or relatively narrow—"Party struggles in the French Chambers of the Restoration (1815–1830)." The French compositions in particular seemed to call for the greatest subtlety and judgment, for the candidate was asked to write an imaginative speech that a character or an author might make in a hypothetical situation. Throughout all of the written examinations the candidate had to demonstrate good judgment as well as knowledge in eloquent and precise essays.

The examination in science was divided between the scientific subjects proper and the humanities. In both 1890 and 1901 there were tests in mathematics, physics, and French composition, each six hours in duration. In 1890 the fourth and final test was a four–hour translation of Latin into French, whereas in 1901 the candidate was required to perform two such translations, his choice between Latin, German, and English. It was possible for the candidate in Sciences to avoid Latin completely by 1901, but in return he had to learn *two* other foreign languages rather than one. This was a clear reminder that the establishment hardly thought that the classics and modern languages were on a par. The examinations in mathematics did not include integral or differential calculus but consisted essentially of intricate exercises in analytical geometry and algebraic operations to the third power. Likewise the physics test demanded a thorough understanding of the basic laws and an ability to solve problems using algebra. The French composition, or *dissertation française,* had less a literary than a philosophical character related to the sciences. In 1890 the topic was "the role of science in moral life," and in 1901 it was "the idea of law in the physical and natural sciences." Questions such as these suggest aspects of the Republic's secular ideology such as science, order, and progress.

Once the written examinations had been read and identified, the candidates were summoned to Paris, where they were examined at the Ecole Normale itself by juries consisting (before 1904) of the Ecole's own professors or (after that date) of eminent professors of the University, most often graduates of the Ecole. Traditionally the oral examinations took place in the library of the Ecole, where the examiners took stock of the demeanor of the candidate, his maturity, and personality, in a way which was not possible in the written examinations. Here the candidate could charm and impress his examiners.

As Edouard Herriot recalls, the competition could be capricious as well as keen:

> Such as it was in my day, the entrance exam of the Ecole Normale left a great part to chance . . . . The list of candidates who passed the written exam was composed of around forty–eight names, of which half were sacrificed at the orals. Each year there were over two hundred candidates. To fail one had only to be surprised by a subject in history poorly understood; one might just as well have to treat Marius and Sulla, the relation between Church and State under the old regime, or the eastern question under Louis–Philippe. I saw many of my friends fail who were better qualified than I. When I was admitted in 1891, when I read the notice on the bulletin board, I congratulated myself less on my merit than upon my good fortune.[16]

Chance was favorable to Herriot on his third attempt, after he had become accustomed, or "formed", to the *concours*.

Although Herriot mentioned purely academic excellence and chance as the necessary factors in success at the *concours,* there were other requirements, certain qualities of character, which the University sought as well. Each aspirant had to produce a number of documents, among which was the statement by the Rector of the Academy that the candidate possessed "moral aptitude" for a teaching career, in order for his name to be inscribed officially on the list of candidates.[17] These statements along with those of the principal of the *lycée,* on which they were based, give us a fair sense of the qualities desired by the University establishment. Most of the comments, of course, were favorable. From 1868: "The young man is a brilliant laureate of the *concours général,* in Latin discourse and above all in history . . . good and strong character . . . irreproachable conduct, possesses to a high degree the moral aptitude for teaching. —He is a Protestant." Another from the same year reads: "Educated and hardworking, of gentle character and very good habits—manners and bearing very fine—Catholic—good health although delicate in appearance. The Rector judges that the University will make an excellent recruit of him."[18] In another case from the crop of 1874 a Rector commented that the candidate possessed "all that was needed, except the height perhaps, to succeed in teaching."[19] There are a few records of the candidates who failed to receive favorable letters from their Rectors and were not permitted to take the examinations. "Weak and whimsical nature, which will accomplish, I fear . . . nothing serious." In the same year, 1870, the suspicion of private enterprise could be seen in the negative recommendation of a candidate: "Far from being preoccupied with the Ecole Normale, . . . he is thinking about private industry, and he is right. His character does not offer all of the desirable guarantees, perhaps, for the delicate functions of teaching."[20]

In the twentieth century apparently it was possible to overcome the negative recommendation of the *lycee*'s principal. One *normalien* of 1910 was rated as follows: "his work—irregular, his aptitudes—not very evident, his character—not sufficiently serious, his morality—very good, his successes—____." In another case that year a successful candidate for Normale received the following note from the principal: "Aptitude mediocre, with a certain originality. Work acceptable. Character dissembling, fault–finding, with marked tendencies toward indiscipline. Manners not very cultivated. Holds a medium rank in the class." X____ was a quite successful candidate at the *concours,* but already the principal could identify an independent and troublesome spirit: "Culture already broad and a rare power of spirit . . . dissertations are rather original essays than homework for class or *concours;* they are brilliant and vigorous. Should succeed easily. What a shame that X____ persists in displaying eccentric manners *(allures)* which cause so much trouble."[21]

In the nineteenth century the conduct and personality of the candidate were critical factors in his admission to the *concours.* Fustel de Coulanges, Director of the Ecole from 1880 to 1883, insisted upon decorum as well as scholarship. In the case of one student he weighed deportment against academic brilliance as follows: "This young man was sent home for misconduct first from Sainte Barbe, then from Massin. Such a troublesome fact cannot be compensated by the prize of honor which R____ has obtained in philosophy.[22] Along with his insistence upon absolute seriousness on the part of the candidate,

Fustel displayed a suspicion of wealth. Concerning a student who wished to resign, he wrote to the Minister of Education: "This young man has just been admitted 17th; I have reason to think that, considering the state of wealth in which he finds himself, he aspired rather to the title of student of the Ecole than to the hard work to which each one should be submitted in this house, and that he would not later have accepted the functions of a professor."[23] Modest origins were considered most appropriate for the schoolmaster.

Once admitted to the Ecole the question remained whether the student qualified because of his merit and the relatively modest position of his family for a scholarship—the *trousseau*—to cover clothing and other incidental expenses. Here the Director's comments and those of the Rector were germane. A student of 1868 failed to receive the scholarship because of the Rector's comment: "Son of a man of property, well off, and whose approaching inheritance will increase his fortune still more. An older brother, thirty years old, just married well. —Unfavorable recommendation."[24] In the case of a member of the *promotion* of 1878 we read: "His parents were residents of Paris; his mother died in 1864, and his father, who was a shoemaker, disappeared in 1871."[25] The scholarship was granted in this clear case of need. The son (prom. 1910) of a primary school teacher *(instituteur)* received his *trousseau* scholarship on the mayor's advice: "[the father] made great sacrifices to educate his children, his revenues are going to decline continually since he is retired."[26] In the case of Jean Jaurès many factors contributed to the decision:

> Monsieur Jaurès owns in the region of Faix property whose value the Inspector does not know exactly, but he estimates it to be around 40,000 francs. M. Jaurès has been disabled for several years. He has two sons, one a student at the Ecole Navale, and the other at the Ecole Normale. They studied at the Collège de Castres. . . . While they were at the Collège de Castres, the last two years, the two young men had to walk about six kilometers from the country where they lived to the *collège*. That seems to me to establish sufficiently that M. Jaurès' resources are modest. I will add that Jaurès family is related to the Vice–Admiral and Senator Jaurès.[27]

Had the Jaurès family been wealthier, it was assumed, they would have sent Jean immediately to a boarding institution.

For the *promotions* of the twentieth century we have financial statements from families, from which we can conclude that there was some injustice and bias in the granting of the *trousseau* scholarships.

There are cases in the 1920s, for instance, in which the father himself was a *normalien* on a good salary (over 40,000 francs in one case, and half that—still a generous amount—in another), and in which special pleading by the Rector (also a *normalien*) secured the *trousseau* allowance: "favorable recommendation. I know the situation of M____ and I know that he needs the assistance," or "There are resources, that is true, but at least the financial declaration is sincere. The family responsibilities are heavy, the candidate is a remarkable boy. His father is worthy in all respects."[28] In other cases families which earned far less were turned down or allowed only half a scholarship. Such evidence of social bias and personal influence is hardly surprising. While comments about politics do not appear overtly in the recommendations, officials evidently judged candidates and their families according to well understood standards.

Certain themes such as seriousness, hard work, and sacrifice run throughout the matriculation documents. At the initial meeting of the school year in 1872, Director Ernest Bersot made the following comments to an eminent *normalien,* Jules Simon, then Minister of Education, in which he stressed work and service: "Let me thank you in particular for one of our excellent students who graduates this year, M. Tartinville. His family, a family of *instituteurs,* four of whom account for one hundred and forty–two years of service in primary education in the same school, requested a scholarship for a young son; you granted him a full scholarship to the very *lycée* where his brother was appointed so that the elder would direct him and prepare him for us and for you. That is good democracy."[29] The emphasis upon democratic recruitment and modest origins appears again in the testimony of Georges Perrot in 1899 before the Ribot Commission investigating secondary education:

> Today we still recruit our candidates from the deep beds of worker and rural democracy, where such treasures of energy are amassed, where so many forces germinate, which only ask to be developed; it is to this milieu that we owe our dear and great Pasteur. We accept the sons of workers, of peasants, above all sons of teachers. . . .[30]

As social analysis his statement was misleading at best, but as an indication of a state of mind concerning the Ecole Normale both among university people and among the legislators who were to decide its fate, it is revealing. While the examinations guaranteed that merit would count heavily in the recruitment of *normaliens,* the recommendations of principals, rectors, mayors, and the Director of the

Ecole suggested other standards according to which the students were selected or encouraged as well. Aside from a perfunctory notation that they were Catholic, Protestant, or "Israelite," comments about their religiosity are absent from the records in the Third Republic. Instead, the frequent references to modest origins, hard work, good behavior, sacrifice, and service suggest secular virtues. The *normalien* was a well–behaved and diligent student—the hero of prize day.

For practically all of its history the Ecole Normale has been an all–male institution. The analogous school to prepare women to teach in *lycées* for girls was the Ecole Normale Supérieure de Sèvres, established in 1881. However, between the world wars some women were permitted to attend special classes held at the rue d'Ulm, and finally between 1927 and 1940 thirty–five women were admitted by *concours* as regular students. The practice came abruptly to an end early in the Vichy regime, when Director Jérôme Carcopino (prom. 1901) determined to exclude women and make boarding mandatory (the *internat*). Carcopino was dismayed at what he considered slack discipline in the house and acted swiftly to recreate the secular cloister for males that he knew as a student at the turn of the century.[31] The women were never to return as regular students, but neither were the isolation and discipline of the past ever restored.

3

Social Origins and Careers: The Statistical Evidence

> L'enseignement est la seule carrière qui se recrute presque exclusivement parmi les boursiers, les fils de familles sans fortune . . . Dans les professions libérales, l'enseignement représente rigoureusement la section des hommes nouveaux.—Albert Thibaudet

THE legitimacy of the *normaliens'* claim to interpret democratic and republican themes drawn from the Revolutionary tradition was based in part upon their modest social origins. During the centennial celebrations of 1895, Director Georges Perrot repeated a recurrent theme: "The Ecole has always recruited in large part among families where one lived by daily toil, often manual work, as did this tanner of Arbois to whom we owe M. Pasteur; scholarships facilitate access to the *lycées* for poor young men who have talent and will. It is a democratic institution."[1] It was well known by the turn of the century that the social character of the University differed from that of the legal profession, the army, or business. Albert Thibaudet expressed in the 1920s what was by then common knowledge when he noted that the teaching profession recruited chiefly from among scholarship students, sons of families with no fortune, and "new men."[2] However, the Ecole Normale was not socially identical with the rest of the University—with professors in the *lycées,* for example, whose origins were more modest.[3] Hence we begin to look for causes for the rise of the *normaliens* in the Third Republic by examining their geographical and social origins.[4] They may be described as "new men" as compared with students of the Ecole Polytechnique or the Ecole Libre des Sciences Politiques.[5] At the same time they possessed considerable cultural capital which was a function of their families' social rank and geographical origins.

The particular culture of the village, town, or city where a boy grew up had a bearing upon his future. Provincials who had no prospect of escape to Paris or to a large provincial city tended to retain not only the local patterns and accents of speech, but also the rather limited ambitions of their neighbors. In the provinces resignation and distrust of the capital were based upon long experience of unsuccessful competition with the Parisians. Paris exercised a cultural hegemony over France, and a disproportionately large number of *normaliens* came from there.

Although the total population of the Seine rose from 6.1 per cent of the national population in 1872 to 11.8 per cent in 1931, the *normaliens* of the Third Republic were drawn much more heavily from that department: 35.2 per cent in Letters and 27.9 per cent in Sciences (Table 1).[6] This situation meant that only a limited number of other departments could supply a percentage of *normaliens* proportionate to their percentage of the total population. In addition to Paris the strong areas were in the East—in particular Meurthe–et–Moselle and Côte d'Or—the Southeast—especially Rhône, Puy–de–Dome, and Isère— and the southern coast from Marseille west to Toulouse. The West was generally weaker as a source of *normaliens* except for the Gironde, Charente, and Vienne. Consistently weaker than other regions were the industrial North (Nord and Pas–de–Calais), the Massif Central region, and the Catholic West and Northwest. By the Third Republic France was divided into two parts: a republican, freethinking, industrializing, and literate East and a culturally retrograde and economically backward West. Statistically a *normalien* was more likely to have grown up in the East or in Paris than in the West.[7]

Other geographical evidence casts light on the distinctive pattern of the *normaliens'* social origins. For instance not all cities of roughly the same size were equally prolific in *normaliens.* Lille, a highly industrial and very Catholic city in the department of the Nord, was notable for its lack of *normaliens.* For instance, the young hero of a novel about an industrial family of that city is tempted by a brilliant university career via the Ecole Normale Supérieure. Instead he remains true to the traditions of his family and of that region by deciding to pursue wealth and power in the family firm.[8] For the industrial capitalist bourgeoisie the Ecole Normale had scant attraction. On the other

TABLE 1. Population of *Normaliens'* Cities of Origin: *Promotions* of 1868–1941 (Per Cent)

	Size of City (Thousands)						
	Paris-Seine	Over 100	30–100	20–30	10–20	5–10	Under 5
Division of Letters							
Birthplace	22.1	11.1	13.7	7.3	8.3	8.3	29.2
Address at Matriculation	35.2	13.5	14.9	6.2	6.9	4.8	18.6
Division of Sciences							
Birthplace	17.9	10.8	15.8	4.8	8.2	7.3	35.3
Address at Matriculation	27.9	11.6	16.7	4.7	8.5	6.6	24.0
France							
Census of 1901	9.4	4.4	7.0	3.3	5.1	6.2	64.6

Letters N = 1766
Sciences N = 1217

hand the reverse was the case in cities such as Paris or Lyon which contained an important older cultivated bourgeoisie of high officials, lawyers, and other liberal professionals. This class, and thus the cities where they lived, furnished a high proportion of the *normaliens.*

This being the case, we should expect that *normaliens* tended to

TABLE 2. Origins from Cities Over 20,000 Population and from Capitals of Departments (Per Cent)

	Promotions						
	1868–79	1880–89	1890–99	1900–09	1910–19	1920–29	1930–41
From Cities Over 20,000							
Letters	70	60	72	69	67	69	77
Sciences	54	46	54	62	66	62	75
France	18	19	20	25	30	33	37
From Capitals Of Departments, Including Paris							
Letters	73	65	70	64	64	62	75
Sciences	52	50	57	53	61	62	73
Excluding Paris							
Letters	50	44	49	48	49	50	57
Sciences	37	35	36	37	46	44	53

Letters N = 1766
Sciences N = 1217

come from the larger cities which were centers of culture and government administration. In fact about two thirds of them were born in towns and cities with a population exceeding 5,000, and their home addresses by the time they matriculated at Normale indicate an even more pronounced urban concentration. Furthermore, those who came from cities of over 20,000 consistently amounted to more than double the national average, and a consistently high proportion came from the capital of the department (Tables 1 and 2).

Teachers and officials, as they advanced in their careers, invariably moved from small towns to provincial cities, and finally perhaps to Paris. Comparing the *normaliens'* residence at birth and at matriculation eighteen or twenty years later, it is clear that their families rated well above the national average in mobility. And the direction of that movement, again well above the national average, was toward larger cities. No doubt the particular profession exercised by their fathers—who were most frequently teachers or officials—made it inevitable that in a normal career the family should move several times from smaller to progressively more important cities (Table 3).

TABLE 3. Family Mobility: Born in Different Department from Current Family Address (Per Cent)

				Promotions			
	1868–79	1880–89	1890–99	1900–09	1910–19	1920–29	1930–41
Letters	34	41	44	39	31	38	45
Sciences	33	30	30	22	32	42	46
France	15	15	17	20	21	23	25

Letters N = 1766
Sciences N = 1217

Another factor which influenced the geographical pattern of recruitment was the location of preparatory classes for the Ecole. The *cagnes* and *taupes* of Paris, Lyon, and Marseille were excellent, and these *lycées* always had good success in placing their students. The existence in a given city of a *cagne* or *taupe* furnished for the entire surrounding area a special opportunity for advancement to sons of families on the lower end of the social scale, that is families who could not imagine or afford sending the son to Paris. Psychologically it was no small matter for a family to send a son in his early teens off to a distant city to a boarding *lycée*. If the *lycée* were close at hand the student could live at home. In this way the location of *lycées* and the existence in certain of them of *cagnes* and *taupes* which prepared for

TABLE 4. Social Origins and Access to the Ecole Normale: *Promotions* of 1868–1941

Profession of Father	Approximate Active Male Population (1872)[a]	Division of Letters			Division of Sciences		
		N = 1598 Per Cent	Student/ Population Ratio[b]	Rank[c]	N = 1033 Per Cent	Student/ Population Ratio[b]	Rank[c]
Owners of Capital, Businessmen	9.2	10.8	1.2	7	10.3	1.1	7
Higher Officials	1.0	5.1	5.1	5	3.6	3.6	6
Liberal Professions	0.8	14.3	17.9	4	8.6	10.8	4
Commissioned Officers	0.2	3.9	19.5	3	4.2	21.0	3
Secondary and University Professors and Officials	0.1	19.6	196.0	1	17.2	172.0	1
Total Upper Class	11.3	53.7	4.8		43.9	3.9	
Primary and Technical Teachers and Administrators	0.5	12.8	25.6	2	12.1	24.2	2
Middle, Lower Officials	—	12.8			12.0		
White Collar	—	7.9			9.1		
Total Officials and White Collar	4.5	20.7	4.6	6	21.1	4.7	5
Artisans, Shopkeepers, and Tradesmen	6.7	4.3	0.6	8	6.6	1.0	8
Total Middle Class	11.7	37.8	3.2		39.8	3.4	
Police and Non-commissioned Officers	1.1	0.8	0.7		1.3	1.2	
Skilled Labor	19.9	3.1	0.2		8.3	0.4	
Unskilled Labor	6.7	0.4	0.1		1.2	0.2	
Farmers	35.0	4.3	0.1		5.6	0.2	
Agricultural Workers	14.3	0.0	0.0		0.0	0.0	
Total Lower Class	77.0	8.6	0.1	9	16.4	0.2	9

[a]These estimates are taken directly from Victor Karady, "Normaliens et autres enseignants. . . ," pp. 40–41.
[b]Percentage of that category at the Ecole Normale divided by the percentage in the active male population.
[c]This is the rank order of the student/population ratios.

the *grandes écoles* was a significant factor in the continuing strength of certain cities as a source of *normaliens.*

In this geographical comparison of all the *normaliens* of the Third Republic with statistics for the nation as a whole, the *normaliens* emerge as distinctly more Parisian, urban, and mobile. Destined to become the elite of their profession, they rate even higher in these categories than *lycée* professors in general.[9] The *normaliens* on the whole were further removed than were the ordinary professors from their rural and agricultural roots.

Although in the nineteenth century the geographical distribution by departments was about the same in the Ecole's two divisions, Letters and Science, the literary students were distinctly more urban than the scientists and more likely to have moved (to a larger city) between birth and matriculation at the rue d'Ulm. This difference reflected social origins which were not identical. Furthermore, we shall observe that whereas in the nineteenth century the *littéraires* were of higher social rank as well as more urban, in the twentieth century the *scientifiques* resembled them quite closely in these respects.

Profession, since it implied a certain education and culture, was a far more important determinant of social rank than wealth. Although the French Revolution marked and sped the decline of the aristocratic class, it could not efface the memory of a social order based upon qualities, ranks, and privileges. Through the educational system in particular this memory soon expressed the new dualism of *bourgeois* and *peuple,* replacing the old one of nobility and Third Estate. Distinctions of status both between and within the major social categories continued to be based upon the familiar criteria of profession, culture, and manners. Some acquired qualities and social rank by their wealth or noble birth, but most *normaliens* had to rely upon another viable route—education.[10]

It is significant that neither the very poor nor the very rich turned up at the Ecole Normale in great numbers. For the poor there were practical obstacles, and for the rich the rue d'Ulm did not seem to be a particularly worthy goal (see Table 4).

Owners of land or other capital, industrialists, financiers, and other businessmen were able to furnish to their offspring all of the cultural benefits that money could provide. Their sons could attend the best boarding *collèges* and *lycées.* But in fact the percentage of *normaliens* from such families (9–10%) was barely higher than the percentage of these families in the nation as a whole. By contrast, at the Ecole Polytechnique this percentage was four to five times higher depending upon the decade, and at the faculties of medicine and law from scarce data we can estimate that it was between twice and three times as high.[11] Normale prepared for public service—for a post as a *fonctionnaire*—and that sort of career demanded a different discipline and offered different rewards from what the industrial bourgeoisie in particular valued or understood. Families of *fonctionnaires* were ten times over–represented at the Ecole Normale compared with families in the private sector. The business class saw no particular advantage in deserting business even if it were to join the educational establishment. From their perspective higher status commensurate with wealth was within reach in other careers.

People at the other end of the social scale saw the Ecole Normale in a different light. Farmers, workers, non–commissioned officers, and policemen make up what we have called the Lower Class,[12] and although in almost every case a son's passage through Normale would represent a social (and material) advance, this class was under–represented. Comprising about 77 per cent of the entire population, the Lower Class supplied only 8.6 per cent of the literary students and 16.4 per cent of the scientists (See Table 4). However the Lower Class was not less well represented at Normale than it was elsewhere. At Polytechnique between 1880 and 1914 it accounted for 10 per cent of the students, slightly more than Normale's Division of Letters, but 8 per cent *less* than Normale's Division of Sciences. During the same period at the Ecole Libre des Sciences Politiques (an expensive private institution known as "Sciences Po"), the Lower Class contributed less than one per cent of the students.[13] Normale–Sciences may have attracted more students from the Lower Class because teaching represented a more credible change in social status than did the coveted civil service careers of graduates of Polytechnique and Sciences Po. No matter what his goal was, any student from the Lower Class who pursued his studies beyond the legal school leaving age risked feeling like an outcast sitting on benches beside his social betters. Jean Guéhenno (prom. 1911), the son of a poor shoe worker, has described both the financial and psychological difficulties that he experienced:

> . . . my father had certain plans for me. He wanted me to go to the *collège* even though tuition had to be paid. I was not happy there. I was ill at ease. I remained there up to the age of fourteen, each year, in September, my parents asking themselves if they would continue [to make] such a sacrifice. My classmates were sons of industrialists, small merchants, and officials, and, the social and

> political quarrels of the small industrial city resounding even into the *collège,* I was aware, [being] among them, of my commoner's status and unworthiness.[14]

Guéhenno was fortunate to have had the encouragement of his family and subsequently that of some of his teachers. Special encouragement is what a child of the Lower Class required, for he was *expected* by his peers and the society to quit school early and enter the work force. Students of higher social status were expected to continue their education: they had the financial means, the encouragement of teachers,[15] and self–assurance.

Artisans, shopkeepers, and small tradesmen were marginally better able to send a son to Normale than the Lower Class as a whole. They had about the same rate of success as non–commissioned officers and policemen (*See* Table 4). But consistently, if the *normalien* came from the lower end of the social scale, he was more likely to have entered the Division of Sciences than Letters. Altogether in the Division of Sciences in the Third Republic 23.0 per cent of the students were from the six lowest social categories; in the Division of Letters the figure was 12.9 per cent. The difference, which is minimal in the middle of our scale and which is reversed in favor of the Division of Letters for the Upper Class (except for businssmen), can be explained in several ways. First, in the lower categories rural dispersion was far greater, and hence since the *taupes* were more dispersed than the *cagnes,* preparation for the science track was more feasible than letters for families with low incomes. Probably far more important was the intrinsic difference between the two fields: literary studies place a greater premium upon taste and language which usually require careful nurture in the family, whereas science is more accessible to poor students who, although perhaps weaker in the manipulation of literary symbols because of their families' lack of education, find themselves on an equal footing with their "betters" in the use of another abstract language, mathematics.

Taking into account the relative size of socio–professional categories in the entire population, next in order of ascending importance as a source of *normaliens,* after the farmers, workers, policemen, artisans, and small tradesmen on the one hand and the capitalists on the other, were higher officials (of the Upper Class) and the middle and petty officials and white collar employees (of the Middle Class). The Division of Letters attracted a larger percentage of students from the higher category, the Division of Sciences more from the lower. Letters was the royal path. The relative weakness of the Ecole's recruitment from these two groups in relation to their national importance arose from different causes. Higher officials aspired to what they considered to be better careers for their sons than teaching; if nevertheless the son ended up at Normale, he most probably undertook literary studies, which, more plausibly than science, led elsewhere than to a teaching career during most of the Third Republic. Paul Bastid (prom. 1910) is a brilliant example of a *normalien* who came from this group of the Upper Class. He came from a prominent republican family. Both his father Adrien and his grandfather Raymond were republican deputies during the early Third Republic. His uncle Pierre Devès (1837–1899) was a Minister of Agriculture in Gambetta's government and later Minister of Justice under Duclerc and Fallières. All of Bastid's ancestors seem to have been lawyers, and their connection with big business is suggested by the fact that Devès was president of the Bône to Guelma railroad and an administrator of the Crédit Foncier of France. In fact it was, according to Bastid,[16] somewhat of an accident that he went to the Ecole Normale. Under normal circumstances he would have taken his law degree immediately after the baccalaureate and then proceeded to take his place in public life, but a temporary decline in the family's fortunes caused him to prepare for a university career as a sort of insurance policy. As a scholar his accomplishments included two *agrégations,* three doctorates, and books of poetry, fiction, biography, law, and public affairs. Yet rather than choosing the University as a career he entered politics and became a Radical deputy from Cantal. This case illustrates that social origins take on their full significance only when they are seen in the light of the different expectations and intentions of the social groups. Thus for the lower white collar class Normale represented a way to rise in the world, but they were neither so predominantly urban nor so well educated as the higher officials; although they perceived that the Ecole Normale offered them cultural and financial rewards, they faced stiff competition from other social groups.

Those families most attracted by the Ecole Normale and sufficiently endowed financially and culturally to prepare their sons for it were affiliated with either the teaching or the military profession. Families of teachers and educational administrators of all kinds, although they comprised less than one per cent of the population, supplied almost a third of the *normaliens* during the entire Third

Republic. These families were over–represented at the Ecole Normale by a ratio of 35:1. Like artists, lawyers, or officials, teachers passed on skills and general ideas about the world to their children from generation to generation. Like many other professions, teaching could become a mission rather than merely an occupation, and loyalty to the profession could permeate the entire family. Archival records are full of comments by mayors and rectors that sisters or brothers of the *normalien* were school teachers or that they had married school teachers. The Delbos family sent two of its sons to the Ecole Normale: Victor (prom. 1882), who became a professor of philosophy at the Sorbonne, and Yvon (prom. 1907), the Radical politican and Minister of Foreign Affairs under the Popular Front. Both the father and a grandfather had been primary school teachers—*instituteurs.* Their mother operated a bookstore, but she was the daughter of a director of a primary school. Raymond Badiou (prom. 1924) came from a similar background. His grandfather was of peasant origin and taught primary school in a village in the Massif Central during the Second Empire. Badiou's father was one of seven children, each of whom became either a primary or secondary teacher. After his studies at the Ecole Normale, Badiou married a secondary school teacher and became one himself before becoming Mayor of Toulouse and a Socialist deputy.[17] Pierre Brossolette (prom. 1922) likewise came from a family committed to the teaching profession in the service of the Radical republic. His father Léon, the son of a small farmer, as a boy walked back and forth to the local school four or five kilometers away. There the *instituteur* recognized his high intelligence and encouraged him to continue his studies at the primary teachers' college at Troyes. He became an *instituteur,* then a professor at the primary teachers' college in Paris, and finally an Inspector of Primary Education. His wife, the daughter of an *instituteur,* also became a professor at a primary teachers' college. Her eldest brother, Francisque Vial (prom. 1890), had attended the Ecole Normale Supérieure and later became Director of Secondary Education. [18] For the son of such parents the Ecole Normale was attractive: its curriculum suited his family's professional aspirations, and its political tradition corresponded with their own. There were many other cases such as these in which the *normalien* became the pride of an entire clan of teachers.

It is important to distinguish, however, between professors of either secondary or higher education, who shared the higher status of *universitaires,* and *instituteurs,* who taught in the primary schools. *Normaliens* never served at the primary level, but instead became professors. Their fathers, moreover, were more likely to have been professors than *instituteurs.* Although during the Third Republic there were approximately five times as many *instituteurs* as there were professors of both secondary and higher education, at the rue d'Ulm the sons of professors were fifty per cent more numerous than sons of *instituteurs.* At Normale professors' sons were over–represented according to their number in the population by a factor of 196 in the case of Letters and 172 in the case of Sciences. *Instituteurs'* sons grew up with some sense of the possibilities of making a career as an educator and possessed some cultural refinement, but they were over–represented at Normale by factors of only 26 in Letters and 24 in Sciences. For both groups the Ecole Normale represented the summit of a hierarchy where their fathers had already found places. But primary school teachers were inferior to professors in both salary and status. To rise furher in the social system required imagination, effort, and sacrifice on the part of the family as well as good luck. In addition, an *instituteur* was far more likely than a professor to live in a rural area. To take full advantage of government scholarships (of which sons of teachers were favored recipients), the rural student had to leave home and become a boarding student at a distant *lycée.* The son of a professor rarely had to leave home at an early age: he could attend the *lycée* near home where his father taught. Only when it was finally time to enter a *cagne* or *taupe,* most likely in Paris, would the provincial professor's son have to leave the nest. In this way it was not the father's profession alone, but also where he exercised it, which played a part in determining the likelihood that his son would be a *normalien.* Lower social status and rural origins, both detriments to becoming a *normalien,* tended to go hand in hand (See Table 5).

That sons of generals and other commissioned officers were second after teachers in numbers at Normale according to their number in the population may seem incongruous, but several factors suggest an explanation. This class was relatively well traveled, well educated, and favored as *fonctionnaires* in the competition for scholarships.[19] Most of the commissioned officers were not graduates of Saint Cyr, but instead, like Edouard Herriot's father, had risen from the ranks. Many officers in fact came from quite humble origins and were not averse to a school which prepared for another branch of state service, even teaching. Nor did every son of an officer share his father's taste for soldiering. Edouard Herriot (prom. 1891) may well as a youth have embarked willingly upon a military career had he not caught Inspector Glachant's attention. "My grandfather," Herriot writes,

TABLE 5. Urban-rural Distribution by Father's Social Class: *Promotions* of 1868–1941

	Family's Residence (Per Cent)			
	Paris	Larger Cities: Over 30,000	Smaller Cities: 5,000–30,000	Towns and Villages Under 5,000
Upper Class				
Letters	42	30	17	11
Sciences	35	32	21	12
Middle Class				
Letters	26	28	20	26
Sciences	23	26	15	31
Lower Class				
Letters	22	20	14	44
Sciences	14	20	20	46
France-1901 Census All Social Categories	9	11	15	65

Letters N = 1524
Sciences N = 979

"the son of the laborer Quirin, retired as a corporal . . . married a washerwoman who was herself the daughter of a carpenter. . . . Of this marriage was born in the Saint–Seven barracks, the one to whom I owe so much, Jean–François, my father. Until my seventeenth year I lived among soldiers. No one could imagine, in my family, that a son could choose a profession other than the army."[20] But the elder Herriot, during his service in Napoleon III's Italian wars, developed a deep interest in classical literature which he passed on to his son. When Inspector Glachant (prom. 1845) discovered the young Herriot and proposed to the family that he prepare for Normale, the Herriots were able to perceive that an educational career via the rue d'Ulm was an honorable and safe alternative to the military. In either case it would be a career of public service in a major corps.

The liberal professions accounted for a larger absolute percentage of the *normaliens* than the military, but ranked slightly lower when their number in the population is taken into account (See Table 4). Composed mainly of doctors, lawyers, clergymen, musicians, artists, pharmacists, and engineers (in that order), this group was important as a source of *normaliens* because of its education and its economic security. But whereas in the case of the higher military there was no significant preference for either the Division of Letters or Sciences, the liberal professions had almost twice the percentage in Letters that

TABLE 6. Evolution of *Normaliens'* Social Origins: *Promotions* of 1868–1941 (Per Cent)

Division of Letters = L; Division of Sciences = S

Profession of Father	1868–79		1880–89		1890–99		1900–09		1910–19		1920–29		1930–41	
	L	S	L	S	L	S	L	S	L	S	L	S	L	S
Owners of Capital, Businessmen	12	14	14	21	13	14	8	7	7	8	10	6	12	5
Higher Officials	3	3	8	2	9	4	3	7	4	2	6	5	4	2
Liberal Professions	17	8	16	9	13	8	15	4	11	8	16	9	13	12
Commissioned Officers	3	2	3	1	3	4	4	4	4	7	5	7	5	4
Secondary and University Professors and Officials	25	22	20	13	19	16	21	14	26	17	14	17	15	20
Total Upper Class	60	49	61	46	57	46	51	36	52	42	51	44	49	43
Primary and Technical Teachers and Administrators	6	12	8	8	7	8	14	11	20	14	19	19	13	11
Middle, Lower Officials and White Collar	19	12	16	14	17	17	25	28	20	25	19	19	26	29
Artisans, Shopkeepers, and Tradesmen	6	8	4	10	4	8	4	10	2	2	3	5	6	4
Total Middle Class	31	32	28	32	28	33	43	49	42	41	41	43	45	44
Total Lower Class	9	19	11	22	15	21	6	15	6	17	8	13	6	13
N =	218	131	209	143	190	121	210	141	220	130	250	172	301	195

Total Letters N = 1598
Total Sciences N = 1033

they had in Sciences. As in the case of the higher officials, perhaps, the Ecole Normale itself was acceptable in certain cases only on the condition that one chose the Division that offered the better possibility of a career in some field other than education, such as journalism, literature, politics, or government administration. There was another important reason that students in the Ecole Normale's Division of Sciences were more Lower Class than those in the Division of Letters. Upper Class science students were recruited by the Ecole Polytechnique and other scientific *grandes écoles,* whereas the Upper Class literary students had no such attractive alternative. The Ecole Normale's recruitment reflected in part the opportunities for higher education available elsewhere to the various social classes. Thus although the Middle Class was about equally well represented at Normale in Letters and Sciences, the Lower Class was more numerous in Science and the Upper Class more numerous in Letters (See Table 4). One should not forget that the intelligence and the will of the candidate played an essential part in his admission to Normale, but there was no question that on the whole the most desirable places—at Normale or elsewhere in the educational system—would be filled by those groups which possessed a rich combination of cultural and economic capital. For others the future was far less assured.

To this point I have considered the "whole universe" of this study, that is all of the *promotions* of the Third Republic as if they existed at one moment in time. However, the recruitment of *normaliens* was hardly impervious to social change: a modest but discernible evolution in the representation of social classes at the rue d'Ulm took place over the course of the Third Republic (See Table 6). This evolution is unfortunately far easier to describe than to explain.

Was it the republican character of the Third Republic's educational crusade at the end of the nineteenth century which accounted for the rising percentage of *normaliens* from the Lower Class? Representation of the Lower Class in the Division of Letters rose steadily until the turn of the century. In the Division of Sciences it was even higher, but in both cases the twentieth century brought a decline rather than a further democratization of Normale's recruitment. As France became more urban and despite the rise in literacy and the implementation of compulsory elementary education, at the Ecole Normale the predominantly rural Lower Class was less able to compete with urban social groups. It is possible that the Lower Class scholarship holders who previously had turned up at Normale went instead to the "New Sorbonne," but we have no data to support this.

The Middle Class made about a ten per cent gain in representation at the Ecole in the twentieth century in each Division, but it was not due to its more modest members, the artisans and shopkeepers, who, like the Lower Class, suffered a decline.[21] The expansion of the Middle Class at Normale represented the urbanization and numerical growth of petty officials, white collar personnel, and primary teachers. *Instituteurs*, who were about as rural as the population as a whole, were not left in the country as the nation moved to cities: they moved to urban primary schools and an urban environment, thus improving their chances of access to the Ecole Normale. The petty bureaucratic and white collar class represented at the Ecole were from the beginning of the Republic almost as urban in origin as the professors and the rest of the Upper Class, and hence they were exposed to cosmopolitan culture and to the *lycées* preparing for the rue d'Ulm. Urbanization swelled the fraction of this class which could compete successfully with groups in the Upper Class for admission to the Ecole (although it is doubtful that their increase at Normale was sharper than it was in the entire population or in urban areas). Sons of the professors were not helped in their access to the rue d'Ulm by the rise in the urban population since they themselves were already city dwellers; urbanization helped newly arrived urban groups at their expense. Perhaps a sign of this fact was that after the First World War the professors were better represented in Sciences—the Division of lower prestige—than in Letters, where their percentage dropped precipitously. But another factor, which we have not been able to weigh, was the manner in which science was perceived by professors and other professional groups from decade to decade. Gradually, in the twentieth century in any case, literary studies ceased to be the one true path to glory that it was earlier.

The representation of the Upper Class in the Division of Letters declined by ten per cent during the Third Republic. In Sciences likewise there was a gradual decline from the 1870s through the 1900s, but thereafter an increase in liberal professions and secondary and higher education partially compensated for dwindling percentages in other categories of the Upper Class. One reason that the 1900s was the nadir for representation of the Upper Class may have been the Reform of 1904, which was widely regarded as a measure which would undermine the Ecole's claim to elite status. The reform eliminated the special separate faculty, the students henceforth would take all of their courses with other students at the Sorbonne, and the few special classes at the Ecole, which were to be open to certain non-

normaliens as well, stressed what many considered to be the rather humble arts of school–mastering.[22]

To sum up, the Ecole Normale became slightly more representative of the nation over the course of the Third Republic in a special way. The urban Middle Class made gains chiefly at the expense of the Lower Class and secondarily at the expense of the Upper Class. Although the Upper Class retreated slightly in the twentieth century, it is not clear whether this was due to increased competition from elements of the Middle Class or whether greater numbers of bourgeois simply sought to avoid the teaching profession as they had in the past in favor of "nobler" pursuits. Urbanization swelled the Middle Class, but it also presented new opportunities for the Upper Class. As increasing numbers of urban white collar families were able to entertain thoughts of the rue d'Ulm for a bright son, Upper Class families continued to regard Normale equivocally. They saw equal or better opportunities at the Ecole Polytechnique or the Ecole Libre des Sciences Politiques, and in business, the professions, and the higher government bureaucracies. For them despite Normale's growing fame as the alma mater of politicians and statesmen, it retained some of the ancient stigma associated with the teaching profession. Normale suited the social ambitions of the Middle Class and the Lower Class far better.

Other evidence in addition to geographic and social data helps to describe and explain the *normaliens'* origins. As the potential *normalien* grew up, a fact as important as his family's social rank was its size and his own rank among the siblings. Although our evidence comes exclusively from the *promotions* of 1905–1941, probably our conclusions would apply to earlier *promotions* as well. The pattern shows small

TABLE 7. Family Size and Age Rank: *Promotions* of 1905–1941 (Per Cent)

	One/ Eldest	Two/ Second	Three/ Third	Four/ Fourth	Five or More/ Fifth or Lower
Division of Letters					
Number of Children	23	35	22	12	8
Normaliens' Expected Age Ranks	52	29	12	5	2
Normaliens' Actual Age Ranks	63	23	9	3	2
Division of Sciences					
Number of Children	25	35	21	8	10
Normaliens' Expected Age Ranks	54	29	11	4	2
Normaliens' Actual Age Ranks	62	27	7	2	3

Letters: Family Size N = 994; Age Rank N = 983
Sciences: Family Size N = 634; Age Rank N = 624

TABLE 8. Number of Children in *Normaliens'* Families According to Profession of Father: *Promotions* of 1905–1941 (Per Cent)

Division of Letters = L; Division of Sciences = S

Profession of Father	One		Two		Three		Four		Five or More		N=	
	L	S	L	S	L	S	L	S	L	S	L	S
Owners of Capital, Businessmen	19	25	28	29	26	14	12	14	16	18	69	28
Higher Officials	12	19	35	33	28	23	15	13	11	13	110	48
Liberal Professions	17	15	41	38	22	27	14	4	5	15	63	26
Commissioned Officers	17	23	34	23	24	29	24	23	15	3	41	31
Secondary and University Professors and Officials	21	21	29	36	19	19	19	13	12	11	170	110
Primary and Technical Teachers and Administrators	26	22	41	35	21	25	7	8	6	10	106	60
Middle, Lower Officials and White Collar	29	27	39	37	21	19	7	7	5	9	209	139
Artisans, Shopkeepers, and Tradesmen	15	27	42	19	24	35	15	15	3	4	33	26
Police and Non-commissioned Officers	33	38	17	50	33	0	17	0	0	13	6	8
Skilled Labor	52	32	32	45	12	16	4	5	0	3	25	38
Unskilled Labor	40	20	30	20	30	20	0	10	0	30	10	10
Farmers	21	24	29	41	14	18	14	0	21	18	14	17

family size and eldest or next to eldest rank for the *normalien* (See Table 7). The few larger families and cases of lower age rank were more common among the wealthy than among the more modest groups, for whom a large family would practically eliminate chances for savings and sacrifices for the education of one child (See Tables 8, 9).[23] The high frequency of the *normalien's* being the eldest (over 60 per cent) is all the more remarkable when we consider that the Ecole, despite the admission of a few women in the interwar years, was essentially a male institution: our data did not exclude female children. Thus the *normalien* was most typically the eldest male sibling in a family of one, two, or three children. The family made its sacrifices for him first, as if it were carrying out ancient traditions of inheritance. The young heir bore a heavy burden. As Director Gustave Lanson noted in 1926, ". . . recruitment [was] assured principally by that lower bourgeoisie which . . . bled itself to educate the only son. . . ."[24]

TABLE 9. Age Ranks of the *Normaliens* Among Their Siblings According to Profession of Father: *Promotions* of 1905–1941 (Per Cent)

Division of Letters = L; Division of Sciences = S

Profession of Father	Eldest L	Eldest S	Second L	Second S	Third L	Third S	Fourth L	Fourth S	Fifth or Lower L	Fifth or Lower S	N= L	N= S
Owners of Capital, Businessmen	55	70	30	15	9	4	3	7	3	4	67	27
Higher Officials	57	51	23	36	12	9	5	4	3	0	108	45
Liberal Professions	64	48	26	36	7	8	3	0	0	8	61	25
Commissioned Officers	60	59	32	31	5	3	0	7	3	0	40	29
Secondary and University Professors and Officials	60	62	25	32	9	5	5	1	1	0	169	104
Primary and Technical Teachers and Administrators	64	61	24	23	9	14	1	0	3	2	105	57
Middle, Lower Officials and White Collar	73	61	18	27	7	6	1	2	1	3	207	128
Artisans, Shopkeepers, and Tradesmen	64	58	24	21	9	17	3	4	0	0	33	24
Police and Non-commissioned Officers	50	62	33	25	17	0	0	0	0	13	6	8
Skilled Labor	84	58	8	42	4	0	4	0	0	0	25	38
Unskilled Labor	50	40	50	20	0	20	0	0	0	20	4	10
Farmers	64	87	7	13	7	0	14	0	7	0	14	15

If the father or another relative had been a *normalien,* then the pressure upon the candidate to succeed had still another dimension. Evidence from the paternal side of families indicates that 4.8 per cent of the *normaliens* were preceded at the rue d'Ulm by a relative, usually the father (3.7 per cent). Although this percentage appears small, in fact it indicates that the likelihood that a *normalien* would be followed at the Ecole Normale by a descendant was about 430 times greater than for a non–*normalien.* Search in the *normaliens'* maternal ancestry would certainly have increased these percentages. For instance, M____ (prom. 1900s) was the father–in–law of S____ (prom. 1930s) and the grandfather of S____ (prom. 1950s). And predecessors of C____ (prom. 1870s) included an uncle, a great uncle, a grandfather, and a cousin, all on the maternal side of the family. These examples suggest dynasties: that of the Debidours, perhaps the most impressive, was unbroken from the Second Empire to the Fifth Republic, consisting of: E. (prom. 1866), L. (prom. 1895), his brother Elie (prom. 1908), Antonin (prom. 1921), Victor–Henri (prom. 1929), and Michel (prom. 1966)—all of the Division of Letters. Further, two Debidour women married *normaliens:* René Lugand (prom. 1921) and Etienne Rey (prom. 1901).[25] Although highly competitive examinations sifted the candidates each year according to their merit, the traditions of certain families imparted great urgency to the success of their sons. How many such sons were driven during their studies in *cagne* or *taupe* as much by the fear of failing the family as by personal ambition?

Inevitably the social categories which we have used in this inquiry have concealed important details of individual family histories. There was at least one *instituteur,* for instance, who was from the old ruined aristocracy. Other *normaliens* (relatively few) were from aristocratic families, but their fathers' professions did not reveal this fact. Some fathers had only recently achieved prominent places in government administration or one of the liberal professions after long struggles in modest circumstances, while others carried on a long family tradition. The category of "skilled worker" in our study does less than full justice to the culture of the family. The high incidence in this study of trades such as locksmith, watchmaker, and cabinetmaker suggests traditions of respect for learning and education among artisans and the working class. The family's cultural history as well as its contemporary social status bore upon the mentality of its members.

Religion and politics were also important in shaping and narrowing the field of candidates. After the Revolution of 1848 many bourgeois rallied to the Catholic Church and its schools, which competed well with public schools until the twentieth century. In practice the approximately equal division of secondary students in France between Church and public schools meant that half of Normale's potential candidates were excluded, for those who came directly from Catholic institutions were statistically insignificant.[26] Of course the preparation of a candidate for Normale was highly specialized and monopolized by the state's *lycèes,* but we note further that students who had attended a Catholic school immediately before the *cagne* or *taupe* classes given in the *lycées* were exceedingly rare.[27] Typically the *normalien* attended a Catholic primary school, but switched to the state's institutions for his secondary education. Proper schooling for the young scholar was often cause for a cultural and political debate within the family. Raoul Blanchard (prom. 1897) was the son of an inspector of lighting and waterworks in Orléans, and all of his family and ancestors were of the working class or petty bourgeoisie. Although for economic and political reasons his father preferred that he attend a public school, his mother had her way first, and at the age of three he began his education at a private school directed by the Sisters of Wisdom. When it was time to choose a new school his father prevailed:

> My father's mind had been set for a long time; the public primary school cost nothing except for a few school supplies, and that pleased him very much; on the other hand it satisfied his republican taste, for my father was sincerely for the Republic, which in 1884 still meant something.[28]

This pattern recurs in the biographies of deceased *normaliens* which appear in the alumni association's yearbooks: early lessons at the hands of religious orders and then "serious" studies in the public schools. Support for the Republic and for the public school system went together. The biographical notices covering *promotions* of the early Third Republic have a particularly republican flavor. The *normalien's* father is often described as a "republican under the Empire," a "republican in the tradition of 1848," or a "republican and a Gambettist." Such rhetoric, however, should not lead us to conclude that during the Second Empire any more than a small minority of *normaliens* actually professed republican sympathies.[29]

Religion was another factor which seemed to influence the pool of candidates. We know the declared religion of 17 per cent of the *normaliens* of the 1870s through the 1890s, and of this group 9.9 per cent were Protestant and 9.2 per cent were Jewish. This compares with national figures of about 3 and 1 percent respectively. Interviews with alumni confirm that for the *promotions* of the twentieth century as well, the proportions of Jews and Protestants were relatively high. The reasons for the strength of these groups at Normale were no doubt their high average cultural level, their own strong traditions in the University, and the suspicion and hostility of many devout Catholics toward a University identified with anti–clericalism.

We have seen that the *normaliens* came from higher social strata on the average than the myth of the Ecole admits. During the First World War Ernest Lavisse mourned the loss of so many *normaliens* at the front—almost half of the students of the immediately pre–war classes had been killed in the conflict—and he dramatized their loss by stressing their humble origins: "But that is only a number," he said, "it says nothing of the value of the dead; we know ourselves, by what sacrifices the poor parents—nearly all . . . were born of poor parents—have introduced their children to the high intellectual life."[30] In fact few of the *normaliens* were from truly poor families. In the vast majority of cases their fathers enjoyed job security as *fonctionnaires,* a good education, and at least a moderate income. Later Gustave Lanson gave a considerably more accurate description of recruitment:

> The Ecole Normale . . . is perhaps and has always been, the most plebian *(populaire),* the most democratic of the *grandes écoles.* Nowhere, I believe, has the proportion of young men from the laboring classes of the nation compared with the total number of students been higher. Assuredly from time to time sons of high officials or surgeons of the hospitals, of lawyers, of financiers, of industrialists [are admitted]. But the recruitment is assuredly principally by that lower bourgeoisie which has bled itself to instruct the only son: ordinary town or country doctors, petty officials, modest men of the law, employees of all kinds, retailers and artisans of all categories; Duruy was the son of a worker at the Gobelins; Pasteur was the son of a tanner of a small town. The sons of professors have always been very numerous, but above all sons of primary teachers.[31]

The mere presence of workingmen's sons in that rarefied atmosphere led other-wise sincere republicans to exaggerate their importance. Although the Ecole had a higher percentage of them than did the other *grandes écoles,* that percentage was quite small. And it was the sons of professors and not primary teachers who were "numerous . . . above all."

The careers of the *normaliens,* predictably, were not so diverse as their origins: three fourths of the alumni during the Third Republic devoted most of their lives to teaching or educational administration, and another five per cent accepted other related government posts.[32] A decline in this percentage over the course of the Third Republic, the Division of Letters falling from 89 to 74 per cent and the Division of Sciences from 98 to 85 per cent (Table 10), coincided with an increasing preference for careers in higher rather than secondary education. As the *lycées* and universities expanded in the twentieth century, the proportion of *normaliens* in these institutions declined. Yet at the same time they moved higher in the ranks. Their scarcity in education seemed objectively to enhance their position. The trend is comparatively gradual in the case of the *littéraires,* traditionally the lords of the university, whereas it is abrupt in the case of the

TABLE 10. Careers Predominantly in Education: *Promotions* of 1868–1941 (Per Cent)

Division of Letters = L; Division of Sciences = S

	1868–79		1880–89		1890–99		1900–09		1910–19		1920–29		1930–41	
	L	S	L	S	L	S	L	S	L	S	L	S	L	S
Secondary Teaching	39	58	47	54	39	58	47	55	27	54	35	40	26	32
University Teaching	34	23	30	30	32	26	29	25	34	24	36	37	42	47
Secondary Administration	12	13	6	6	8	7	5	7	13	9	11	9	5	5
University Administration	4	4	1	3	3	2	1	1	2	2	3	1	1	1
Educational Careers, Total:	89	98	84	93	82	93	82	89	76	89	85	87	74	85
N =	212	156	217	170	215	150	244	151	211	116	256	178	301	211

scientifiques, as the re–evaluation of pure science in the nation, the expansion of laboratories in the universities, and the increase in scientific posts in the 1930s and in the post–war period gave them opportunities to advance.

Until the rapid increase in opportunities for pure research from the 1930s, the scientists of the rue d'Ulm had far fewer opportunities outside of the teaching field than did their counterparts in Letters (Table 11). Jobs in engineering and research in business were traditionally filled by graduates of other scientific *grandes écoles,* such as the Ecole Polytechnique, the Ecole Centrale, or the Ecole des Mines. Faced with severe competition, the scientists from Normale remained in the *lycées* and Faculties. They could not count upon an informal alumni network to place them in attractive jobs outside the University, jobs which were taken usually by the graduates of Polytechnique.

The demand for literary *normaliens* outside the University, however, had long been more brisk. Normale–Letters was preeminent in its field and more prestigious than the Sorbonne. Although the Ecole Libre des Science Politiques was highly successful in placing its graduates in government posts,[33] it became increasingly common from the late nineteenth century for *normaliens* to take courses at the Ecole Libre if they wished to compete for those government posts. They could be found in particular serving the League of Nations,

TABLE 11. Careers Predominantly Outside of Education: *Promotions* of 1868–1941 (Per Cent)

	1868–79	1880–89	1890–99	1900–09	1910–19	1920–29	1930–41
Division of Letters							
Literature and Journalism	2.8	5.5	6.9	4.5	5.6	3.5	3.3
Politics	2.2	2.3	3.1	3.2	2.3	1.5	1.9
Government Administration	0.9	1.3	1.3	0.8	2.8	1.9	2.6
Cultural or Diplomatic Posts	0.0	0.0	0.9	3.2	2.7	3.7	7.4
Business	0.4	0.4	0.4	1.6	3.3	0.7	0.9
Other	4.4	6.4	5.4	4.2	7.2	0.8	9.9
Total	10.7	15.9	18.0	17.8	23.9	15.4	26.0
N =	212	217	215	244	211	256	301
Division of Sciences							
Research	1.2	3.3	1.9	4.5	3.3	6.6	9.8
Politics	0.0	2.3	0.6	0.6	2.5	0.5	0.0
Business	0.0	0.0	2.0	1.9	0.8	2.2	0.9
Other	0.9	1.7	2.9	4.5	4.9	3.3	4.2
Total	2.1	7.3	7.4	11.5	11.5	12.6	14.9
N =	156	170	150	151	116	178	211

various diplomatic missions, and the United Nations. One alumnus observed that in the twentieth century the cultural counsellorships associated with French embassies became practically their exclusive preserve.[34] What better diplomatic candidates could one imagine in the post–aristocratic age than these exemplars of classical humanism? Moreover the accession to political power of Herriot and a host of other *normaliens* facilitated their entry into government jobs. Stiffening competition for important positions in education also caused departures for opportunities elsewhere.

Social origins, despite a common experience at the rue d'Ulm, had a bearing upon which *normaliens* were likely to seize opportunities outside the field of education. We have already noticed differences in geographical and social origins between scientific and literary *normaliens,* the latter being more urban and upper class. This undoubtedly was *one* factor which caused some literary *normaliens* to leave careers in education. Two facts support this explanation. Families of higher status than "professor" (Table 4) had declining rather than ascending

TABLE 12. Profession of Normalien (Letters and Sciences) According to Profession of Father: *Promotions* of 1868–1941 (Per Cent)

	Profession of Normalien				
Profession of Father	Education	Government	Liberal Profession	Other	N =
Owners of Capital, Businessmen	80	11	7	2	243
Higher Officials	72	15	11	2	152
Liberal Professions	70	12	14	4	284
Commissioned Officers	75	12	9	4	85
Secondary and University Professors and Officials	83	10	5	2	457
Primary and Technical Teachers and Administrators	81	14	4	1	206
Middle, Lower Officials and White Collar	84	10	4	2	492
Artisans, Shopkeepers, and Tradesmen	85	11	4	0	123
Police and Non-commissioned Officers	91	9	0	0	22
Skilled Labor	82	10	8	0	101
Unskilled Labor	92	8	0	0	12
Farmers	85	7	7	1	107

ratios of representation at the Ecole: these families had, in a sense already started to "avoid" educational careers for their off-spring by the fact that they were represented at the Ecole in inverse proportion to their status. The second fact, which reinforces the meaning of the first, is that the sons of higher status families (above "professor") deserted education as a career in greater numbers (Table 12). Considering both literary and scientific *normaliens* for the classes of the entire Third Republic, we note that sons of professors, primary school teachers, and other categories lower on the socio–professional scale (Table 4) were all over 80 per cent in remaining in educational careers. In the case of the higher social categories—generals, commissioned officers, liberal professions, higher bureaucrats, owners of capital—the rate of continuance in education was uniformly below 80 per cent. Liberal professions ranked lowest at 70.0 per cent and landowner–capitalist ranked highest at 79.8 per cent. This last category, however, is misleading for we have probably not been very successful in discerning which *propriétaire* was wealthy and which was actually a small farmer. It turns out that 92.5 per cent of the rural *propriétaires'* sons remained in education whereas for the sons of the Parisian *propriétaires* the figure was 68.7 per cent. A similar pattern is exhibited for the next two highest social categories. Sons of 68.2 per cent (N = 63) of the Parisian higher bureaucrats remained in teaching, whereas the figure for the small town was 75.0 per cent (N = 16, inevitably small since higher bureaucrats were instrinsically urban). In the case of the liberal professions, sons of 64.4 per cent of the Parisians (N = 121) remained in education, as against 76.3 per cent (N = 55) of rural origin.

We have already seen that Fustel de Coulanges had a certain conception of the ideal candidate for the Ecole—humble origins would guarantee hard work and loyalty to the teaching profession.[35] Later Perrot, Lavisse, and Lanson repeated that the Ecole was democratic, for it recruited its students in Perrot's words, from "deep beds of worker democracy." Lying behind this model of the ideal *normalien* were the exigencies of democratic rhetoric in the Republic, but also the assumption, based upon experience, that the teaching profession did not confer the status which would attract and hold the sons of Upper-middle and Upper Classes. Despite the efforts of republicans like Lavisse to bestow upon the teacher a mystique, to make of him a lay priest of the nation, in fact the Upper Classes continued to prefer more "glorious" pursuits. André Francois–Poncet and René Massigli, both of the promotion of 1907, are prominent examples of *normaliens* who went on to brilliant careers outside of the University.[36] Both became distinguished diplomats and statesmen; both came from upper class Parisian families connected with the law.

A congeries of factors within the field of education also influenced both the choice and the patterns of careers. Throughout the nineteenth century and even in the twentieth the Ecole Normale occupied a privileged position in French education. By its rigorous *concours* it skimmed off many of the nation's best students. There was no doubt that the high quality of its students gave it an initial advantage in producing graduates who would excel in their careers. Another advantage was the three years at the Ecole itself, when the student, relieved of financial worries, was at liberty to study for the *licence* and the *agrégation* in the very best of circumstances in terms of instruction, comrades engaged in a similar enterprise, and resources such as the library and laboratories. The *normalien* then passed the *agrégation* at an early age, at twenty–three or twenty–four. At the beginning of the Republic, the non–*normaliens* who passed the *agrégation* were older by about six or seven years, but as scholarships became more plentiful, this age differential decreased to one or two years by 1945. Early passage of the *agrégation* for the *normalien* gave him a better chance to advance further in the University than his non–*normalien* competitor.[37] As this advantage diminished, careers outside the University became more attractive.

The phenomenon of the Ecole Normale existed within a far larger relevant social as well as cultural field. Social origins and career choices, for which we have offered largely hypothetical explanations, were partly functions of competition for entry into all of the *grandes écoles* and competition for related employment and careers. Although our description of social origins and career choices is warranted by empirical evidence, our explanations for these patterns are tentative, for they depend upon incomplete knowledge of a wider field which is only partly explored.

It is clear in any case that we should not accept at face value the refrain that Normale recruited from "deep beds of worker democracy." The Middle and Upper Classes, as we have defined them, were steeped in classical culture and were richer sources of students. On the other hand, compared with the Ecole Polytechnique, the Ecole Libre, and probably most other *grandes écoles,* the Ecole Normale appeared indeed to be a democratic institution. Perceptions of contemporaries concerning the *normaliens'* origins went largely unchallenged. Sociologically they bore a sufficient resemblance to their myth that they were credible to themselves and others as they worked to forge the democratic ideology of the Third Republic. Yet in addition to their social origins, it was the character of their intellectual tradition which made it possible for them to play a broad and unaccustomed national role.

4

The Intellectual Tradition: Continuity and Change

> Le principe de l'Ecole, son dogme, c'est la nécessité d'une forte culture classique . . .–Georges Perrot

THE military disaster of 1870 called into question far more than the army. The French were inferior to the Germans in geography and linguistics as well as artillery. An aphorism credited victory to the German schoolmaster and the primary school curriculum, but Ernest Renan had already observed in 1868 that the Prussian success at Sadowa was due rather to university professors and German science at the highest level.[1] In the *Revue des Deux–Mondes* Gaston Boissier (prom. 1843) concurred with Renan that the French should reform their system of higher education and noted in passing that the Ecole Normale was already preparing learned professors. Boissier added, however, that the *normaliens* were not above reproach, for they " . . . had not always held the rank in philology and erudition that they occupy in letters, and that they have remained outside that scientific movement of which Germany is the center."[2] In a century preoccupied with scientific discovery and analysis the French and the Ecole Normale were criticized for preferring graceful form over substance, aesthetic values over practical ones, and classical over modern subjects. It was the challenge of German research that prompted Minister of Education Victor Duruy (prom. 1830) to set up the Ecole Pratique des Hautes Etudes in 1868 to support advanced research.[3] Yet, however much German competition worried some French academics during the Second Empire it did not spur the government to reexamine higher education as a whole. Only after 1870 did there begin in earnest a broad cultural debate concerning the extent to which the French should emulate their neighbors from across the Rhine.[4] As national survival became associated with education, *normaliens* were drawn to the center of the discussion. In the Third Republic, finally, their specialty became central to the national purpose.

Jules Simon (prom. 1833), Minister of Education from 1871 to 1873, assembled a group of alumni of the Ecole Normale "who met in [his] office every Saturday, and who, without official title, out of friendship for the Minister, and above all out of attachment to solid studies, worked with [Simon] on all the reforms [he] tried or which [he] was projecting."[5] The Saturday group included the politician Alfred Mézières (prom. 1845), the philosopher Paul Janet (prom. 1841), the linguist and professor at the Collège de France, Michel Bréal (prom. 1852), and Ernest Bersot (prom. 1836), a personal friend of Adolphe Thiers. Like many other liberal professors, Bersot had left the University rather than swear allegiance to Napoleon III. But under the Republic, this man of letters became Director of the Ecole Normale, a post which brought him into close contact with members of the political establishment.

Although Bersot had a reputation as a liberal and a free–thinker, in some respects he was culturally conservative. He was not so eager as others in the Saturday group to have the French University imitate German models. Among Jules Simon's brain trust of *normaliens* it was Michel Bréal who led the attack on the unscientific literary tradition which was enshrined in the French University and at the Ecole Normale.[6] He considered hypocritical the argument that Latin helped students to understand their own language, for in fact students studied little outside the Latin of Cicero and the French of the seventeenth century. The centuries of barbarism which led progressively from Latin to French were ignored lest students be charmed by barbarisms. Bréal contended that students long bored by the classics, which were taught as eternal and perfect models, would be fascinated to learn how their language actually evolved. Their curiosity would awaken, and they would be eager to make their own discoveries. Education at every level should emphasize understanding rather than memory work. The current French backwardness was due, moreover, to the influence of the Ecole Normale itself. "While in other countries a scientific movement without equal was transforming the study of antiquity, establishing textual criticism, renewing historical methods and philology, the maxim which prevailed at the Ecole Normale was that it was necessary to learn to think and write well and to avoid vain curiosities."[7] The result of this stultifying formalism at the highest level of the University was that enthusiasm for discovery was stifled throughout the educational system, and therefore France had fallen behind Germany and the rest of Europe in scientific progress.

Bersot's support of more traditional classical studies was challenged immediately by a student who responded as follows to his opening address:

> We do not wish to claim that the purpose of our activity is simply the repetition of what we did in the *collège,* confining our horizon to the prescribed tests punctually taken, wise compositions written according to the formula. We set our ideal higher. Still quivering from the great national disaster, we intend to work for the intellectual revenge, the precondition of political revenge. For that we have resolved to break with the old formalism to which our traditional education is too much associated. We would defeat Germany in learning from her, here as elsewhere, to surpass her. To write up discreet elegancies is no longer education. Germany arrogates to herself the empire of science; we will dispute it with her. Her thought is strong; we have faith in our thought.[8]

Bucking the tide, Bersot lamented that critics found the Ecole Normale to be "... too preoccupied with good taste, to speak and write well ... They propose to us, then as a remedy for our faults, the exclusive diet of erudition and philology ... The Ecole Normale is not the Ecole des Chartes."[9] Beloved by the *normaliens* for his personal qualities, Bersot the philosopher and wise essayist took his own inspiration from the French literary tradition, which stressed personal reflection.[10] His fears that the *normaliens* might become simply scientific pedants were not entirely justified, for philosophy at least was to remain a haven for personal reflection upon general ideas.

After Bersot's death in 1880 Jules Ferry chose the historian Fustel de Coulanges to replace him as Normale's Director.[11] Fustel was less of a politician than Bersot, but certain premises of his scholarly work had political implications. Instead of tracing all virtue to primitive German forests, Fustel saw French history from a French perspective as the story of Gauls reacting to challenges generation after generation.[12] He was a social conservative who admired aristocracy, whether in Germany or France, and who refused to enlist history in the service of an increasingly fashionable liberal idealism. His elitism applied to the Ecole Normale as well as to the nation, for he wished the Ecole to staff the Faculties rather than the *lycées* and to remain small in order to preserve its high quality. He compared the small classes in literature, philosophy, history, or mathematics with the famed German seminars in which discussion and criticism yielded new discoveries.[13] Alumni would serve best in the Faculties, where they would instruct *lycée* teachers, who would go forth with true knowledge and rejuvenate the nation. "In our conferences," he observed, "the students speak; they discuss; we wish that they always be active. In the sections of Letters they do their lessons in turn; in the sections of Sciences, they do lessons and experiments. It is rather evident that the greater the number of students, the more seldom each student will do the lesson or the experiment."[14]

Fustel was an elitist in another sense as well. Like Bersot and like his successor, Georges Perrot, he favored the classics as the core of general education.[15] He insisted that the *normaliens* take the old *licence* in letters (which stressed the classics) rather than any of the other options, and that they should all pursue the same studies in their first year. Although he was a skillful historian and philologist who appreciated the advances made by specialized research, he believed that solid classical studies remained essential for students in letters. Broad learning, he hoped, would check the intellectual arrogance of the narrow specialist, while depth in certain areas would impose limits upon the romantic and unscientific litterateur.

When Fustel gave up his post at Normale in 1883 to return to historical research, Jules Ferry appointed in his place a man who was similarly committed to the classics, to scientific research, and to the notion that the *normaliens* should comprise a small elite. Georges Perrot (prom. 1852) became Normale's Director for the next twenty years, but was not the persistent or dominant intellectual force that his two predecessors had been.[16] He left much of the day to day operation of the school in the hands of his subordinates, and his personal contacts with the students were not frequent. Yet his tolerance contributed to a liberal atmosphere during his regime, as Charles Andler recalled:

> He was linked by family alliances with the most well known republican aristocracy. He had been persecuted as a republican at the beginning of the Empire. He well understood that each generation had its political dream. The generation before 1870 had its dream of the republic. Without approving of us, he did not find it strange that some of us had as our ideal the social republic. His solid good sense was not shaken by our utopia.[17]

Perrot's own republican views are evident in his statement that the Ecole's " . . . fortune was always tied to that of the liberal party and of the cause which it defended."[18] He noted that under the Second Empire the Ecole Normale was one of the last places where liberalism and the critical spirit flourished and that the *normaliens* had cooperated with and served the Republic from its inception. Writing in this spirit in 1895 on the occasion of the Ecole's centennial celebration, Perrot maintained further that, "Democracy needs an elite which is made up of the only superiority which it recognizes, that of the mind. It is for us to recruit that elite, or to speak more modestly, to work at furnishing some of the elements which will make it up."[19] Two decades earlier Emile Boutmy had founded the Ecole Libre in part to defend the political power of a privileged class menaced by democracy.[20] Now Perrot presided over a public institution after the Republic was well established, and so he justified its elite character by pointing to the diversity of its recruitment. As we have seen, this claim was relatively well founded. Yet the classical studies which Perrot insisted should be the core of the curriculum limited any further broadening of Normale's recruitment.[21] Thus, consciously or not, the liberal republican paid his dues to aristocracy in cultural coin.

The teaching faculty even more than the Directors created the intellectual climate at the Ecole Normale, and this seemed especially to be the case during Perrot's directorship from 1883 to 1903. During this period the masters of history, philosophy, and literature largely defined the range and character of intellectual life at the rue d'Ulm. Although one of the leading issues of the period was whether and how to make humanistic scholarship scientific, the pure scientists themselves did their own work in the background without speculating in public about its larger meaning. The professor as prophet, moralist, or political statesman was almost inevitably a teacher of the humanities.

The historians were particularly visible in this role in the late nineteenth century. As they worked to change the methods and broaden the scope of their discipline, they insisted that it was central to the renewal of the nation. Ernest Lavisse (prom. 1862) taught history at Normale only from 1876 to 1880 before taking a post at Sorbonne, but for over thirty years he had a wide influence which was apparent to the community at the rue d'Ulm. In a letter to Bersot in 1879 he asserted the importance to the nation of higher education and history:

> I am mistaken, perhaps, in placing all my hopes in higher education . . . In spite of myself I have always looked to higher education . . . True history can only be discovered in higher education, from whence it will pass on to primary and secondary school. The teaching of history, well done, would introduce calm and reason into our minds, which are ready to become excited; it would teach us not to be limited by our admiration or hatred of the past, not to have sacred dates, to find Charlemagne good for his time and the regime we have good for ours. There is not an elementary book in Germany where the idea of continuous development is not found, an idea which we have so much trouble understanding.[22]

Lavisse assumed that truth in culture or politics depended upon historical circumstances. Through his history textbooks for the primary schools he sought to lay the foundation for republican citizenship, for loyalty to the Republic as well as to the nation.[23] The Ferry laws of 1880–1882, which made primary education obligatory, free, and laical, posed many questions. Perhaps foremost among them was whether a child could attend one of the government schools and come out of the experience a good Catholic. In an atmosphere of apprehension Lavisse's little texts on French history were marvels of conciliation, for they avoided political quarrels and concentrated upon the greatness of the *patrie* and the duties of the citizen to defend and cherish it. Lavisse refrained from judging whether the crusades were good or bad in themselves, or whether the Albigensians were righteously or barbarously slaughtered by agents of the Inquisition. Some political judgment, nevertheless, could not be avoided. Thus in successive editions of one text Louis XVI becomes culpable of conspiring with a foreign power and meets a just end. Robespierre is the architect of brutality, Danton a patriot who roused the people to defend France against the invader. Throughout Lavisse's manuals partisan politics is subordinate to national integrity. As far as abstract political principles were concerned, Lavisse was a relativist. He sought to show how different political forms were appropriate to their times. There were good kings and bad, but now France lived under a beneficent republic.

Lavisse's adherence to a national rather than a political ideology grew out of his own experiences. While he was a student at the Ecole Normale during the Liberal Empire, he was not interested in politics. But soon after leaving Normale he became the *chef de cabinet* for Victor Duruy, the Minister of Education, and then upon Duruy's recommendation he became the preceptor of the Prince Imperial. Hardly a republican under the Empire (in contrast to so many other *normaliens*), only in 1878 did he begin to turn to republicanism. After the elections of 1879 Lavisse the political loyalist saw that history had wrought change, and he shifted his own political allegiance. But he remained more of a nationalist than a partisan politician, for neither during the Boulanger Affair nor the Dreyfus Affair did he openly take a stand.

During a three year sojourn in Germany immediately following the Franco–Prussian War Lavisse wrote a doctoral thesis on the origins of the Prussian monarchy. His real purpose, however, was to understand the defeat of France by exploring the reasons for the rise of Prussia. His subsequent historical writing was of a more general nature and intended to burnish the image of the French nation rather than to probe the frontiers of historical knowledge. He remained a spokesman for educational reform to fortify France against future challenges from across the Rhine. At the turn of the century he supported university expansion and reform and argued for modern studies against classicists like Perrot.[24] His influence in government, the university, and education in general was pervasive.

When Lavisse was called from Normale to the Sorbonne in 1880, Director Fustel de Coulanges asked Gabriel Monod to replace him. Monod (prom. 1862) had already made a name for himself as a professor in the new critical tradition at the Ecole Pratique des Hautes Etudes and as the founder and editor of the *Revue historique*.[25] Like Lavisse, Monod was a republican, but his background and outlook were different. Monod had studied in Germany before rather than after the Franco–Prussian war, and he had returned to France an admirer of German scholarship and culture. Furthermore he was instinctively cosmopolitan rather than nationalistic, and this was consistent with a liberal idealist philosophy which is implicit in his correspondence. It was not surprising, given his principles, that in 1897 he became the first of the academic intellectuals publicly to call for the revision of the Dreyfus case.[26] However, during the two decades that Monod taught at Normale his contribution to the intellectual climate there was more scholarly than political.

Two other professors renowned for the high quality of their scholarship and teaching were Gustave Bloch (prom. 1868), the historian of ancient Rome, and Paul Vidal de la Blache (prom. 1863), the geographer. Bloch, a republican and a Dreyfusard, was respected particularly by his students as an exacting teacher in the tradition of Fustel de Coulanges.[27] Vidal was a similar case. Vice Rector of Normale's Division of Letters from 1881 to 1898, and the founder of an entire geographical school, Vidal de la Blache was eager for French monographic scholarship to catch up with that of the Germans by replacing the traditional emphasis upon classical humanism with rigorous scientific analysis.[28] But like Fustel he cautioned against premature specialization and insisted that his geography students gain a broader understanding of their subject by studying geology, history, and other allied disciplines. Thus although among the masters of history and geography there were differences of emphasis in research and in political assumptions, there was no one who still considered history essentially a branch of literature. German erudition had made it deepest penetration here.

Philosophy at the rue d'Ulm eventually came to grips with scientific questions without, however, passing through a phase of materialism, positivism, or scientism. No Littré taught at the Ecole Normale. The influence of Victor Cousin, represented by Jules Simon, Caro, Ollé–Laprune, and others, gave way during the Third Republic to that of Kant, whose thought was introduced and developed by Lachelier and Boutroux.[29] Léon Ollé–Laprune (prom. 1858) represented a Catholic variant of spiritualism at the Ecole from 1875 until his death in 1898. Romain Rolland (prom. 1886) described one of his lectures as a Roman Catholic apologia which made the free–thinkers and Jews in the classroom squirm in their seats.[30] It was because of the metaphysical tradition at the Ecole that Rolland avoided philosophy in favor of history, where his masters were Guiraud, Monod, and Vidal de la Blache, men who demanded exact knowledge and the critical appraisal of facts.[31] Edouard Herriot (prom. 1891) suggested that by the 1890's neo-Kantianism was a strong influence among the philosophers despite the presence of Ollé–Laprune:

> . . . M. Ollé–Laprune did nothing to direct us toward German thought. . . . His influence was due less to his teaching, dominated by a religious preoccupation, than to his good will. Quite often, Sunday evenings, he invited us to his apartment on Place Saint Sulpice to have us taste his wine of Jurançon. A long time ago Jules Lachelier ceased to teach at the Ecole, but his influence remained. His metaphysical spiritualism, inspired by Kant, had reacted against the ideas of Cousin. And we continued to read with interest . . . his vigorous thesis on the *Fondement de l'Induction.* A new young star was

> rising, that of Henri Bergson; his *Essai sur les données immédiates de la Conscience* as yet reached only a small elite. On the whole we remained, my comrades and I, Cartesians.[32]

From 1877 to 1887 Emile Boutroux (prom. 1865) introduced *normaliens* to German philosophy in general as he developed the line of Kantian idealism held by his teacher Lachelier (prom. 1851).[33] In an era enthralled by science, Boutroux defined a realm of spirit and of freedom where the laws of necessity did not apply.[34] In somewhat the same spirit, but as an opponent of Kantianism, Henri Bergson (prom. 1878) argued for the priority of mind and intuition over matter and physical events.[35] Although he taught at Normale only from February 1898 to May 1900, *normaliens* were among the crowds which flocked to his lectures at the Collège de France before the First World War.

Among themselves the *normaliens* certainly discussed the prophets of a knowable, causally connected, material world—Saint-Simon, Comte, Darwin, and Spencer—but the official philosophies at the Ecole Normale from Cousin during the July Monarchy to Bergson at the turn of the century all placed great emphasis upon individual freedom, action, and will. The individual was not an epiphenomenon of either Nature or Society, they maintained, but free and responsible. This, of course, had been the core of the liberal faith since the Enlightenment. It justified democratic politics, the importance of ideas (and intellectuals), and the urgency of education.

In the field of French literature there was less consensus among the masters. Ferdinand de la Coulonche (prom. 1847) taught literature from 1867 to 1893, when his students' protests over his dogmatic characterizations of authors and works led to his resignation.[36] Several years before Coulonche left, Ferdinand Brunetière, who was not himself a *normalien,* arrived and immediately brought excitement and distinction to literary studies at the rue d'Ulm.[37] Eloquent, learned, and combative, he preferred the seventeenth century over the eighteenth because he saw in it more of eternal rather than merely passing value. Contrary to the naturalists, who were preoccupied with reflecting their time, Brunetière thought that true art evoked universal human themes that were not bound by their time. For example he considered Zola a vulgar and shallow journalist whose works depicted only a limited series of human experiences. Although he had read Darwin and Comte, he denied that science could solve all human problems or penetrate all mysteries. The scientific mode of thought was valid, he thought, but it contributed little to the understanding of individuals or societies. Religion was a major inspiration of his overall perspective. Despite having grown up a non–practicing Catholic, he was always interested in religious experience, Buddhism and Christianity in particular. As a result of his readings in Pascal and Bossuet and his audience with Pope Leo XIII in 1893, he moved closer to Catholicism and finally joined the Church during the Dreyfus Affair. For Brunetière the Dreyfusards represented modern individualism, which was harmful to social life. The Church represented eternal values and the priority of groups such as the family, the community, or the nation, over the individual. Thus Brunetière offered a theory of politics, religion, and culture which was out of favor with the establishment of the University and the Republic.

On the other hand, Joseph Bédier (prom. 1883) and Gustave Lanson (prom. 1876), who also taught literature at Normale in the 1890s, placed their emphasis upon textual criticism. They were the literary counterparts of Monod and Bloch in history. Bédier had studied at the University of Halle, and in France his mentor was the great philologist Gaston Paris, who had also studied in Germany.[38] A free–thinker, a Dreyfusard, and a friend of Lucien Herr and Jean Jaurès, Bédier was nevertheless not a socialist. Lanson was also a Dreyfusard, but in addition he joined Herr, Charles Andler, Daniel Halévy, and others in collaboration with Jaurès when he founded *Humanité* in 1904.

Most eminent among the classical scholars was Gaston Boissier (prom. 1843), who taught Latin literature at Normale from 1865 to 1898.[39] Boissier was a member of the French Academy and the Collège de France and was, like Bréal, Lavisse, and Monod, a figure of considerable authority and influence in the University. He believed that French classical scholars should emulate the Germans in devoting attention to archaeology and epigraphy, but he himself was more interested in Latin literary texts. Edouard Herriot suggests that Boissier the teacher was even anti–intellectual in his analysis of texts:

> When one asked him for the reasons for an interpretation he would respond: "I have consorted very much with the author of the *Odes*. I know how he thinks. He wanted to say this." And this intuitive critique was worth more than all the peremptory demonstrations of the pedants.[40]

Herriot was evidently much impressed by the charm of this man who put great stock in manners and style which suggested real but inexplicit inner qualities. "Humanity consists above all," Boissier wrote, "in the charm of a spiritual conversation, the finesse of the ideas, the distinction of the manners, a humanity based on knowledge and which ends up in *savoir–vivre*."[41] The very basis of such an ideal for Boissier, Perrot, and most of the older scholars was the classics, which remained the subliminal refuge of an aristocratic sensibility. Politically Bossier was a skeptic who preferred regimes in place to visions of better ones. He joined other conservatives in the French Academy in opposition to revision of the Dreyfus case. By that time, however, younger scholars such as Bédier, Lanson, and Andler far better reflected the intellectual atmosphere at the Ecole.

Charles Andler (prom. 1884) took over the chair of German studies in 1893 from Arthur Chuquet (prom. 1870), who went to the Collège de France.[42] Andler became one of the leading German scholars in France at the end of the nineteenth century and was a staunch champion of modern languages in the secondary school curriculum. His reasons for advocating modern languages in place of the classics were linked to his social and political philosophy. "A farmer who wished to instruct his son, but who intended him to become a farmer like himself, put him into modern education (based upon modern languages)."[43] Latin and Greek seemed to be impractical luxuries which would yield rewards only if the student could afford long years of study, higher degrees, and a professional career. Hence a modern curriculum would be more democratic since from the start it would attract students from all social classes. Andler was both a socialist and a Dreyfusard, a friend and political ally of Normale's famous librarian.

Lucien Herr became a legendary intellectual force at the Ecole Normale in the late nineteenth century although he was neither a director nor a professor.[44] He entered Normale as a student in 1883, became an *agrégé* in philosophy three years later, and then accepted a state scholarship to study in Germany. Although he was an exceptional student, his deepest wish was neither to teach nor to write but rather to become Normale's librarian. The following letter addressed to Georges Perrot suggests the force of his determination and character:

Paris, Wednesday, December 11, 1887

Monsieur le Directeur,

I am, unfortunately, exceptionally timid. You asked me yesterday, with your infinite benevolence, what I desire, what I dream of. My visit had no other object but to tell you, but I did not.

Lucien Herr at his desk
Courtesy of the Bibliotèque, Ecole Normale Supérieure.

You know already. I wrote you of it six months ago. My whole dream, my whole ambition, is the library of the Ecole. When I applied in a letter sent from Germany, I did not receive any answer from you about this question. I did not dare to insist. It was M. Boutroux, whom I told of my ambitions, who encouraged me to speak to you again about it.

It is the only thing that I desire; I have dreamed about it, I have wanted it for years. Please take my request into consideration with all the goodness which you have never ceased to show me. I tell you very naively that you will cause me infinite distress in answering my request with a categorical refusal. If my hope cannot be fulfilled in the very near future, leave it open to me for later. I will wait very patiently.

I have perhaps a few references. M. Rébelliau would be able to tell you that I know the library very well, and that I have used it extensively. Then, since I would not consider this position as temporary, but rather as permanent, at least for many years, I would accept in advance to undertake the long task of bringing the catalogue up to date—a thing which I know to be very necessary. All of my devotion is, or would be, acquired in advance.

Do you require degrees other than those which I possess? If you absolutely wish that my thesis be completed when the vacancy is announced, I accept this condition in advance. Are there other conditions which you would consider necessary? I accept them in advance: I am prepared for anything.

You must sense very well, Monsieur le Directeur, how seriously I desire this post. You would not believe the price which I assign to it. For months and years I have lived in this hope. I ask you, in the name of your benevolence on my behalf, not to put this beyond my reach with only a word. I ask you to take my request into consideration, and to consider my very sincere intentions, which you well know, for serious work.

I commend myself to you with confidence; but you cannot guess my anxiety in waiting for your answer.

Lucien Herr
11, rue du Val–de–Grace[45]

Herr won the post that he so earnestly sought; he was the Ecole Normale's librarian from 1888 until his death in 1926. In addition to being a librarian he was also an intellectual and political mentor. In each of these roles he was formidable.

Usually Herr could be found seated behind his desk in the library, peering over piles of books and journals which he was in the process of reading and classifying. Tall, well built, bearing a full mustache, possessing a strong face with penetrating blue eyes, he was impressive by his force and intelligence.

> Cordial, rough, pleasant, informed, set on sound critical methods, horrified by rhetoric and all its derivatives [such as] art and poetry, socialist, anticlerical, Herr possessed succinct and absolute judgments about people and things. The force of his statements, his very size gave him great authority.[46]

Herr's intellectual influence upon the students was great but not absolute. Raoul Blanchard (prom. 1897) even suggests that his influence—a difficult thing to measure in any case—has been exaggerated:

> Bourgin and Andler have made of Herr in their books the *directeur de conscience* of the *normaliens,* the one who inspired our thoughts and actions. He was nothing of the sort; we made much fun of him, without malice, however, and in particular we joked about his admiration for German science; we liked and respected him, but we did not follow him.[47]

On the other hand Edouard Herriot (prom. 1891) acknowledged Herr's impact upon generations of *normaliens* although he himself did not fall under his spell:

> In my day the librarian was M. Lucien Herr, who exercised a profound influence on numerous generations of *normaliens.* He, it seems to me, assured the transition from Jaurès, whose disciple he claimed to be, to Péguy, to whom he was the first guide. I should say that I completely avoided his influence; I admired his intellectual integrity, but his abruptness shocked my feelings.[48]

Herr tended to alienate students who were more committed to aesthetic values than to critical ones. Students were also either attracted or repelled by his socialist politics or his stern manner, but he remained nevertheless a central figure in the intellectual life of the Ecole while he was its librarian.

This brief description of the ideas of Normale's Directors from 1871 to 1903, of a selection of the more important teachers, and of the librarian Lucien Herr, suggests several conclusions about Normale's intellectual climate during this period. Although German scholarship enjoyed high prestige following the Franco-Prussian War, even those like Monod who admired it were not uncritical imitators. Typically the French pursued erudition not for its own sake but to achieve some broad new synthesis. The legacy of philosophy and *culture générale* in France was particularly profound at the rue d'Ulm.[49] This was the case in part because the purpose of *culture générale* had always been the personal cultivation of an elite. Some professors such as Andler and Lanson attacked the classical basis of *culture générale* as undemocratic. And Lavisse charged that the old classical curriculum which stressed personal refinement was impractical in a modern state; France needed instead men who had a precise knowledge of facts. But men of an older generation such as Boissier and Perrot defended the classics undoubtedly for unstated (and even unconscious) social reasons as well as for cultural or pedagogical ones. Alumni of the rue d'Ulm were to be found on both sides of the quarrel between the "ancients" and the "moderns" around the turn of the century.[50] By that time, however, modernism had gained the upper hand among the professors at the Ecole Normale. The younger scholars in particular, many of whom had studied in Germany, sought to create a "New Sorbonne" which would emphasize empirical research in a wide range of subjects. Their success—for the revival of the Sorbonne was indeed dramatic—soon led to a reassessment of the place of the Ecole Normale itself in French higher education.

The Sorbonne and the Ecole Normale prepared students for the same examinations— the *licence,* the *diplôme d'études supérieures,* and the *agrégation.*[51] Even the practice of sending candidates for the *agrégation* into a *lycée* to teach for several weeks under the supervision of an experienced professor was common to both the Ecole Normale and the Sorbonne.[52] Why should the Ecole Normale have a separate faculty to teach most of the courses—essentially the same courses as those taught at the Sorbonne? What was the special and unique purpose which continued to justify Normale's privileges?

Ernest Lavisse had called attention to the Ecole's anomalous situation as early as 1885 and sought to transform it into a pedagogical institute.[53] Georges Perrot tried unsuccessfully in the 1890s to persuade the Ministry of Education to require that entering *normaliens* already possess the *licence.*[54] This would have made Normale essentially a research institution except for the preparation of the *agrégation* in the third year. It would have differentiated the Ecole functionally from the Sorbonne when many powerful voices in the University were asking why this elite institution should exist at all.

Public opinion, moreover, began to see the *normalien* as a journalist and man of the world rather than a dedicated teacher. In 1892 the

Ministry of Education saw fit to clip and save the following column from *Le Matin:*

> "Holy Routine"
>
> Two days ago I met a good young man who is trying for the Ecole Normale, and for whom it is, naturally, a serious undertaking. The prestige which the Ecole enjoys is real, but it would be a mistake to be proud of it, for it is not for itself that it is loved. If one said to all of these young men who put themselves through so much trouble to get in that at the end of their pains there was a good job as professor in a *lycée* of Paris, more than one of them would frown. For most the Ecole Normale is simply a waiting room, a first class waiting room, however, for journalism, Parliament, and Institut, for all careers, in a word, except teaching. The famous *promotion* of Edmond About, of Weiss, of Prévost Paradol, of Challemel–Lacour, of Taine, of Sarcey, has completely transformed the character of the Ecole Normale in the eyes of following generations, and it is perfectly certain that a *normalien* who, on leaving the Ecole, contents himself with entering the University and making his career there, is, for his comrades, a failure, an unhappy man who has taken many pains for nothing!
>
> . . . At Polytechnique, they ask one another during the recreations: "What are you going into when you get out?" And it is generally into [government agencies of] mines, or tobaccos, or officer corps. At the Ecole Normale, it is into journalism: the first to the *Revue des Deux-Mondes,* the others scattered everywhere"[55]

By 1895, the year of the centennial, Georges Perrot saw that the Ecole was menaced, and he correctly surmised that its principal antagonist was Lavisse. During the broad investigation of secondary education which produced the Ribot report of 1899, the two men testified in turn about the Ecole Normale. Lavisse agreed with Perrot that the institution should differentiate itself from the Sorbonne, that it should not be permitted to continue to do the same things in the same ways:

> For a long time the Ecole Normale was alone in preparing for the *licence* and above all the *agrégation.* The Faculties had only the general public as auditors; they had no students; today, at the Sorbonne, the Faculty of Letters numbers 1500 students. It produces the largest number of *agrégés* who enter into University circulation. At the present time the Ecole Normale duplicates the work of the

> Faculties of Letters of the universities. We should find a means for it to differentiate itself in one fashion or another.[56]

But whereas Perrot wanted Normale to become a school for advanced research, Lavisse wished to transform it into an institute of theoretical pedagogy which would be accessible even to students at the Sorbonne. Perrot saw more in Lavisse's attack than simply an attempt to eliminate a case of duplication in the University. A partisan of "modern" studies, Lavisse was an opponent of the old Ecole Normale because it was the bastion of classicism. Perrot defended the classics because of their clarity and the Ecole Normale because of its proven excellence in classical studies. He was scornful of Lavisse's suggestion that the Ecole become a pedagogical institute:

> One of the ideas—I will not say one of the errors: I would wish to find a more polite word—one of the unconsidered infatuations which have been manifest since 1870, an epoch in which they think they should take everything from Germany, has been this enthusiasm for theoretical pedagogy.[57]

Perrot believed that the best way to learn to teach was to teach; students had ample opportunity to learn pedagogy indirectly by watching their professors. In a report which he circulated and sent to the Minister of Education, Perrot maintained that the Ecole had never lost sight of its dual role of "pedagogical institute" and "school of advanced studies."[58] Whereas the classes at the Sorbonne were large and formal, he argued, those at Normale were small and informal; while there was no chance at the Sorbonne for students to ask questions, at the Ecole Normale discussion and criticism were the rule. In the process of learning to defend their ideas, the *normaliens* learned to produce coherent lessons for their students. Perrot's ideas gained the support of eminent scholars of the older generation such as Paul Girard, Boissier, and Monod.[59]

Nevertheless, architects of the "New Sorbonne" went ahead with their reforms despite opposition. The Minister of Education, Chaumié, issued a decree in 1903 which made specific the parliamentary resolutions of the previous year. The Ecole would be "reunited" to the University of Paris in that the *normaliens* would take all of their academic work there with the other students. Normale's separate teaching faculty was abolished; with the exception of Brunetière,[60] the masters were given posts instead at the Sorbonne or the Collège de France. The Reform also abolished the *internat;* henceforth, students were at liberty to leave the rue d'Ulm and return whenever they wished. This was no small matter, since the *internat* was a venerable tradition which had its adherents as well as its critics. Whereas the students favored this aspect of the reform, many alumni feared that the elusive *esprit normalien* would now simply dissolve into thin air and the Ecole would become merely a dormitory. Perrot was at the age of retirement, and he resigned after having directed the Ecole for twenty years. Lavisse, his adversary, replaced him.

On 23 November 1904, Lavisse explained the rationale and purpose of the reform to skeptical students. It was urgent, thought Lavisse, that the Ecole Normale differentiate itself from the Sorbonne by assuming the leadership in national renewal through education. The old Ecole Normale was undemocratic in that a small elite had its own faculty while all other students at the Sorbonne were forced to learn in inferior conditions with proportionately fewer faculty members if not inferior ones. Lavisse reproached the *normaliens* for snobbery: students in the 1850s signed hotel registers with an additional description of themselves as "voyagers of the house of Taine, About, Prévost–Paradol and Company." The Ecole had acquired a social significance to which Lavisse objected. "The public thought of the Ecole Normale quite as we did . . . the *normalien* was the author who wrote well, who had wit, fine irony, elegance . . . "*normalien*" did not make one think of a professor. The *normalien* of a *lycée,* who devoted himself to generations of students, lived in a deep shadow." Lavisse wanted to make certain that his students were sincerely interested in the teaching profession rather than in literary glory. In his eyes the teacher had a critical national role to play: "My young comrades, to be an educator is to work at building France."[61]

The principal target of the reform was the Division of Letters. Since the scientists had always taken much of their academic work at the Sorbonne, they had enjoyed more freedom from the constraints of the *internat.* Furthermore criticism of the *normaliens'* pride and their desertion of the University for journalism or politics applied almost exclusively to the literary rather than the scientific students.

After much controversy, the reform changed less at the Ecole Normale than had been feared or hoped.[62] The difficult entrance examination continued to assure a student body of great talent. The prestige of former students such as Jaurès, Herriot, Painlevé, and Blum continued to lure candidates who did not intend to make teaching their life's work.[63] More than ever in the twentieth century *normaliens* left the classroom for journalism, politics, or government administration. Despite the fact that academic instruction became less homogeneous, there was sufficient continuity between the old regime and the new so that *normaliens* remained a proud, envied, and self--conscious community. Although Director Lavisse was even more withdrawn from the school's daily affairs than his predecessor was, Lucien Herr and Paul Dupuy, the fabled *surveillant général* (roughly the equivalent of an American Dean of Students), were fixtures until the mid–1920s.[64] Dupuy and Georges Perrot had permitted the gradual liberalization of the *internat* in the nineteenth century, and so the abolition of parietal rules proved to be no upsetting revolution. The Ecole did not become simply a hotel for students taking courses at the Sorbonne. The community of the rue d'Ulm retained much of its coherence because of shared intellectual interests and a common effort to prepare for examinations.

Yet the reform seemed explicitly to limit the teaching of formal classes at the rue d'Ulm. Second year students in both Letters and Sciences were required to attend the sole lecture course that was permitted at the Ecole. Consistent with Lavisse's wish to make Normale a pedagogical institute, this course dealt with the science of pedagogy.[65] In theory all other courses were held at the Sorbonne, but in practice, according to Pierre Jeannin, the situation immediately following the reform was in flux:

> Concerning the distribution of courses between the Sorbonne and the Ecole, the formula changed according to the disciplines, according to the years, depending upon possibilities offered by accommodations and above all by the personal preferences of the professors. Certain [professors] persisted in coming to the Ecole because they were *maîtres de conférences* there before 1904 or simply out of affection for the old house.[66]

Progressively the first year curriculum in the Division of Letters was reconstituted at the Sorbonne. Henceforth the Ecole's particular contribution to its literary students' education was the pedagogical course in second year and various seminars in the third year taught by professors of the University of Paris hired on a temporary basis. At the same time it became a practice for adjunct professors to teach subjects at the rue d'Ulm not directly related to the *licence*. Although these small discussion groups were open to students of the Sorbonne by permission of the instructor, in fact they were directed at the *normaliens*. In short, after the reform literary *normaliens* had greater freedom to choose their courses from offerings at the Sorbonne and at Normale. They were required to take three courses at the Sorbonne in their first year, at the end of which they were expected to pass the *licence;* in their second year they studied for the *diplôme* under the supervision of a professor of their choice and at the same time took Normale's course on pedagogy; in the third year they prepared for the *agrégation* by attending courses of their choice at the Sorbonne or the Ecole Normale.

The scientists were accustomed to taking their basic courses at the Sorbonne and working in small groups in laboratories and seminars at the rue d'Ulm. The reform merely caused the directors of the laboratories to deal with teaching as well as research and to request more and better equipped laboratories so that pedagogical instruction could be more effective. The laboratories and their directors helped to maintain an esprit de corps among scientists and assure continuity between the old Ecole Normale and the new. For instance Henri Abraham (prom. 1886) directed the physics laboratory for forty years beginning in 1900 and had an enormous influence upon the scientists.[67] The laboratories carefully nurtured an elite in small groups, and so produced social as well as scientific results.[68]

Gustave Lanson became the new Director when Lavisse retired in December 1919. Both men had played important roles in assuring that science and erudition dominated the intellectual climate of the New Sorbonne. Lanson in particular was a favorite target for critics of the Sorbonne's reigning philosophy; his appointment to the Ecole Normale demonstrated that his ideas still prevailed at the Sorbonne and were influential at the Ministry of Education. His immediate task as Director was to defend the independence of the Ecole Normale against the attempts of the Rector of the University of Paris to enforce the letter of the Reform of 1903. The Ministry's decree of November 1920 was a victory for Lanson. It permitted certain classes to be set up for first and second year students at the Ecole Normale in cases where the subject was treated nowhere else in the University. Students at the University of Paris might be admitted to these courses with the permission of the instructor depending upon space. In the third year special courses given at the Ecole by professors delegated from the University of Paris were likewise open to students at the Sorbonne who were preparing for the *agrégation.* The decree guaranteed the Ecole's continuing teaching function independent of the Sorbonne.[69] The ultimate result of the Reform of 1903 amended by the decree of 1920 was that the Ecole gained in breadth of curriculum without losing its right to conduct special classes for its own students.

Since Normale's faculty no longer constituted a discrete corps, whatever distinctive intellectual climate there was at the rue d'Ulm as opposed to the Sorbonne was produced by administrators, students, and the weight of tradition. The new director was dour and authoritarian and had difficulty enforcing discipline among men who had just returned from the trenches. His role of task-master prevented him from becoming an intellectual mentor for the *normaliens.* Dupuy and Herr best embodied Normale's social and scholarly traditions that went back to the 1880s, but they soon departed. Dupuy retired in 1925 after forty years of service. A historian of the institution and deeply attached to its students, he had long exercised a benevolent influence. Lucien Herr's death in 1926 created a tremendous void. Known in histories of the Third Republic chiefly as the grey eminence who sent *normaliens* into the Socialist Party and inspired them during the Dreyfus Affair, to generations of *normaliens* he was also a generous intellectual mentor competent in a wide range of subjects. He could hardly have been more influential as a *maître de conférence.* He had become a legend.

Soon after the departure of Herr and Dupuy there arrived at the rue d'Ulm another figure who embodied old traditions as well as the school's spirit in the 1930s. Célestin Bouglé (prom. 1890) was Vice Director from 1928 to 1935 and Director from 1935 to his death in 1940.[70] He was beloved by the students, who appreciated his sincere concern for their welfare.[71] A Radical–Socialist with close ties to socialists of Durkheim's circle, Bouglé was at the same time a vessel of the classical *normalien* tradition.[72] In 1938 he extolled *culture générale* at Normale based upon the classics and emphasized personal reflection and literary form as well as the mastery of facts and logic:

> I must mention a fine trump card that is now in the hands of those who defend classical humanism. That is the great School which I have the honor to direct, the Ecole Normale Supérieure. Its literary section does not, by any means, provide the majority of secondary school teachers who have obtained the *agrégation,* but it provides a considerable number, and they, as my forerunner, Monsieur Gustave Lanson, used to say, "set the pace." Now those who leave the Ecole Normale with their *agrégation* have a greater chance than anyone else to soak themselves in the traditional classical culture, by the very nature of the examination they must pass in order to be admitted to this school. Out of seven written papers, there is a Latin translation, a Latin composition, a Greek translation (which may be replaced by the translation from a modern language by the

> minority who intend to teach modern languages in a secondary school), then three essays, one on French literature, one on philosophy, and one on a historical subject. It is expressly understood, even in the case of the historical essay, which presupposes a certain factual knowledge, that the examiners should pay attention, above all, to the quality of the composition and of the exposition, for they reveal the activity of a mind capable of rising superior to the facts at its disposal by means of personal reflection.
>
> It is hardly necessary to add that, though the students may specialize within the Ecole Normale itself, though, for example, during their second year, they may undertake specialized research for the diploma of higher studies, which will lead perhaps to a thesis for the doctor's degree, nevertheless they are continually encouraged to look beyond the confines of their particular subjects. An excellent library containing all the authors they are obliged to explain in detail, comrades of varied origin and outlook with whom ideas are exchanged and bouts of intellectual criticism indulged in—all that is more than sufficient to feed the sacred flame, and to make the School an unrivaled center of general culture.
>
> Those who have had the privilege to pass through this center never lose, it seems to us, however diverse the situations they occupy, something that sets them apart, both in the educational system and outside it. They seek to defend and to develop that general culture by adapting it to the demands of the day, for it is far beyond a doubt, one of the charms and one of the vital forces of our country.[73]

The scientific movement emanating from Germany after Sedan made deep and fruitful inroads into the Ecole Normale's literary tradition of scholarship. Fustel de Coulanges, Monod, Bédier, Lanson, Durkheim, and their students had fundamentally changed their disciplines and the intellectual climate of the Sorbonne. But although they had broadened and achieved official recognition for several aspects of the Cartesian tradition, they could not eliminate the persistent and widespread Pascalian sensibility which hesitated to generalize about individuals and human affairs and which proceeded by intuition and an *esprit de finesse* rather than by geometric logic. Each tradition tended to define itself in relation to the other, creating a dialogue in the history of French thought. Intellectuals pursued this dialogue within themselves as well as with each other. Bouglé was a case in point. Although he was a member of Durkheim's circle at the *Année socioloqique,* he tended to place less emphasis than these colleagues upon the priority of social facts over the individual will.[74] For Bouglé the classics yielded clear models for the mind "rising superior to the facts." Important philosophers in the Ecole Normale's intellectual tradition such as Lachelier, Boutroux, and Bergson agreed that thought was essentially autonomous rather than the mirror, however creative, of the material world. Sartrean existentialism would spring from the same root.

New ideas from the social sciences and even from philosophy itself which argued on the contrary that social facts determined individual thought gained ground steadily at the rue d'Ulm. But the priority and independence of the mind remained the central strand of Normale's intellectual tradition during the Third Republic. It was supported by the weight of classical and Christian literature, which consumed the largest part of the *normaliens*' energies. This doctrine was particularly attractive to an intellectual aristocracy, for it implied the social and political precedence of those who gained their livelihood by thought. Like the old aristocracy, this elite claimed to serve high ideals which it alone fully understood, ideals most truly expressed in classical and French literature. Hence the *normalien* embodied social and intellectual traditions which were often antithetical. The tension which arose between lower or middle class origins and upper class culture contributed in individual cases to a wide variety of responses, from the socialism of Jaurès to the fascism of Déat. But it is possible to make some generalizations about all of the *normaliens* of the Third Republic. The following chapters attempt to explain how cultural traditions shaped political ideas—how the social–cultural tension which was implicit in the institution was expressed politically by many of the *normaliens* during their years at the rue d'Ulm and afterwards in the public arena.

5
Society and Politics at the Rue d'Ulm

On est normalien comme on est prince du sang.—Georges Pompidou

L'Ecole ne cessa pas de s'intéresser aux efforts des hommes d'Etat qui . . . travaillaient à fonder la République.—Georges Perrot

SOCIAL and political ideas at the Ecole Normale developed from elitist as well as democratic traditions. Like students at other leading *grandes écoles,* the *normaliens* had survived intense competition for admission, and their success at the *concours* seemed to proclaim their superiority over other mortals. By rituals and folklore which excluded the unwashed, they let it be known that theirs was a closed society. Special customs which grew out of their daily life at the rue d'Ulm contributed to the shaping of their more consciously held liberal political ideas.

Normaliens resembled students elsewhere who were constrained by strict rules of conduct. To maintain their integrity and a feeling of independence, they resorted to subterfuge and revolt. Although in broad outline their behavior was not particularly original, they convinced themselves and the general public that it had unique characteristics which were specifically *normalien.* They were especially proud of their sense of humor.[1]

Throughout most of the nineteenth century the students waged a whimsical war against officials who attempted to enforce house rules. Louis Pasteur, a Vice–Rector during the Second Empire, was a strict disciplinarian who tracked down the smokers in the cellars or in the roof gutters and decreed their confinement to the building.[2] Students responded by disobeying either the letter or the spirit of rules which governed their daily life. Compulsory attendance at chapel was a prime occasion for sabotage. Once the entire student body hid in the cellars of the Ecole during the service. Albert Duruy (son of the Minister of Education) was sent home in 1864 for his impious reading of a prayer: he had read "Pierre, Paul, et Baptiste" instead of "Saint Pierre, Saint Paul, et Saint Jean–Baptiste." Nor would Pasteur easily permit a student to declare his conversion to another faith:

> It is absolutely impossible that I should permit a Catholic student suddenly to cease to take part in Catholic services on his affirmation pure and simple that he has ceased to be a Catholic. If he is really a Protestant, let him testify so by the affirmation to that effect of a minister of the religion; if he is of a mind to affirm that he adheres to no religion recognized by the state, he should be expelled from the Ecole.[3]

After 1881 religious observance finally ceased to be an issue, for Fustel de Coulanges abolished the post of chaplain and had the chapel divided up into study rooms, called *turnes.*

Yet throughout the 1880s, although some of the house rules were relaxed, the daily schedule was full of constraints:

> "Arise at 6 AM in winter; 5 AM in summer (beginning May 1) except for the day following a *sortie* (6AM) or a permission to stay out until midnight (7AM). Leave the dormitory 20 minutes after the bell rings. Breakfast at 7:30 AM. Study or Class, 8–12. Dinner at noon, recreation until 1:30 PM. Study or class from 1:30 to 4:30 PM. Snack 4:30, recreation until 5:00. Study from 5 to 8 PM. Supper at 8, recreation until 9, optional *veillée* (general meeting) from 9:10. Thursday, permission to leave the Ecole at noon, return by 10:00. Dinner at 6:30. Sunday, permission to leave at 8 AM, return at 10 PM in winter, at 10:30 PM in summer. "Midnight permission" the last Saturday of each month: leave at 5 PM and return by 12:30 AM."[4]

Although this schedule does not seem unreasonable as a general guide, the administration tried to assure that it would be followed to the letter. Conviviality which took time away from studies was discouraged: "The students of third year have developed the bad habit of getting together for tea in the evenings—this will be forbidden."

Nor was it permitted to nap during the day: "Five students of the second year in Letters turned down the gas in their study to sleep. They were warned already that they would be punished." And there was something suspect about making snacks during study hours: "Dejean made chocolate in his study yesterday evening at 6 PM."[5] Like confined students anywhere, the *normaliens* let off steam at opportune moments: "The students of the Sciences section have created a great deal of disorder in the dormitory, and for the second time. The students in this section of first and second year are very undisciplined." The dining hall frequently was an arena for festive revolt: "Desrousseaux made a disturbance Saturday in the dining hall with unseemly exclamations." Nor were the requirements of decorum lifted during recreation: "[a list of students], all of third year Letters, created disorder yesterday during evening recreation and met during study time to drink." One was not even safe from sanction in the public street: "First year students in Letters last Thursday returning from the exams for the *licence* created disorder. They made a procession in the street, singing.—Monsieur the Director decided that the students would be kept in school two extra days at the end of the *licence*."[6]

During his one year at the Ecole Normale (1890–1891) Léon Blum refused to conform, as Dupuy's log book reveals:

> November 20, 1890
> Blum created disorder in the dormitory
> December 8
> Blum returns at 11:15 PM (late)
> February 14
> Blum rises late
> March 2
> Blum is absent without authorization from Saturday evening to Sunday morning
> March 5
> Returned late, 11:25, Eisenmann and Blum
> March 7
> Late, Blum
> March 16
> Blum did not return Saturday night
> Confined to the Ecole for two days
> March 21
> Neither Blum nor Berthelot observe their confinement

Blum soon left this secular cloister, which another *normalien* described as follows:

> Extreme claustration: one could go out only on Thursday afternoon and Sunday; those who took a course at the Sorbonne had to go there in a body along a prescribed route. Forbidden to talk in the study rooms . . . or else-where, for "all movements are carried out in order and silence;" forbidden to smoke, forbidden to read newspapers. "Respect for religion and public authority."[7]

Gradually, however, during the 1890s the rules were honored more in the breach than the observance due to the benevolent regime of Georges Perrot and Paul Dupuy. It became possible to study all night and to sleep in the daytime. Dupuy pretended not to notice. Permission to leave the Ecole during the week to go "into the city" was still required, but good reasons or pretexts were almost equally satisfactory. Toward the end of the century it was no longer difficult for a *normalien* to obtain permission to stay out late or even overnight. Every other Saturday students had the right to an overnight permission; the Saturdays in between required special, often whimsical, pleading:

> Every two weeks the *Cacique Général* went to see the Director on Friday to present to him a motive which justified an extraordinary *sortie.* The motives were pure nonsense *(canular)*; sometimes the anniversary of the arrival of a professor, sometimes the coming to power of a new government ministry, or a birth at the home of a *normalien,* it did not matter as long as it was whimsical; the Director listened with benevolent gravity and granted the permission. Only once a year, to indicate that his entire authority remained intact, he refused.[8]

In the Ecole Normale's deliberately distinctive slang, the *cacique* of each *promotion* was that student who was first on the list of those accepted to the Ecole; the *cacique général* was the *cacique* of the third year class.[9] The cement of language endured even as the house rules became less severe. Paul Dimoff (prom. 1899) records an incident which was indicative of the relaxing of discipline. Dupuy announced to a student who had made a disturbance that he would be deprived of his right to leave the Ecole the following Sunday, to which the student responded with convulsive laughter. Taken aback, Dupuy said ironically, "You make fun of your denial of permission: therefore you will not have it."[10] Dupuy and other officials so relaxed the old discipline that by the turn of the century the Ecole Normale was hardly an *internat* in practice.

As parietal rules fell by the wayside students still found ways to behave like a delinquent band within the walls. The dining hall continued to provide a stage for collective action and ritualistic revolt. Unappetizing food became the pretext for disruption. Upon the signal, "Chicken!" a tumult would erupt and dishes and food would be thrown to the floor. Alternatively the *cacique général* might decide that it was time for a "Quel Khon au Pot!" At a signal the *cacique* would direct one hundred and fifty *normaliens* in unison: "Quel . . . Khon!"[11] *Pot* could indicate the dining hall, the food, or the business manager, who was responsible for both. So a common rallying cry when the meat was tough was a high pitched "Mort au Pot!" The standard recessional hymn for such rites was the *Internationale,* in which only the true believers in the Revolution, fearful of sacrilege, abstained from taking part. Eminent alumni fondly recall their castigation of the *Pot.* If there was genuine anger when the food was bad, there was also exhilaration in the act of revolt. Herriot delighted in the retelling of an episode in this tradition which ended in the students' breaking into the kitchen and stealing the stores. "A certain number of us learned the next day that we were not 'well bred young men.' I cannot say what injustice or merit there was in this; but I well know that for several weeks in our *turnes* wê ate a delicious strawberry jam . . ." The ritual appears in Jules Romains' epic *Men of Good Will:*

> "What is going on?"
>
> "We are, Messieurs, at the moment which precedes a 'Quel Khon au pot.' Quite literally."
>
> "Jallez and Jerphanion had heard a great deal said about this legendary rite without daring to hope to witness it for weeks or perhaps months."[13]

When former ambassador François–Poncet spoke at the celebration of the Ecole's one hundred and fiftieth anniversary, he cast a haze of mystification over it:

> In the fracas of plates and glasses there is a magical transformation. Controversies begun in the *turnes* grow in intensity toward their zenith; stimulated by the eagerness of empty stomachs, spirits rival each other in profundity and subtlety; convictions expand at the same time that humors relax; partisanship is tempered by be-

> nevolence; the fantastic and the serious, the sublime and the absurd, intermingle in a web which is inextricably and specifically *normalien.*[14]

A romantic custom pursued alone or in small groups was to walk the forbidden gutters at the edge of the roof. "Our administration, for which all the schools envy us, had in its indulgence, the good humor to forbid some small things so that they still have some attraction. The gutter was such. Thus we found in our discreet walks the illusion of doing something which one should not do, and we took stock of our liberty . . ."[15] In the evening after dinner the third year student would take to his perch on the roof, survey all of the Left Bank, talk with friends, dream, or even sing long into the night.

Participation in a common rite formed an "inextricable web" of feeling and conduct. Ritual lawlessness affirmed membership in a historic band. Romantic, boorish, or brilliantly humorous, the customs served to define the scholarly *normaliens* in more human terms to each other and to the outside world. This aspect of the school seemed to have been threatened by the reform of 1904. The cloistral rules were lifted, and inevitably some of the old atmosphere of a closed brotherhood disappeared. Now there were a number of externs, who could not have shared the same life at the school as the interns. Gaston Boissier regretted the change he foresaw in student life:

> The most serious innovation, and the one which should disturb us most in the new decree, is the one which augments the number of students of the Ecole Normale and which introduces a group of externs. At this time boarding school is not in fashion; public opinion is against it, and no one dares defend it. It is however the boarding school regime which has given the Ecole its character and which has produced its strength.[16]

Boissier was correct in observing that the reform would alter the spirit of the Ecole, but it did so in ways that he could not anticipate. Locked up like juveniles, the *normaliens* had little choice but to behave like obedient, cunning, or rebellious children. The new situation left them free to amuse each other with their pranks, to joust humorously with the naive general public, or to pursue the adult game of politics.

The *canular* served each of these purposes. Like *pot* and other words in *normalien* slang, *canular* had more than one meaning. Strictly speaking it referred to the initiation rites inflicted upon the newcomers at the start of the school year. Since the rites were ribald and humorous, the word came to mean any elaborate prank which took advantage of the naïveté of an individual, the administration, or the public. Or further, something might be strictly *canular* which was merely witty or ironic, such as a request for permission to leave the Ecole to celebrate the anniversary of the Peace of Westphalia.

The *canular* as initiation rite for new students had the same elements as hazing in some American college fraternities: anxiety, humiliation, and humor were a prelude to warm fraternal greetings.[17] Other kinds of *canulars* seemed to serve chiefly to proclaim the sophistication and superiority of the *normaliens.* On one occasion in the 1920s, nervous candidates who had just passed their writtens were conducted to the Ecole to take their orals. Unwary, some fell prey to a false jury made up of older students, struggled with bizzare questions, and submitted to extravagant compliments for banal answers. Forewarned, at least one candidate mistook the correct jury for the false one.[18] First year students were easy targets early in the school year. The fictitious Russian mathematical genius, Professor Bourbaki, appeared in 1923.[19] This picturesque bearded figure (an older student in disguise) mystified first year science students with a fantastic and totally nonsensical lecture complete with charts, graphs, and vectors. Not wishing to seem ignorant in mathematics, the students did not confess their incomprehension to each other and thus remained *canulés* for several days until the hoax was revealed. Bourbaki returned in 1946 as a false Assistant Director in charge of the Ecole's Science Section to welcome and preside over a lecture given by a real Russian physicist.

The care which went into the building of a *canular* could be as great as the naiveté which was its target. In the late 1920s a visiting student from Albania was an unfortunate victim. Certain *normaliens* told Peppo of an oppressed people, the Poldevians, who lived on the border of his country. The elaborate farce which ensued included false Poldevian identification papers for false Poldevians and false calling cards from eminent parliamentary and university personalities who claimed to support the Poldevian cause. The hapless Peppo accepted an invitation to lecture at the Sorbonne, where he made an impassioned plea for the Poldevians, whom he had "seen with his own eyes."[20]

When Charles Lindberg landed at Le Bourget in 1927 the stage was set for a *canular* aimed at the general public. A group of *normaliens* announced in the press that the brave American pilot would be made an honorary student of the Ecole Normale and would be received at the rue d'Ulm. On the appointed day a large crowd gathered and filled the adjoining streets. The credulous police arrived to keep order, a sure sign, some thought, that it was no hoax. Soon a tall blond student made up to resemble the flier arrived in a large Citroën, and the students carried him into the Ecole in triumph.[21]

The transition in the folkways of *normaliens* from pranks to politics was a gradual one, and certain *canulars* had elements of both. In the inter-war period, for instance, a group of *normaliens* dressed as priests and led by their "bishop" entered a large lecture hall at the Sorbonne. Sitting where they could be seen, they listened to part of the lecture. Then at a signal from the bishop they took out their breviaries in unison. Finally, they pretended indignation at one of the professor's remarks, the bishop intoned in a loud voice, "Come, my brothers, we must hear no more of this," and they made a formal exit. The left wing press failed to check the story before it criticized Cardinal Suhard for "sending one of his capitulary vicars to commit this attempt upon the imprescriptible rights of laicism, of the school, and of the state."[22] Thus the ultimate, but unintended, victim of this lampoon on the Church was the political left.

Although *normaliens* had more opportunities after the reform of 1904 to express political opinions of their own, open political activity did not entirely replace elaborate pranks. *Canulars* and archaic customs were convenient indirect methods to express conscious or even subconscious political or social feelings. Folkways at the rue d'Ulm grew in a shared atmosphere which underscored both liberal political values and assumptions of cultural superiority.

Whereas most students participated in rituals devised to sabotage the infantalizing boarding school regime, a significant number also held, expressed, or acted upon explicit political ideas. The *normaliens* were never unanimous in their political opinions, but on the whole throughout the nineteenth century they were men of the moderate left. At the beginning of the Third Republic the students at the rue d'Ulm held a variety of political views. Auguste Gérard (prom. 1872), a lifelong Gambettist, recalled that "the Ecole was, like the country itself, divided into parties and groups. There were . . . monarchists and republicans, Catholics and free–thinkers; and in each of these categories, how many varieties and nuances!"[23] Republicanism solidified at the Ecole Normale gradually as it became more general in the country;. Gendarme de Bévotte and Romain Rolland, both of the promotion of 1886, indicated that in their day the Ecole was liberal. Bévotte added that although the students were mostly Gambettists, there were also royalists, radicals, and perhaps a few socialists as well. In religion the students were predominantly free–thinkers, but there was also a minority of practicing Catholics and Protestants.[24] Rolland provides us with a statistic concerning the *normaliens'* opposition to Boulanger. They supported taking part in anti–Boulangist demonstrations in the Latin Quarter by a margin of 83 to 20, with 24 abstentions.[25] Personal opposition to Boulanger may have been more pronounced than these figures suggest, for some of the students must have feared to jeopardize their careers by joining street demonstrations or by proclaiming their views openly. A Napoleonic decree insisted that teachers demonstrate obedience to the regime, and under successsive regimes teachers as well as the Ecole Normale itself were penalized for expressing unofficial political views.[26] Most overt political expression on the part of *normaliens* during the first decades of the Third Republic consisted of a prudent liberalism which rejected socialism, monarchy, anarchism, or Caesarism. Probably typical of his generation, Elie Halévy (prom. 1889) explained that he arrived at the Ecole too early to be attracted to socialism. "I was anticlerical, democrat, republican, let us say with a single word which was, however, full of meaning: a Dreyfusard . . . in the course of those years (1889–1892) I did not know a single socialist at the Ecole Normale."[27] Lucien Herr had just become the librarian in 1888 and would not begin to recruit genuine socialists among the *normaliens* until the mid–1890s.

When Charles Péguy entered the Ecole in 1894, Herr had begun to preside over anticlerical political discussions which took place in the library in the afternoons.[28] Jaurès himself attended from time to time and gave these discussions added prestige. At the same time Péguy's *turne* became a socialist cell. Tharaud recalled that Péguy shared his *turne* with Mathiez, Albert Lévy, and Weulersse,

> . . . all three of a fiercely socialist orthodoxy [a puzzling statement in light of the state of French socialism]. On the cardboard which covered the diamond shaped window over their door they had cut with a knife: *Utopie*. Was it an irony about themselves? Was it rather a challenge which they presented to their comrades who did not share their faith? It was rapidly established that the *turne Utopie* was the citadel of socialism at the Ecole, of an informed, scientific, and integral socialism.[29]

Yet most of the *normaliens* remained preoccupied with studies and examinations. According to Félicien Challaye (prom. 1894) students with serious and time consuming political commitments were rare.

"Petty bourgeois as most of us were, we generally had no political opinions. Péguy had one: he was a socialist."[30] The Dreyfus Affair, however, soon stirred many other *normaliens* to political activity.

Herr and Gabriel Monod made the rue d'Ulm one of the earliest and most prominent centers of Dreyfusard activity. Challaye was an assistant in the library of the Ecole when he overheard an excited conversation between Sorbonne Professor Lucien Lévy–Bruhl (prom. 1876) and Herr. Lévy–Bruhl assurred Herr that it was out of the question that his cousin, Dreyfus, could have committed treason. Dreyfus was innocent, and the real criminal was still at large.[31] This conversation took place soon after Dreyfus was sentenced in 1894. So from the beginning Herr was aware of the possibility of a miscarriage of justice.[32] Monod too was suspicious that Dreyfus had been condemned unjustly. In a December 1894 interview, his former pupil Gabriel Hanotaux, the Minister of Foreign Affairs, was abrupt and evasive on the subject of Dreyfus.[33] Yet it was more than two years before evidence appeared which would permit the skeptics to challenge the verdict which had sent Dreyfus to Devil's Island. In 1897 Herr declared bluntly to Blum that Dreyfus was innocent. The work of Bernard Lazare had convinced him, and he was determined to try to convince others.[34]

Soon the Affair exploded. Senator Scheurer–Kestner asked Joseph Reinach in October to try to restrain Monod from an open declaration that Dreyfus was innocent: "I understand . . . the impatience of Monod, for he is, like me, like you, a man to whom conscience speaks imperiously. . . ."[35] But the following month Monod was unable to remain silent and argued for revision of the Dreyfus case in a letter of *Le Temps:* "I can be mistaken, I will even say that I wish one would demonstrate that I am mistaken, for I would thus escape this torture of thinking that my country had condemned an innocent man to such pain for such a crime."[36] At first Monod was alone to face violent attacks from the press, for the Dreyfusard party had not yet formed. But the *normaliens,* unanimous in Monod's favor, sent the following letter to *Le Temps:*

> Paris, November 15, 1897
>
> To the Director of *Le Temps:*
>
> The students of the Ecole Normale Supérieure have addressed the following letter to M. Gabriel Monod, which they would be grateful if you would insert:
>
> "Monsieur:
>
> Indignant at the injurious attack of which you have been the

> object in different newspapers, the students of the Ecole Normale Supérieure wish to express to you their respectful sympathy, which they have for you and your character."
>
> (The names of all the students of the Ecole Normale follow, and it is signed by "Cl. E. Maitre, Third Year Student.")[37]

As the Dreyfus Affair developed Monod continued to use his influence to try to persuade prominent academics to support the cause of revision of the case.[38]

Early in 1898 the revisionists seemed to have been checked by the government and the army. The probable real culprit, Esterhazy, was declared innocent at his court martial on January 11, and Colonel Picquart, whose accusation had led to Esterhazy's trial, was placed under arrest. But Zola immediately shook the nation by publishing his letter *J'accuse,*[39] and it became difficult for intellectuals to remain neutral as discussion of the Dreyfus case became heated. Monod and Herr led the campaign for signatures from prominent figures in the academic and literary worlds to petition in favor of a new trial for Dreyfus.

In the *Revue blanche* Herr accused the anti–Dreyfusard Maurice Barrès of racism and claimed that the idea that the integrity of France was being weakened by her critics was only a smoke screen to protect the army.[40] Herr saw the military establishment as irrational, imperialistic, politically repressive, and fundamentally antidemocratic. In his articles in *La Volonté* he wrote that the same empty rhetoric and stolid intransigence which supported French imperialism in Africa also prevented an honest reassessment of Dreyfus' conviction. A visionary as well as a practical political activist, Herr claimed to see a new generation which, . . .

> though weak and awkward, was alive and generous and sure to triumph. . . . The truth and also the marvel of this epoch is that in a narrow, dried up, and hardened France, a small number of men, for a work of justice, humanity, and honor, have been able to undertake the struggle against the sovereign force of organized brutality, syndicated interests, and the coalition of elementary force, secular passion, the ruling hierarchies of the world, egotistical dastardliness and indifference; these few men have been able in daily battle to fire people up one by one, to awaken consciences . . . to crystalize an active hope in an ideal of human justice. . . This spirit of emancipating generosity is perhaps the sole nobility and unique honor of our time.[41]

Thus the Dreyfus Affair was for Herr the awakening of the conscience of a more ethical France in which intellectuals would play an important part.

Yet intellectuals like Herr, who were *fonctionnaires,* risked their jobs when they proclaimed their support for Dreyfus. Especially since he was so thoroughly committed to his profession and to his post as librarian at Normale, Herr showed his mettle when he declared himself a Dreyfusard, allowed his name to appear on posters of the League of the Rights of Man and Citizen, and worked in other ways for the cause.[42] On one occasion he took part in a street demonstration. Upon the invitation of the League of the Rights of Man and Citizen, crowds filled the streets around Longchamps on June 11th, 1899. The air was still charged with excitement over the Affair. Only one week previously at Auteuil President Loubet received a caning at the hands of a rightist youth, and many blamed the Minister of the Interior for not providing adequate protection. So Herr headed toward Longchamps with some of his friends, including the two *normaliens* Simiand and Bahon. They were waylaid by rightists who threw bottles and an iron chair, but Herr restrained his followers from pursuing the attackers and prevented a riot from developing on the spot. When Herr's small troupe reached the Avenue du Bois, they joined a crowd already gathered chanting "Vive Loubet! Vive Picquart! Vive Dreyfus!" in the faces of the police. During the demonstration Herr persuaded the crowd not to lynch a police officer fallen from his horse and separated from his brigade. On the following day in an address to the Chamber of Deputies Edouard Vaillant quoted Herr's letter which described the brutality of the police during the demonstration.[43] The Dupuy ministry soon fell, and the new government of Waldeck–Rousseau ordered the retrial of Dreyfus. Herr was a self-effacing man, but he was never far from the center of political activity on behalf of Dreyfus.

In addition to Monod and Herr other active Dreyfusards on Normale's faculty included Bloch, Lanson, Dupuy, Tannery, and Andler. It was Dupuy who, following Loubet's caning at Auteuil, led a group of six *normaliens* to the Elysée to assure the President of the support of the Ecole Normale.[44] In the other camp were Boissier, Brunetière, and Ollé–Laprune. Boissier instinctively opposed any movement which challenged the authority of an established government,[45] whereas Ollé–Laprune and Brunetière saw the Dreyfusard movement as a threat to Catholicism. Brunetière was an aggressive

Catholic who declared, "The Christian idea, that is the absolute. . . . Catholicism, that is France, and France, that is Catholicism."[46] At the same time he condemed anti–Semitism in all its forms along with those who accused him of being an anti–Semite. He claimed that the very pre-condition of democracy and freedom was an army capable of defending the national soil. It was individualism and anarchy, not the army, which endangered the Republic, and the so–called "intellectuals" were most at fault since they claimed falsely to be competent in all areas including military subjects. Such rampant individualism as the intellectual party displayed was the road to tyranny. He warned individual scholars not to question the word of generals, who, he asserted, were specialists in their own field.[47]

Director Georges Perrot maintained an impeccable public silence during the Affair, but there is evidence that privately he gave aid and comfort to the Dreyfusards. In a routine letter to the Minister of Education concerning the selection of a jury for the entrance examination in philosophy, he noted in passing that Lucien Herr was particularly tired that year, 1899, and asked whether the Minister could not find someone else to serve.[48] Perrot understood that Herr, deeply involved in the Affair, had good reason to be tired. In March of 1901 on the occasion of President Loubet's visit to the school, Perrot delivered an address which contained hints that he was more in sympathy with the liberal triumph than his position at Normale would allow him to admit:

> If there is anywhere in France an institution where the President of the Republic, above all when he understands his task as you understand yours, is certain to meet to welcome him only sentiments of keen and respectful sympathy, it is indeed the Ecole Normale. The Ecole, before the Third Republic was proclaimed, was already republican by tendancy and instinct.[49]

After Perrot had resigned from his position at the Ecole, he wrote the following flattering letter to the Dreyfusard deputy Joseph Reinach:

> May 23, 1906
>
> Dear Sir,
>
> I am very happy at your success. You are returning to that Chamber which you should never have left and where there will be more than one combat to carry on, for the defense of principles, of that tradition of Gambetta and Ferry of which you are one of the

> most faithful and last representatives. You carry into these battles your usual courage.
> Bien à vous
> Georges Perrot[50]

Although this expression of admiration followed Reinach's recent grant of a favor, Perrot had expressed similar ideas before in more general terms. Furthermore there is no evidence that he objected when Herr, Dupuy, Monod, Andler, and others implicated the Ecole Normale in the Affair from its beginning.

The students favored the cause of Dreyfus, Picquart, and Zola as decisively as their masters did. Raoul Blanchard (prom. 1897) recalled that during 1897–1898 "emotion mounted [at Normale] among professors and leaders" and that critical discussion of the facts of the Dreyful case took place in the library under the direction of Lucien Herr. Early in 1898, just after the publication of Zola's famous letter, about half of the students signed the petition for revision immediately.[51] After the death of Henry the following year the Ecole became "one of the citadels of Dreyfusism, where Jaurès, Herr, Péguy, and Seignobos met." Charged with collecting signatures from his class, Blanchard obtained thirteen or fourteen out of twenty–one.[52] Some students who were sympathetic toward Dreyfus refused to risk their careers by signing the petition. Félicien Challaye estimated that "well over half" of the students were for revision, while Albert Cans (prom. 1896) recalled that they were "all Dreyfusards, with very few exceptions."[53]

There were three basic reasons for Dreyfusism at Normale. In the first place, the *normaliens* were not sympathetic toward the military, whose instincts and reasoning were far removed from their freely critical attitude. Secondly, the students were largely unreligious or anticlerical, and the Church's alliance with the Army only tended to increase their distrust of the Church. Gabriel Monod noted that those families who sent their children to private Catholic schools typically preferred them to aspire to Saint–Cyr or the Ecole Polytechnique and a military career.[54] But only a handful of the *normaliens* came from Catholic secondary schools. Parents of a large percentage of *normaliens* were involved in state public education (which was laic), the government, the liberal professions, and business, all of which were favorable to the republican regime. In the third place, the *normaliens* opposed anti–Semitism, which they assumed was the basis of the condemnation of Dreyfus. Their Jewish comrades were thoroughly assimilated into the mainstream of French culture.It would be difficult to imagine a recent East European Jewish immigrant, however brilliant, at the rue d'Ulm. But it was the *normaliens'* eighteenth century humanistic universalism as well as their daily association with Jewish friends which caused their rejection of anti-Semitism and provided a further reason to support Dreyfus. Jean Jaurès remarked that there were many Jews at Normale when he was a student there in the 1870s. "They were excellent comrades as well as distinguished minds; indeed, they were almost always in the first ranks [as scholars]. The two *promotions* which preceded mine had Jews as *caciques,* that is as heads of the class. . . . Nearly all [of the Jewish students] were not only mystical but of largely Christian sentiments. They had a special affection for those of us who were brought up in religious [elementary] schools, and they had long 'spiritual' conversations with us."[55] Tharaud also relates that the *normaliens* lived with their Jewish comrades "in the same close friendship" as with their Christian friends. "It never entered our minds that they could be different from us, and the idea that a man should suffer for his religion and race seemed intolerable to us. Also, even among the *talas* [students who were practicing Catholics in *normalien* slang], very few of us refused to sign the petitions which demanded the revision of the [Dreyfus] case."[56]

As the Dreyfus Affair progressed, socialism grew in importance among students at the Ecole Normale in large part because of the combined influence of Herr, Jaurès, and Péguy. With the constant advice of Herr, Jaurès shaped the political ideas which gained acceptance among most of the university socialists. Like Jules Guesde, he accepted the reality of the Marxian formula of class struggle, but unlike Guesde he entertained the possibility of cooperating with the bourgeoisie to achieve ends sought by the oppressed. The socialism of Jaurès was a mixture of democratic idealism and social realism in that it sought to guarantee freedom for the individual as it defined the needs of society as a whole. Students with different political ideas in points of detail found in Jaurès an intellectual like themselves as well as the creator of a broad political synthesis.[57]

During the Dreyfus Affair Péguy was a follower of Jaurès, a friend of Herr, and a political leader of students in the University.[58] Like Herr and Jaurès, he was no doctrinaire Marxist. He did not see the Affair as a mere quarrel between two factions of the bourgeoisie. He shared the belief of leading Dreyfusards that the central issue was whether the state would render justice to one of its citizens. But Péguy was more romantic than most of his socialist friends. During a year's leave of absence from the Ecole Normale, he helped to form a socialist cell in Orléans, but he also wrote a mystical play about Joan of Arc.[59] At first the romantic side of Péguy's nature drew him to the defense of the martyr Dreyfus, but later it led to a bitter break with his old Dreyfusard allies.

Péguy was married in October 1897 and as a result had to resign from the Ecole Normale. Yet he maintained his associations at the rue d'Ulm, for Director Perrot arranged for a scholarship so that he could audit courses and prepare for the *agrégation*.[60] Events soon bore out, however, that Péguy was far more a man of letters and action than he was a student and a scholar. In the summer of 1898 he opened a bookshop in the Latin Quarter with money from his wife's dowry.[61] The Librairie Bellais became a gathering place for his friends and for students in general who were interested in socialist literature.[62] From his shop Péguy, cane in hand, led his followers to repel anti–Semitic bands who menaced Dreyfusard professors at the Sorbonne such as Aulard, Buisson, and Seignobos. Léon Blum, who stopped at the Librairie every morning at the height of the Dreyfus Affair, called it the "general center of Dreyfusism in the Latin Quarter," where "students of the Ecole Normale met with free students, with their elders of recent classes, with their professors."[63] For instance, there Blum first met the *normalien* socialists Albert Thomas (prom. 1899), Jean Perrin (prom. 1891) and Paul Langevin (prom. 1894).

Enthusiasm among university socialists and Dreyfusards did not prevent the Librairie from approaching bankruptcy at the end of the first year. In this situation Péguy sought help from Herr, who had tried to dissuade him from the venture in the first place. Despite his earlier opposition to the project, Herr asked his friends to contribute to a reorganized Librairie which would be a joint enterprise under new management to publish and distribute socialist and scholarly literature. The stockholders first met on 2 August 1899, and a few days later they elected a Board of Directors consisting of Léon Blum, Hubert Bourgin, Herr, Mario Roques, and François Simiand. Except for Herr the members of the Board had all been *normaliens* during the 1890s. They comprised Herr's circle. Péguy was excluded from even a voice in the new enterprise and quickly turned against Herr and his collaborators; in his *Cahiers de la Quinzaine,* he attacked the Sorbonne, Jaurès, and many other old socialist comrades.[64]

Most of Normale's socialists remained faithful to Herr and Jaurès, and their support of the new publishing enterprise is one

TABLE 13. Stockholders in the Société Nouvelle de Librairie et d'Edition: AUGUST 2, 1899[a]

Promotion at the Ecole Normale	Name	Shares	Capital	Payments
1884	Charles Andler	5	500	125.00
1893	Carle Bahon	5	500	125.00
1890	Léon Blum	50	5000	1250.00
1895	Hubert Bourgin	45	4500	1125.00
1893	Louis Bourilly	1	100	62.50
1894	Etienne Burnet	45	4500	1125.00
—	Paul Fauconnet	1	100	31.25
1895	Lucien Foulet	40	4000	1000.00
1883	Lucien Herr	68	6800	1700.00
—	Jules Isaac[b]	1	100	62.50
1894	Paul Langevin	1	100	31.25
—	Louis Lazard	2	200	62.50
1894	Albert Lévy	1	100	31.25
—	Maurice Loewé	5	500	125.00
—	Edgard Milhaud	1	100	31.25
1896	Albert Monod	45	4500	1125.00
1895	Charles Pérez	2	200	62.50
1891	Jean Perrin	1	100	25.00
1894	Mario Roques	45	4500	1125.00
1894	Désiré Roustan	45	4500	1125.00
1893	François Simiand	45	4500	1125.00
1898	Ernest Tonnelat	1	100	31.25
1895	Antoine Vacher	45	4500	1125.00

[a]Source: A.N. 40 AQ 1.

[b]A student at the Sorbonne and the only stockholder who did not own shares in the enterprise in 1929. He died in 1963.

index of their strength. There were twenty–three original stockholders in Herr's "Société Nouvelle de Librairie et d'Edition" (*see* Table 13). Two, Herr and Andler, held posts at Normale; sixteen were *normaliens* of the 1890s, thirteen in Letters and three in Science. Only five of the twenty–three were not *normaliens.* Andler suggests that the members, that is the stockholders, were strictly socialist.

> Herr wished that the whole group [of subscribers to the Société's publications] would become firm adherents of socialism. Not that he refused to inform whoever wanted to take up other doctrines. . . . Each one being informed, it was our task to say why we [the stockholders] chose, for our part, the way of socialism.[65]

Ownership of stock in the Société, therefore, appears to be a useful rough index of socialist leanings.

TABLE 14. Stockholders in the Société Nouvelle de Librairie et d'Edition: FEBRUARY 10, 1929[a]

Promotion	Name	Shares	*Promotion*	Name	Shares
1884	Andler[b]	55	—	Lazard[b]	2
1898	Aubert	3	1894	Lévy, Albert[b]	1
1893	Bahon	1	—	Lévy, Emmanuel	1
—	Bauer	1	—	Lévy, Isidore	1
1900	Berthod	1	1894	Litalien	1
1890	Blum[b]	50	—	Loewé[b]	5
—	Bourgin, Georges	51	1895	Maître	1
1895	Bourgin, Hubert[b]	44	1901	Marais	1
1893	Bourilly[b]	1	—	Mater	1
1901	Boutry	1	—	Mauss	1
1894	Burnet[b]	45	—	Milhaud[b]	1
—	Caron	10	1896	Monod[b]	45
1894	Challaye	1	1895	Pérez[b]	50
1900	Comert	1	1891	Perrin[b]	1
—	Créhange	1	1911	Petit	30
1899	Daudin	1	—	Picquenard	2
1892	Demangeon	1	1894	Poirot	2
1898	Dupouey	1	1898	Prévot	1
—	Fagnot	1	1900	Réau	1
—	Fauconnet[b]	1	1895	Rey	1
1895	Foulet[b]	40	—	Rodrigues	1
—	Frémont (Mlle.)	1	1894	Roques	45
1900	Frossard	1	1896	Roussel	1
1894	Gaillet-Billoteau	1	1894	Roustan[b]	45
1902	Gernet	1	1891	Sagnac	1
1900	Goineau	1	1893	Simiand[b]	45
—	Gorodichze	2	1899	Sion	1
—	Grunebaum	16	—	Spire	1
1898	Halbwachs	1	1899	Thomas, Albert	2
1883	Herr[b]	675	—	Tondelier	1
1901	Hertz	6	1898	Tonnelat[b]	1
—	Hesse	1	1895	Vacher[b]	45
1905	Hubert	60	1883	Weill, (Geo.?)	1
1894	Langevin[b]	1	1894	Weulersse	1

[a]Source: A.N. 40 AQ 1.
[b]Indicates an original stockholder.

In 1929 when the Société was liquidated at a general meeting of stockholders, the records still revealed a high proportion of *normaliens*—forty–six out of sixty–nine (see Table 14). By this time nine out of twenty–eight in Péguy's class (1894) held stock in the enterprise. Other evidence suggests that five more members of this class were socialists or probably sympathetic to socialist ideas but not members of the Société. Probably as many as half of the members of Péguy's class at Normale had become members of the Socialist Party or voted with that Party in elections. The class of 1898 had only one original stockholder (Tonnelat) in 1899, but it had five by 1929; other evidence allows us to speculate that a total of six literary students out of eighteen that year were socialists. Similar surveys of other classes since 1900 show that less than one quarter were either socialists or involved in the Société.[66]

There is no doubt that socialism was widespread at the Ecole Normale at the end of the century, but Sorbonne professor Alphonse Aulard (prom. 1867) exaggerated when he wrote in 1903 that "most [of the *normaliens*] were inclined to the socialism of the type of M. Jaurès."[67] Although Herr did lead the majority of *normaliens* into the Dreyfusard camp, he was not able to make socialists out of all the Dreyfusards. Other political doctrines of the moderate left—radicalism in particular—had their place. The *normaliens'* modest bourgeois origins posed no problem for them to enter the Dreyfusard army, for they were already republican, anticlerical, antimilitarist, and antiracist. But only a minority were likely to advocate, even if only in theory, the destruction of a bourgeois social ladder which they had begun so successfully to climb. It was a real achievement for Lucien Herr to have guided as many *normaliens* to socialism as he did.

During the decade which preceded the First World War some *normaliens* reacted against socialism and the scientific spirit of the New Sorbonne, and many were attracted to Bergson, to the so-called "new nationalism," and to religion. Lavisse, who said, "You are now leaving the hands of distinguished humanists, whose lessons you must now forget in order to become scientists," was a convenient object of their ridicule.[68] Some students sought a new faith to replace agnosticism, internationalism, and science. It is not certain whether a majority of *normaliens* followed the new intellectual and political fashion. Agathon judged that half of the *normaliens* of 1913 shared the "patriotic spirit," but that this tendency was far stronger in schools like the Ecole Libre des Sciences Politiques and the Ecole Polytechnique which recruited from higher strata in the middle class.[69] Nationalism, of course, was consistent with Radicalism and the Jacobin tradition as well as with French Catholicism. Gambetta was a nationalist and a hero of *normaliens* of the 1870s. Massis records that in 1912 one third of the *normaliens* were practicing Catholics,[70] perhaps slightly more than in the previous generation, but not a dramatic change. What is more significant is that these Catholics were drawn primarily to Christian socialism and the Sillon rather than to right wing doctrines. Massis noted that there were only two members of Action Française at the Ecole in 1912.[71] During the same pre–war decade, Herr continued to preside over a socialist cell (we lack membership figures).[72] Some of the very few students who survived the war were later to be associated either with left wing politics or the Communist Party, namely: Etienne Weill–Raynal, Jean Guéhenno, René Maublanc, Marcel Prenant, Marcel Bataillon, Charles Parain, and Jean Pommier. What seems clear is that following the Dreyfus Affair the broad political consensus at the rue d'Ulm broke down. Although the political center of gravity remained left of center, a greater variety of political opinions emerged during the twentieth century. In part this was a legacy of the reform of 1904, which had opened the Ecole far more than before to the outside world. It was also due to political developments in France and beyond.

During the First World War and the months which followed the Ecole was united in grief. Of slightly over 800 *normaliens* who were mobilized, 239 were killed. Of the 240 members of the *promotions* of 1910–1913 who went to the front, 120 were killed and 97 wounded.[73] As lieutenants leading their men, the *normaliens* had faced a terrifying duty. Inevitably the shock of the carnage produced long term political results. Georges Cogniot (prom. 1921) and Jean Prévost (prom. 1919) read Romain Rolland's *Au dessus de la mêlée* and were decisively influenced by it to turn to socialism.[74] Many students at Normale and elsewhere became disillusioned with European liberal civilization.[75]

To replace those lost in the war, the government authorized the creation in 1919 of a special *promotion* approximately twice the size of the normal class. As compared with the typical *normalien,* these men were older, many had been to war, and all had seen more of life. They were not so willing to accept the usual humble apprenticeships in provincial *lycées,* which might, with luck and good conduct, one day lead to a post in Paris. As Jean Mistler related, many of his generation saw the Ecole as only a stepping stone to careers outside the University: ". . . after the break of four years which occurred in my life, I could no longer consider Normale to be more than one step and I set about to prepare my *agrégation* to be done with it as soon as possible. My comrades did not reason otherwise: of 80 students of our class hardly half were to remain in the University. . . . This flight from the University was due to the disproportion between the intellectual level of the *concours* and the material rewards of the career to which it led."[76] Although Mistler exaggerates the numbers who left the University (about three quarters remained), it was true that more *normaliens* than in the past looked elsewhere for employment. Intellectual talent which survived the war was in short supply everywhere, and thus *normaliens* began to prepare themselves for such careers as the Inspectorate of Finance. In interviews some alumni admitted that they abandoned teaching at the very beginning of their careers because of the drudgery of correcting students' papers, a task they believed to be beneath their abilities. Some students planned for a career outside the University even as they attended the Ecole Normale. One day a week they would leave the bohemian atmosphere of the rue d'Ulm to attend courses at the Ecole Libre des Sciences Politiques, where they were exposed to different social and political ideas as well as to a different curriculum.[77]

An increase in careerism outside the University on the part of the post war generation did not necessarily mean that they had changed their political orientation while they were students at the rue d'Ulm. Jean Prévost (prom. 1919) insisted that he and his friends in the *cagne* of Henri IV were different from the students of Saint Cyr, Polytechnique, and the Ecole Agronomique, for they were not nationalistic: they supported Wilson and a peace without revenge.[78] But Raymond Aron (prom. 1924) recalled that in the mid–twenties there was not much political feeling at the Ecole Normale. Except for Brasillach and Bardèche, Action Française was weak. Nor was there much real Marxism either; Aron himself read Marx in depth only after he had completed his studies at the rue d'Ulm.[79] According to Raymond Badiou (prom. 1924, Division of Sciences) the scientists were more decisively "on the left" than their literary comrades. They were solidly for the Cartel des Gauches, and there was only one *tala* in the *promotion.*[80] Father Jean Ribaillier (prom. 1927) testified to the existence of a strong minority (30–40 students) of *talas* in the school as a whole in the late 1920s; but instead of affiliating themselves with Action Française, these students supported Christian socialism and democracy.[81] Like the pre–war *talas,* those of the 1920s considered themselves to be men of the left. Robert Brasillach (prom. 1928) was a monarchist and an adherent of Action Française impatient with the political moderation of his classmates. He wrote that in the late 1920s the Ecole had not strayed from its traditional political orientation to the left of center: "The Ecole at that time was seen as revolutionary. Actually half a dozen comrades were more talk than deeds, and most adhered to a righteous radical and socialist mediocrity."[82] For the mid–thirties, one alumnus (prom. 1932) believed that a majority of his class was socialist, another (prom. 1933) remembered his comrades as being "to the left," with a few scattered on the far left and the far right, and a third (prom. 1933) claimed that there were seven or eight Communists and an equal number of Action Française; but over half of the students subscribed to the national Vigilance Committee against Fascism led by men of the left.

The interwar period differed from the 1890s in that both the far right and the far left had gained force and clarity. The newspaper *Action Française* had consistently attracted readers at the Ecole because of its literary criticism if not always for its political stance. Only a handful of students took its political line seriously. On the far left there arose the Communists, who were riveted by the drama of the Russian Revolution. For both the 1920s and the 1930s it is far easier to identify *normaliens* who as students were Communists or "fellow travelers" than men of the far right. This lends support to the repeated statements of alumni of those years that politically the Ecole remained on the left. Although the right wing appeared to have gained some strength, it was balanced by the Communists on the extreme left. The *talas,* moreover, were moderates of the left.

That the military continued to be treated with scant respect at the rue d'Ulm suggests continuity rather than change in the political balance. One method used to express antimilitarist feelings was the *canular.* After the First World War Normale had received a "75" cannon to illustrate certain lessons in required military instruction. One night in January 1921, students painted the cannon red and covered it with graffiti as well. A week later when General Girard arrived at the Ecole for a ceremonial visit, the gun was painted red again and bore the label "first cannon of the Red Army." To make matters worse, powder strewn in the General's path made light explosions as he strode to the Salle des Actes, where graffiti and a bizarre arrangement of the statues destroyed whatever solemnity might have remained in the occasion. Girard was quoted later as having said "Messieurs, there is an abcess between us. We shall have to drain it. You should go to Moscow if you have such ideas."[83] It is difficult to imagine pranks of such audacity at the Ecole Polytechnique, where military traditions were inherent.

Strained relations with the military continued, and the *normaliens* expressed their antimilitarism openly. A law of 1923 left the *normaliens* without the assurance of a military commission upon graduation, whereas the *polytechniciens* continued to receive their commissions as a matter of course. This meant that Polytechnique enjoyed an advantage in recruiting science students. By 1928 Normale's Director was able to have the law changed so that the *normaliens* would again be given their commissions upon graduation, but at the price of more rigorous military training at the Ecole. Military drill became the only required course for the *normalien,* and in these circumstances absenteeism, already a tradition at military drill, increased. In November 1928, eighty-three students (over half of the student body) wrote to the Minister of Education to request that they not be given the special "privilege" of obtaining a military commission without their individual consent.[84] The Ministry interpreted this as the kind of disloyal political statement which Napoleon I and successive rulers and regimes had forbidden by law. This manifestation of leftism by disobedient civil servants passed, nevertheless, with only a reprimand. What ensued was more serious.

Simone Weil (prom. 1928) was one of the few women who were admitted to the Ecole Normale as regular students from 1927 to 1940. Deepy committed to left wing political causes, she was often the instigator of petitions. Finally, despite the Director's warning, she circulated and then published a petition which officials could not ignore. It concerned students of the Ecole Normale des Instituteurs of Quimper who had just been disciplined by their administration for their opposition to military drill. Weil's open letter, which was signed by twenty–three militants, read as follows:

> We, students of the Ecole Normale Supérieure, protest against the sanctions which have hit our comrades of the Ecole Normale des Instituteurs of Quimper. We declare ourselves entirely in sympathy with their action against obligatory military preparation in fact, and with their struggle for the reform of the regime of the Ecoles Normales.
>
> The manoeuvres of the administration and the pressure put on each student individually to try to obtain denunciations seems to us like police methods which we judge intolerable. We congratulate our comrades for having assured the failure of these methods and we trust they will continue the struggle.
>
> In the face of such conditions, we know of nothing better than to call for the solidarity of the teaching personnel and of the entire proletariat.[85]

The list of names which followed amounted to fifteen per cent of the student body and included students who were later associated with socialist or communist politics. Since the letter appeared in both

L'Humanité and *Le Populaire,* these students did not escape punishment, but the Council of Discipline could agree only on a relatively mild sanction: a verbal reprimand and a notation in each student's dossier.

Over the course of the Third Republic the *normaliens* had become bolder about expressing their political opinions. The Dreyfus Affair caused many of them to look squarely at a political issue, and the Reform of 1904 gave them all greater personal freedom. The First World War, the Russian Revolution, the rise of fascism, and other public issues also provoked some to become active politically. But they did not suddenly give up rituals and customs which helped to assure their distinct identity. The *canular* in particular was a useful mask for political opinions that could not be expressed openly without risk. More often, however, the *canular* was political only in the more indirect sense that it was a social practice which contributed to the identification of this elite.

Small as it was, the Ecole Normale was never a single community of about 150 students, but rather two distinct groups of about 80 and 70. Scientists and literary students usually spent little time in each other's company. Their encounters were limited for the most part to the tennis court, first year military drill, the Catholic group,[86] and, during the twentieth century, to political clubs. Of the twenty–three students who signed Simone Weil's letter in support of the students of Quimper, four were scientists. On the whole the politicians were the literary students, and segregation between Letters and Sciences was the rule. There is much truth in Georges Pompidou's humorous description of the relationship:

> One is a *normalien* in the same sense that one is prince of the blood. Nothing on the exterior marks the fact. But it is known, it is observed, although he be polite and even humane so as not to make others sensitive to it. I will go even further. Even in the heavens there are degrees. When a literary *normalien* speaks familiarly with a *scientifique* and does not hesitate to address him in public with affectionate solicitude, do not be under a misapprehension: that is only a manifestation of his sociability. Thus the descendant of the crusaders, when he has been well brought up, speaks as an equal with the nobility of the Empire. But the reality is different and nothing can change it.[87]

The literary *normalien,* especially, inherited a *persona* which was the product of legend and custom as well as tangible intellectual achievements.

The academic curriculum shaped the mentality of the *normaliens* in important ways by stressing criticism, rationalism, idealism, and classicism. But the extracurricular setting had important social and political ramifications as well. Soon after the students arrived at the rue d'Ulm as brilliant individual scholars, they participated in rites and traditions which confirmed their belonging to an elite with an honorable history. "Former student of the Ecole Normale Supérieure" became a title for a new republican nobility. The rising intensity of political activity among *normaliens* of the Third Republic was evidence of their growing self-consciousness as potential leaders. Lucien Herr was undoubtedly a symptom as well as a cause of this heightened political awareness during his long tenure as librarian. The school became a forum for scholars who learned to assume that they should make important contributions to the Republic even outside the field of education. And indeed, a significant minority of *normaliens* entered the national political arena.

6

The Alumni and the Republic

> Que trois normaliens [Edouard Herriot, Léon Blum, Paul Painlevé] . . . ayant acquis et formé toutes leurs idées et tous leurs sentiments politiques dans la température de l'Affaire Dreyfus, aient succédé en 1924 à de grands avocats, c'était naturel, typique, instructif. . . .—Albert Thibaudet

BEFORE the Third Republic national electoral politics attracted very few *normaliens.* The handful of graduates who became active in public affairs generally pursued careers in administration, literature, or journalism, while the great majority remained in their classrooms, where they exercised social or political influence indirectly or even unconsciously. The state, however, was hardly indifferent to the political influence of the Ecole Normale, for with each change of regime the Director's political reputation became an issue.[1] Yet the *normaliens'* sphere was largely secondary and higher education; in other areas of public life the alumni of the rue d'Ulm comprised only a marginal élite.

After the fall of the Second Empire in 1870 new opportunities beckoned men with political ambitions. Suddenly those who had opposed Napoleon III became prime candidates for political office or other responsibilities under the Republic. Whereas only four *normaliens* had held national political office before 1870, eleven who had attended Normale before that date became legislators in the early years of the Third Republic. Ten of these were republicans (see Table 15).

Jules Simon's career as a legislator and a Minister of the early Third Republic illustrates the essential conservatism and caution of

TABLE 15. Members of Parliament *Promotions* of 1810–1869

Name and Promotion	Journalistic Affiliation	Opposition to Regime	Years in Parliament	Political Affiliation
Renouard, Augustin Charles (1812 L)	*Le Globe*	Liberal during Restoration	1831–37, 1839–42	Conservative Republican
Corneille, Pierre Alexis[a] (1813 L)			1852–68 1876–78	Bonapartist
Wallon, Henri (1831 L)			1849–50, 1871–75 1875–1904	Center-Left
Simon, Jules (1833 L)	*Liberté de Penser, National, Siècle*	Opposes Napoleon III	1848, 1863–70, 1870–75, 1875–	Moderate Republican
Barni, Jules Romain (1837 L)	*Revue de Paris, Avenir, Liberté de Penser*	Refuses Oath to Napoleon III	1872–75, 1876–78	Gambettist
Deschanel, Emile (1839 L)	*Revue des Deux-Mondes, Indépendante, National, Liberté de Penser*	Exiled under Second Empire	1876–1904	Opportunist
Chalamet, Arthur (1842 L)			1876–81, 1883–95	Opportunist
Mézières, Alfred (1845 L)	*Revue des Deux-Mondes, Le Temps*		1881–	Opportunist
Challemel-Lacour, Paul (1846 L)	*Revue des Deux-Mondes, République Française, Le Temps*	Exiled under Second Empire	1872–96	Opportunist
Ordinaire, Louis-Dionys (1848 L)	*République Française, La Petite République*		1880–	Opportunist
Duvaux, Jules (1849 L)			1876–89	Opportunist
Maze, Alexandre (1859 L)			1879–91	Opportunist

[a]A descendant of the poet.

the early republican politicians. Simon ran unsuccessfully for the Chamber of Deputies in 1847 as a candidate of the *gauche modéré* and became a "representative of the people" in 1848 and a member of the Counseil d'Etat in 1849 before the Napoleonic government compelled him to withdraw from politics. The day before the plebiscite held on 10 July 1851 to ratify Napoleon's coup d'état, Simon addressed his philosophy class at the Sorbonne as follows:

> Messieurs, here I am a professor of moral philosophy. I owe you a lesson and an example. The law has just been publicly broken by the one whose duty it is to defend it; and France must say tomorrow in this balloting whether it approves this violation of the law or whether it condemns it. Be there in the ballot boxes but one vote pronouncing condemnation, I announce in advance, it would be mine.[2]

Although he was cheered by his students, Simon lost his posts at the Sorbonne and the Ecole Normale Supérieure. But he returned to the legislature twelve years later as an opposition member of the Corps Législatif and continued his career during the Third Republic as a Minister of Education and a senator.[3]

Jules Simon's characterization of himself as "profoundly republican and profoundly conservative" would apply to his fellow alumni in many respects. Yet he occupied a special place among them, since he was never accepted fully either by the Opportunists around Gambetta and Ferry or by monarchists, clericals, and conservatives. He expressed his social ideas in a small book on free and obligatory education which he wrote just before the fall of the Empire:

> I am not an enemy of what exists, a maker of systems like the Saint–Simonians, and I accept as just and salutary a certain number of laws which do some harm along with much good, and which one should not tamper with because everything would be upset with no improvement. I am not upset by those who are rich and happy without having done anything to achieve it. So much the better for them; I do not envy them; I do not wish to deprive them of any of their pleasure or wealth. But for those who suffer unjustly I request that they be assisted to support and defend themselves by giving them education. That is all I insist upon. . . . Since some instruction is necessary for everybody, it follows that everyone has a right to it. That is, the state owes to each citizen what is necessary, under one condition: provided that it is able to give it. Thus primary education ought to be universal and free.[4]

Although most *normaliens* shared this concept, as Minister of Education, Simon was forced to compromise in 1871 before a hostile legislature by supporting obligatory, but *not* free, primary education. The idea needed another decade and more solid republican strength before it could be transformed into law. Simon by then found himself out of step with the younger republicans of more Jacobin turn of mind who finally carried through the great educational reforms of 1880–1884. In the name of liberty he continued to oppose laws outlawing the religious orders and supported *liberté de l'enseignement* against the *monopole universitaire.* His entire career in fact was a doomed effort to reconcile elements which would not be reconciled, namely the Republic and the Church. His vision of a society led by tolerant republicans and liberal Catholics was not shared by either camp as polemics mounted in the 1880s and 1890s. Late in his career he took over the political direction of the conservative newspaper, *Le Gaulois,* where he hammered at the left wing republicans and opposed such things as amnesty for the Communards (contending that this was a weak placation of forces which were antiliberal), divorce, liberty of the press, and the separation of Church and State. To Simon the adoption of such positions was not inconsistent with his commitment to individual liberty; gradual change was the best guarantee that liberty would expand and that society would not become paralyzed by strife.[5]

Other *normaliens* of this generation who shared Simon's devotion to personal liberty did not always agree with him about the role that the state should play. Arthur Chalamet (prom. 1842), who had been an undersecretary in the Ministry of Education under Paul Bert before becoming a deputy, voted for divorce and partial amnesty of the Communards and spoke in favor of Ferry's Article Seven, which sought to invoke existing laws against religious orders. Yet like Simon, he voted for the Loi Lisbonne restricting liberty of the press. Jules Barni (prom. 1837), a former secretary of Victor Cousin and later a noted Kantian scholar, had joined Jules Simon in 1848 in founding the *Société démocratique des libres pensants* and wrote for the liberal newspaper *Liberté de penser.* In a remarkable article he stressed that the recent provision for universal suffrage presupposed education. Before the people should be permitted to vote directly for the President, they should be turned into proper citizens through education:

> Since certain political rights have been granted to all citizens, they must be made worthy of them. . . . To inculcate and develop in

> young souls, by every means, those principles and those sentiments of liberty, equality, and fraternity, which the Republic has made its motto, and which are in fact the attributes of a truly republican soul; to initiate them to the knowledge and inspire in them the love of their rights and duties as men and citizens, and at the same time to protect them against all the false doctrines which threaten the social order today: such is the goal of primary education instituted by the state which should be pursued.[6]

With the fall of the Empire Barni rallied to the government of National Defense and became a Gambettist. His moderate political and social ideas are revealed in his description of a citizen on the Republic as an individual who enjoyed "personal dignity, which included sobriety, independence, and honest labor; devotion to the family and the traditional virtues of the good father and the constant husband; liberty without licence and the untrammeled expression of the individual spirit; equality of opportunity without "brutal leveling," and humanity toward the ill fortune of others and toleration of diverse opinions."[7] Thus Barni participated in the elaboration of a bourgeois republican ideology which stressed democracy and individual freedom but assumed that social hierarchies would be transformed, if at all, very gradually.

In the early days of the Republic the *normaliens* in the legislature were all to be found in the same political camp. Only Jules Simon and Henri Wallon, both of whom led long careers in the Senate, remained independent of Gambetta and Ferry. Wallon is remembered chiefly as the author of an amendment in the National Assembly in January 1875 which led to the drafting of the Third Republic's brief constitution in the face of challenge from monarchists. The *normalien* politicians slightly younger than Simon and Wallon were also more radical and were all clients in some way of Gambetta or Ferry. Challemel-Lacour helped Gambetta to found *La Republique française,* which became the political organ of the Union Républicaine. Louis–Dionys Ordinaire was a regular contributor to this newspaper and became editor–in–chief of *La Petite république,* a more popular paper of the same political line. Jules Duvaux was elected to the city council in Nancy in 1871, expressed republican sympathies, was elected deputy in 1876, became undersecretary of state in the Ministry of Education under Ferry, and succeeded Ferry as Minister. During the 1870s and 1880s the Ecole Normale sent to the legislature no monarchists, no staunch apologists for the Church, nor any Radicals or Socialists. During the high tide of Opportunism, all except Jules Simon and Henri Wallon were Opportunists.

From the *promotions* of 1870 to 1880 five *normaliens* entered the Chamber of Deputies in the 1880s and 1890s, and all, including Jean Jaurès, did so as Opportunists, as had the generation which preceded them. Maurice Barrès lamented in 1898 that rootless intellectuals of this generation, men of Kantian moral principles and republican political ideas, had torn good people from their local traditions, folkways, and loyalties.[8] Bouteiller of *Les Déracinés* was educated at the Ecole Normale, where he became a pious Kantian who claimed to know what the categorical imperative demanded in concrete terms. But he soon left his teaching post in Nancy, compromised his principles, accepted the support of selfish business interests, and entered the legislature in Paris. Barrès was a good observer quite apart from his political message. *Lycées* indeed, like cloisters, shut young men off from the real world, encouraged them to ponder abstract ideas claiming universal validity, and suggested that they deserved to rule because they had special insight into truth. The early Republic was a period when professors of humble origin eager to rise in society helped to develop and expound the new republican ideology.

Auguste Burdeau (prom. 1870) had been Barrès' professor in Nancy and became the model for Bouteiller. His case illustrates how a *normalien* might make a political career in the early Third Republic. The youngest of four children, Burdeau grew up in a poor household. His father died before he was born, and his mother supported the family with difficulty as a seamstress. Burdeau became an apprenticed iron worker at the age of ten, but did well in school and made his way with prizes and scholarships to the *lycée* of Lyon, the *collège* Sainte Barbe of Paris, and the Ecole Normale, and he achieved first place in the *agrégation* of philosophy in 1874. Before entering the Ecole Normale he had served in the army, was captured by the Prussians, and escaped and returned home to a hero's welcome—an experience which afterwards probably contributed to the nationalist tenor of his republicanism. He taught philosophy from 1874 to 1880 at St. Etienne, where he helped to found a republican club and organize resistance to the May 16 movement, which sought to overturn the Republic in favor of a monarchy. After a year in the *lycée* of Nancy, where he helped to found the *Bulletin de correspondance universitaire,* he became *chef de cabinet* (administrative assistant) of Paul Bert, the Minister of Education. In 1885 he entered the Chamber of Deputies from the Republican Opportunist list of the Rhône.

A children's story, which Burdeau published early in his career, testifies to his beliefs about France's frontiers. In the tale a French customs agent is killed by contrabanding Germans, but there is a promise of revenge, for his son vows to rectify the frontier between France and Germany.[9] France should not only reclaim its lost provinces; it should also pursue its civilizing mission abroad lest other nations step in. In domestic politics Burdeau was a moderate. On the one hand he opposed collectivism in the name of freedom and the law of supply and demand, and he defended the rights of capital, inheritance, and property; on the other, he favored lightening taxation on consumption and a progressive income tax.[10] He stressed those traditional virtues which are particularly important to men who govern: work, savings, self–help, and duty towards parents, superiors, and country. The nation should reward work and merit, and social change should take place in good order so that the state and traditional hierarchical institutions would be respected.[11] In all innocence Burdeau admitted that the new army of *instituteurs* was created to fulfill a role of political pacification:

> When a people has universal suffrage, that it can claim to be its master and hold the national purse strings, it cannot be ignorant of what the budget is. Furthermore, since there are orators who publicly denigrate private property, and who lead workers astray, diverting them from saving, those great social truths, those too must have their defenders. It is said that England saved herself from a revolution by founding thirty–five years ago more than four thousand chairs of political economy. The law of 1882 has just founded forty thousand of them in France: they are positions of confidence that the state has turned over to our *instituteurs.*[12]

Given Burdeau's own origins and the role of civic indoctrination which he assigned to the *instituteurs,* it is perhaps not surprising that in the 1880s he should have favored a common primary school, the *école unique* which would elude reformers for another half century. Further, he wished to eliminate the baccalaureate as a requirement for state jobs; he would retain it only for entrance to the university Faculties, but even then with a much lighter emphasis upon Latin and Greek. But the *lycée* should remain the preserve of the elite. After the common primary school,

> . . . the mass of the sons of workers and petty bourgeois, having no more than three or four years before them to devote to studies, would attend higher primary schools, which would be better named the secondary schools. The others, having either more talent already apparent, or having parents who were better off or more

> ambitious, would enter into the *lycée* stream, which ought to be called higher education.[13]

Burdeau applauded a system in which the *lycée* would be reserved for an elite which could actually attain the "bac" and would go on to higher education. Those not fit by evident natural gifts or family fortune should not have false hopes but instead take a shorter route to better organized apprenticeships and jobs. Burdeau's democratic instinct stopped well short of devising programs which would give all children an equal chance to pursue a university career despite the family's fortune. He was a reformer in his time, but a sober realist rather than a visionary of the democratic dream. He well represented those *couches nouvelles* which Gambetta and later Ferry wished to educate, promote, and join to the body politic.

By the 1890s Burdeau's old left, which had struggled for democracy and the Republic against monarchists and Bonapartists, had become the party of order. The politics surrounding the Boulanger Affair and the Ralliement caused former Radical allies to seek alliances with the Socialists, and the Opportunists themselves drifted to the right.[14] With Burdeau (prom. 1870), Delpeuch (prom. 1879), Dejean (prom. 1880), and Legrand (prom. 1876), a certain *normalien* parliamentary tradition which stressed national unity over social change came to an end. Although Opportunists continued to exercise a great deal of influence in the legislature, young *normaliens* ceased to become deputies of that persuasion for about twenty years. Nor did a new generation of *normaliens* suddenly take their places in the Chamber of Deputies as Radicals and Socialists. Jaurès, who became a socialist in 1893, alone provided some continuity between the "old left" of the 1880s and the "new left" after 1900. Legrand, a *Progressiste,* was the only *normalien* in the Chamber who could have witnessed Jaurès' great debate with Clemenceau in 1906 over the repression of strikes. But four years later the tribune was joined by a small army of Radicals and Socialists who had been educated at the rue d'Ulm during the 1880's and 1890's and who would later carry his remains to the Pantheon.

Five Radicals, three Socialists, and one Republican Socialist were victorious in the elections of 1910 and 1912 (*see* Figure 1). Others joined them between the wars, and until the Second World War, Socialists and Radicals led by *normaliens* dominated French politics. The Radicals were led by Herriot, the Socialists by Jaurès and Blum, and the Republican Socialists by Painlevé.[15] Through these men the

Figure 1. Members of Parliament: Political Affiliation and Duration of Service in Parliament (Promotions of 1870–1940)

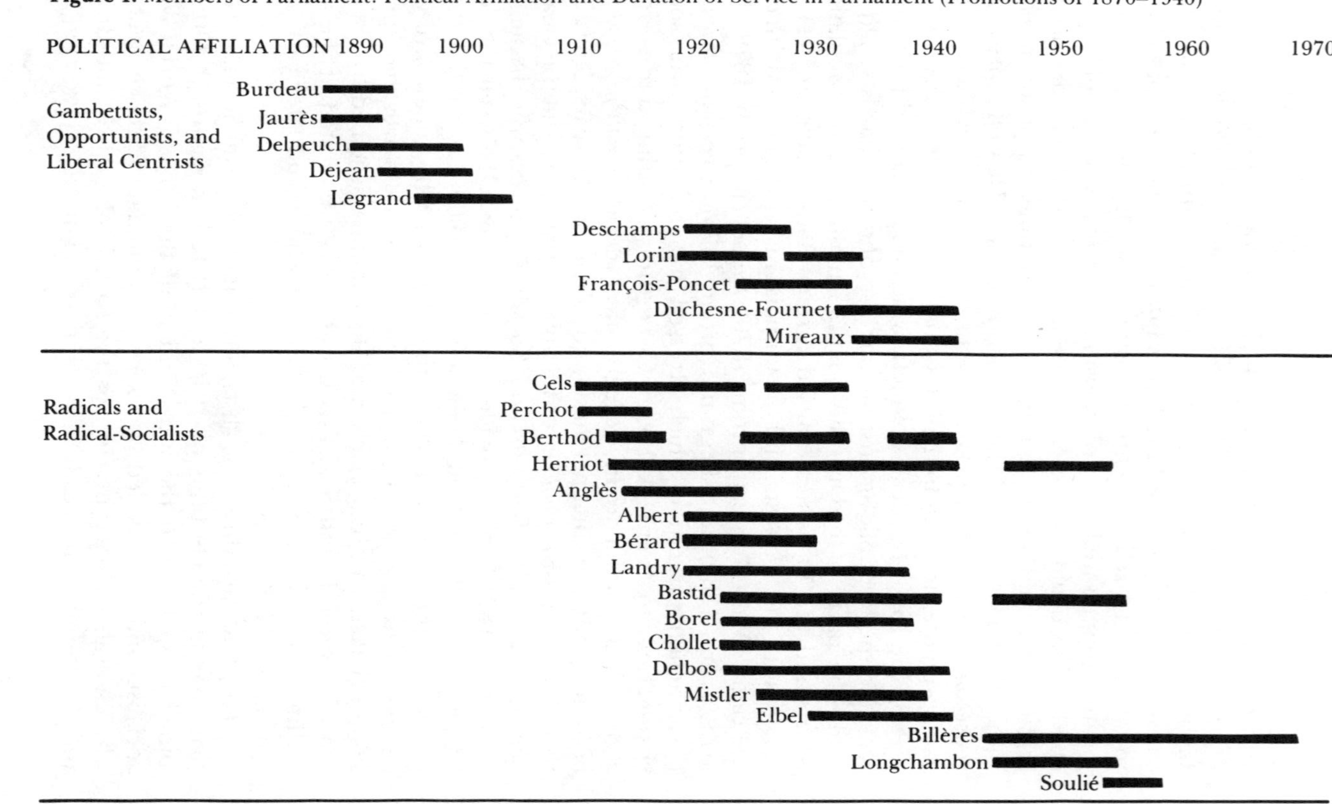

Figure 1. (Continued)

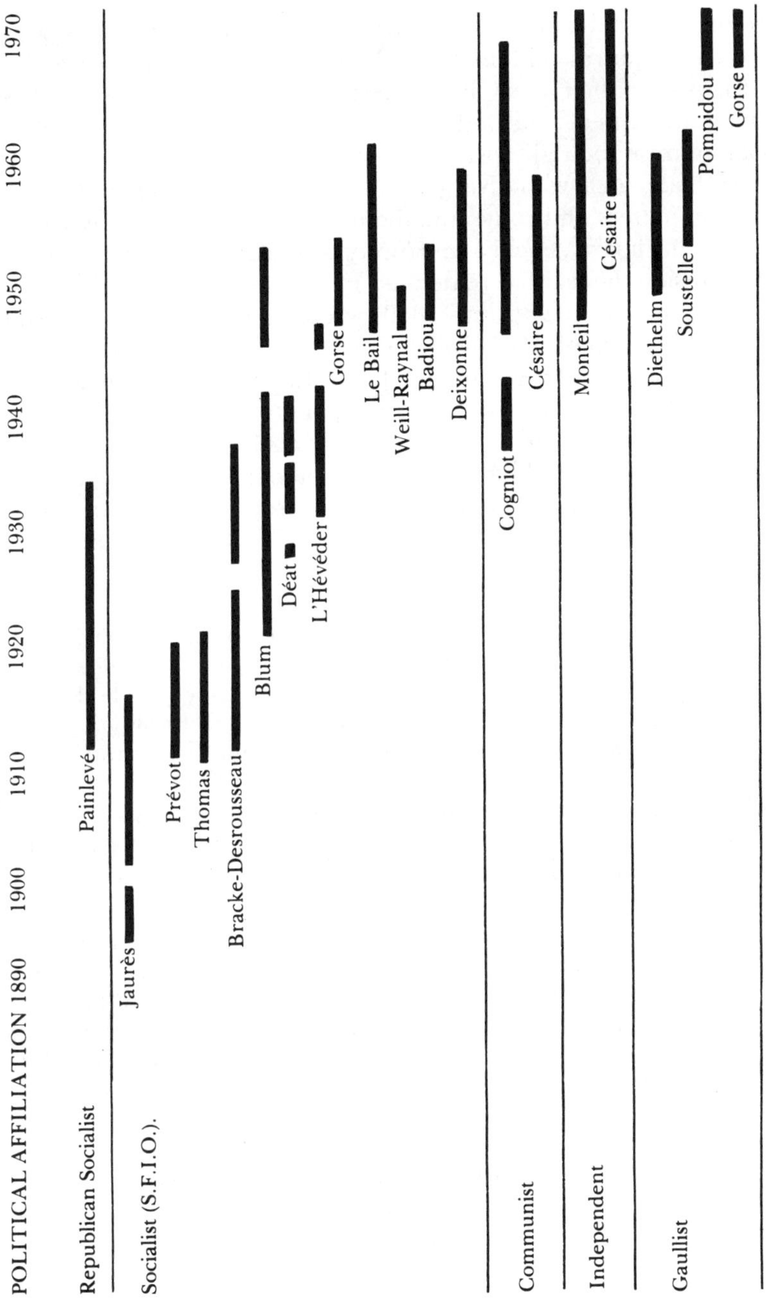

Ecole Normale was clearly visible on the left and left of center of the political stage during the last thirty years of the Third Republic.

Both Jaurès and Blum took considerable pains to define the socialism of their party in intellectual terms both to draw it into a single movement and to differentiate it from anarchism, Caesarism, Communism or radicalism.[16] The leaders of the Radical Party, however, had to deal with divergent tendencies of autonomous local Radical committees and contented themselves with vague formulae about individual liberty, equal opportunity, and the laic Republic.[17] A *normalien* outside the legislature defined radicalism more sharply.

Emile Chartier (prom. 1889) wrote many political essays under the pseudonym of Alain while he taught philosophy at *lycée* Henri IV for the last thirty years of the Third Republic. As both writer and teacher his influence was substantial, and many of his students went on to the Ecole Normale. As a young man Alain had witnessed official corruption surrounding the Panama scandal and the Dreyfus Affair. This must have contributed later to his repeated warnings that the citizen should cede as little power as possible to his representative in government:

> Experience has shown a hundred times that a governing élite, whether it governs from heredity or by acquired knowledge, very quickly deprives citizens of every freedom if the people do not exercise a power of control, of accusation, and finally of recall. When I vote, I do not exercise a right, I defend all my rights.[18]

Alain's individualism did not quite end up as anarchism, but his distrust of government as he knew it or as he thought socialists envisioned it was acute:

> To govern is to do what is necessary and to hand things over to competent people. Each man in the system is a good man if he does his job. . . . What is wrong then? It is this, that the formidable state, composed of military men, diplomats, and administrators, has no master. This blind instrument proceeds by itself. . . . This situation of the reigning bureaucrat is new. We need a government against the state. . . .[19]

He was suspicious of the state as organizer of society no matter whether it was run by military men or by socialists: "The state should not in the least oppose cooperation, mutual assistance, or mutual insurance; but neither can it impose them . . . forced communism is ruinous."[20] Alain's entire political creed was consistent with his opposition to Rousseau concerning the General Will: "To say everything in short, I much distrust a General Will which would emerge from an assembled people. Metaphysical tyrant."[21] Optimistic about human nature, Alain was pessimistic about the state's ability to regulate its expression. He was the philosopher of the individualistic rather than the Jacobin strain of radicalism.

Edouard Herriot (prom. 1891) was an active politician who became the embodiment of the entire Radical movement from 1919, when he was elected President of the Radical Party, until his death in 1957. His rumpled clothes, pipe, and expansive manner all appealed to and reassured the Radical clientele of artisans, small merchants, small farmers, petty officials, and teachers. He had been a scholarship student, his origins were similar to theirs, but he became a Dreyfusard who resisted the attraction of socialism represented by Jaurès. At the Ecole Normale he:

> . . . admired Jean Jaurès; more modestly, I joined that solid infantry of the Republic which I have never abandoned. I took part in the electoral campaign [of 1893] by writing articles signed with transparent pseudonyms. . . . I carried on a polemic with the *Gazette d'Annonay*. When I returned to the Ecole, Director Perrot gave me a severe reprimand.[22]

When he had served the required ten years in the teaching profession, he began his political career in Lyon in 1904 under the sponsorship of the Socialist mayor. He chose, nevertheless, to become a Radical, a decision that he claimed much later was made for intellectual reasons:

> I had studied with great interest the theories of Marx and Engels according to which economic production determined the social class of men, their political and intellectual history. Charles Andler had just published a new translation and commentary of the Communist Manifesto with the Librairie de la rue Cujas . . . I refused to believe in the theory of classes for a country like France where the variety of conditions is so great, property so widely dispersed, the crafts so well developed. I considered too simple and artificial this reduction of society to two fatally hostile elements: bourgeoisie and proletariat. I refused to believe that the degree of civilization of a people was strictly dependent upon its material production. It seemed to me that the history of our country re-

> vealed incessant mutations in men's condition and the rise of the most humble—when the means of instruction were given to them—to positions of control. I persisted to believe in the essential role of the individual, of the person.[23]

The Marxism which Herriot rejected, in which the key elements were materialism, determinism, and class struggle, was interpreted in France principally by Jules Guesde. And since Guesde controlled the Parti Ouvrier, Herriot sought his political fortune elsewhere. Despite his admiration for Jaurès and Blum he remained a Radical, for he believed that some forms of private property should always remain.[24] His France was a nation of small property owners, small farmers, artisans, and petty officials who might rise in the democratic republic provided that they were given the proper opportunities for education. Having risen in status through a scholarship and higher education, Herriot the politician took a deep interest in the further democratization of education.[25]

Radicals disagreed with each other about many things, but a common theme was their anticlericalism. Agnostics themselves, Alain and Herriot granted that others should be free to believe what they wished; to deny this would be inconsistent with liberalism. However, the state should not permit its children to be swayed by a religious world view offered by teachers who were ultimately disloyal to France. The Radical dogma of the laical state stood in the way of lasting alliances with parties of the center and the right. Radicals were forever weighing conflicting demands of their doctrine (however flexible it proved to be), practical reforms, and participation in power.

The Ecole Normale's Radicals and Socialists came from two branches of the same political tree rooted in the Enlightenment. Essential for human happiness were material well being, peace, and knowledge of the world; standing across the path to progress were superstition and violence. Rationalism, the philosophical basis of their anticlericalism, was the secular faith which they sought to spread through the educational system. But whereas the Radicals saw education as a long range instrument of social justice which would enable worthy individuals to fulfill their separate possibilities, Socialists saw it more as a vehicle to fashion a new consciousness explicitly for the coming socialist society. In short, Radicals and Socialists faced different directions: Radicals looked to the past, where the exemplars of humanitarian wisdom and individualism could be found, while Socialists, assuming that individualism was proven bankrupt by the ravages of industrial capitalism, envisioned a new, cooperative humanity unlike any in the past. Radicals were more satisfied with their own society and with human models furnished by history. Socialists, much like early Christians, yearned for a future which would be very different from the past; but they too experienced the difficulty of explaining to heathen what the future would be like or that it would be a substantial improvement upon the present. Yet despite this difference in orientation, Radicals and Socialists of the rue d'Ulm in particular shared the same rational, democratic, and civil libertarian assumptions.

For Radicals, socialism provided the fascinating challenge of a different but allied doctrine. Elie Halévy (prom. 1889), an habitué of Péguy's bookstore of the rue Cujas during the Dreyfus Affair and later a leading authority on the history of socialism, was a critical but sympathetic observer of the movement.[26] He confided to Célestin Bouglé (prom. 1890), one of the philosophers of solidarism, that his lectures on socialism at the Ecole Libre des Sciences Politiques were nervously being heard by Eugène d'Eichtal, "the defender of private property," and by Boutmy himself (Director of the Ecole Libre), who was, however, "more serene."[27] Halévy maintained that he would not be intimidated. In another letter to Bouglé during that same year, 1904, he wondered whether France was ripe or suited for socialism, and by 1913 he had indeed come to believe that socialism contained the secret of the future. Would it take the form of Swiss republics or a European Caesarism? In either case he would keep his distance. "Strange thing, I do not believe that I ever for an instant had the desire to join the Party: the only moments when I wanted to become a cell–member was when, each autumn, I saw on the walls of the Latin Quarter the small notices, in double columns, of the Positivist Church. I ask myself sometimes uneasily if what keeps me from becoming a Comteist is not a vague worldy or rather intellectual aristocratism."[28] An insistence upon independence was typical of the *normaliens*.

Jules Romains (prom. 1906) captured, in his novel *Le Drapeau noir*, the reticence of the young pre–war *normalien* to give up his political independence despite being attracted to socialism. Jerphanion confides to Jallez about his political activity: "I am in touch . . . with a committee. They were kind enough to accept me without requiring formal membership. I made a few speeches. The advantage for me was to experience a living local political milieu. . . ." Jallez interjects: "What committee?" And Jerphanion continues: "You will laugh . . . Radical–Socialist. . . . If I had wished, they would have made me a candidate for the elections next year." Replying to Jallez' question about the presence of Socialists in the area, Jerphanion comes to the heart of the matter: "I feel no estrangement from the Socialists. If I went into active politics one day, I would enter into the best relations with them. But I do not wish to be of their Party. And they have no great need of men like me. If I must absolutely be a member of some organization, I would like much better to be someone very advanced in a Party where the thought is free and where complexity of judgment is no crime. I am convinced that the Socialists are mistaken on a number of points and to their detriment. If I were one of them, they would never allow me to tell them."[29] The Radicals permitted the intellectual to think according to his own rather than the Party's initiative without penalty. Jallez reminds us of Herriot, who also prized his independence and was on good terms with Socialists.

The question of revolution posed a problem for men of reason and humanity like Herriot, Bouglé, or Halévy. In a letter to Bouglé in 1908 after the appearance of Jaurès' *Histoire socialiste de la Révolution Française,* Halévy confessed, "If the Revolution had neither the September massacres nor the drownings of Nantes, nor the guillotinings of Paris, and if . . . it ended with a Washington instead of a Bonaparte, I would like it better."[30] The irrational, the savage, the inhumane in the Revolution of 1789 or an imagined revolution of the future repulsed *normaliens* in general and caused them to prefer gradual change by democratic means. The Russian Revolution was later to provoke an ambivalent or negative response among *normaliens* because of its violence.

Were the Socialists from Normale more willing than the Radicals to contemplate the outbreak of a violent revolution? Probably not, although many of them believed that the persistence of social injustice would make it inevitable. It was an event they neither sought deliberately to provoke nor eagerly awaited. Jaurès himself had no illusions about a peaceful passage to socialism, but he consistently stressed education, persuasion, and peace.[31] George Lichtheim calls our attention to ". . . a distinct line which runs from the minority faction of the 1871 Commune, via Brousse and Malon, to Herr and Jaurès, and finally to Léon Blum and the later S.F.I.O. Those who adhered to this tradition were democrats, though most of them also regarded themselves as Marxists. . . . Ultimately the moral community of the French nation meant more to them than mere working–class solidarity—though in their fashion they tried to be loyal to both. . . . [Their doctrine] rested upon a refusal to separate socialism from humanism. The appeal was not to history but to a distant goal which, in principle at least, all men could share."[32]

The only Socialist deputy of Jaurès' age from the rue d'Ulm to reject this tradition, at least at first, was Alexandre Bracke–Desrousseaux (prom. 1881). Bracke became a follower and close associate of Jules Guesde, Jaurès' long–standing rival. His father had been a military officer, then a worker, and finally a *chansonnier* of considerable renown; his mother was the daughter of a revolutionary Blanquist. As a *normalien* "Bracke" published articles in socialist journals. He became secretary of the Parti Ouvrier Français in 1889, several years before Jaurès became a socialist and only a year after Herr became librarian of the Ecole Normale. Soon he began to write for *Le Travailleur du Nord, Petit sou,* and *Le Socialiste,* which he helped Guesde to found. There had been nothing at Normale in his day which might have challenged the rigid brand of socialism which he learned from Guesde, and he evidently ignored the republican orthodoxy dominant at the school in the 1880s. Eventually, however, he joined socialist comrades of the rue d'Ulm, first in the *Union Sacrée* of the First World War and later in Léon Blum's entourage.

Jaurès was suspect among the Guesdists because of the education and political instincts which he had acquired at the Ecole Normale.[33] He kept one foot in the republican tradition exemplified by Gambetta and Ferry which he had found at the rue d'Ulm in the late 1870s. This was the fundamental reason for his rivalry with Jules Guesde. He and Guesde clashed over the *universités populaires,* for instance, as well as over the Dreyfus Affair, the Millerand case, and other matters. A former professor and at heart always an intellectual, Jaurès ardently supported workers' education immediately, before the expected revolution took place. Guesde also had been a teacher, but he was far more rigid than Jaurès, considered himself an infallible interpreter of Marxist doctrine, and saw the *universités populaires* as an attempt by unreliable intellectuals who evaded the Party's discipline to gain control of the working class movement. Jaurès believed that socialism would profit from a plurality of voices, but there was a limit to his tolerance. In the nervous atmosphere before 1914, when he was trying to maintain solidarity between French and German socialism to preserve the peace in Europe, he seems to have departed from his own principles in a bitter dispute with Charles Andler (prom. 1884) about the character of German socialism.[34]

Jaurès' flexibility permitted him to work with men outside his own Party. He favored cooperation with Radicals for specific goals like the revision of the Dreyfus case. He applauded Millerand's program for social reform and refrained from criticism when Millerand accepted a ministerial portfolio in Waldeck–Rousseau's government in 1899. And from behind the scenes Jaurès as political tactician directed parliamentary strategy for the entire republican left in the Combes era until he was forbidden to do so by his own party in 1905.[35] That year marked the formal joining of the diverse strands of French socialism around the orthodox Marxist formula of Jules Guesde. Yet it required a genius of Jaurès' stature to weave a synthesis which would keep the Party together by reconciling wild hopes and reason, ideals and politics, and the conflicting claims of individuals, the Party, and the nation at large.

The pull of diverse traditions upon Jaurès' own thought is suggested by the listing of Michelet and Plutarch alongside Marx in the preface of his history of the French Revolution. The economy was important, but original creative beings always had the possibility of reacting to it in their own ways: they were never simply its reflection.[36] In this sense Jaurès remained a *normalien* and resembled friends and professors at the Sorbonne whose rationalism and philosophical idealism also had liberal political ramifications.

On 31 July 1914, as assassin put an end to Jaurès' effort to maintain peace in Europe, and as workers, farmers, and bourgeois marched off to war, evidence of his crusade for peace melted away almost overnight. Socialists joined Radicals and others in a *Union Sacrée* to defend the *Patrie.* Jules Guesde became Minister of State, Marcel Sembat accepted the portfolio of Public Works, and Albert Thomas (prom. 1899), summoned from the army ranks to coordinate national transportation, soon assumed the enormous task of directing the production of armaments. What Jaurès would have done must remain a matter for speculation, but since he had always thrown in his lot with the Party rather than abandon it when it failed to correspond to his own conceptions, it is difficult to imagine that he would not have participated in the *Union Sacrée.* At the same time it is difficult to conceive that the history of the war and of Europe would not somehow have been different had he lived through the period of stalemate and the peace initiatives of 1917.

Albert Thomas soon became the most prominent Socialist in the government through his service as Undersecretary and Minister (late in 1916) of Arms Production. Like Jaurès, he had refrained from participating in Radical cabinets out of loyalty to the Party, but his socialism was not the same. Jaurès once accused him of *ouvriérisme*—of believing that the labor movement was the one true source of socialist initiatives.[37] Thomas assumed that he should interpret the aspirations of the reformist wing of the syndicalist movement and transform these aspirations into legislation which affected the workers' well–being. As Minister of Armaments his initiatives on behalf of workers included the improvement of working conditions in factories, working conditions for women, lodging, hygiene, day care centers, and maternity care.[38] He saw the war, curiously enough in retrospect, as an opportunity for the different social classes to know each other better and to prepare for a socialist society. Jaurès too was optimistic by nature, but he was a subtler thinker than Thomas and had few illusions about reforms *per se* unaccompanied by changes in mentality. Intellectuals, Jaurès maintained, were more likely than workers to think independently of their origins or social condition. For this reason they had important work to perform in defining socialist cultural goals and exploring the meaning of current events for the socialist movement. Unlike Jaurès, Thomas focused his attention almost exclusively upon concrete legislation which would benefit the laborer immediately. Even after the war had cast a shadow on his brand of socialism, he remained faithful to reformism as the Director of the International Labor Bureau (B.I.T.) in Geneva, where he worked tirelessly for the improvement of working conditions in the world at large.[39]

Despite differences in political philosophy among politicians of the same party (Jaurès and Thomas) or of different parties (Radicals and Socialists), the *normaliens* in the legislature and outside of it shared a common accord which went far deeper than the political truce of the *Union Sacrée.*[40] They were all humanists and democrats. In the first twenty years of the century the Socialist/Radical–Socialist consensus was the expression of their thought. During the two decades following the war this concensus remained dominant among politicians from the rue d'Ulm, although to a much lesser degree. The Russian Revolution, the peace settlement, the depression, and the rise of fascism gradually placed strains on old assumptions and caused the political spectrum to widen. A few *normaliens,* like a great many other citizens, began to look outside the parties of Blum and Herriot for theoretical ideas and programs for action.

Radicals and Socialists further developed the tactical alliance which had arisen during the Dreyfus Affair and the Combes era. Of the 23 *normaliens* in the legislature between the wars there were 13 Radicals and 4 Socialists (there were also 5 deputies of the center parties and 1 Communist deputy). Personal relationships founded upon shared traditions tied leaders of these parties to the rue d'Ulm and encouraged political careers. Herriot and Painlevé remained on the scene after the war, Jaurès was gone, and Albert Thomas had left national politics for the International Labor Bureau in Geneva. Léon Blum (prom. 1890), already an outstanding literary critic, man of letters, and jurist, assumed the leadership of the S.F.I.O. in 1919.[41]

A close friend and admirer of both Jaurès and Herr, Blum proceeded quickly to rebuild the Socialist Party after 1920, when a majority left it to join the Third International. With enormous courage and dialectical skill Blum explained his position at the Socialist Congress at Tours. He would not give in to those like Albert Thomas on the right wing of the Party who believed that a series of reforms would, of themselves, lead peacefully to socialism; the passage to socialism would mark a revolutionary and painful break with the past. On the other hand he stressed that the mere seizure of power by a small elite in the Russian or Blanquist manner would not produce socialism either, but merely another form of tyranny. As he explained to the hostile audience at Tours, he chose neither Lenin nor Wilson but rather Jaurès.[42]

Of course Jaurès' synthesis of democratic and revolutionary ideas had always been difficult to maintain, and Jaurès himself would have had difficulty reconciling all positions at Tours and afterward. Blum was fully equal to the intellectual task that his mentor had set, but the situation was drastically altered from what it had been before the war. The enthusiasm for the Russian Revolution thwarted his effort at Tours to keep French socialism united and under its own direction. After the majority had left to join the Third International, for the moment all Blum could do was to "guard the old house."[43] Soon afterwards disenchantment with Communism as it was administered by Stalin brought many of the wayward back to the fold—although, significantly, none of the Socialist *normaliens* in the legislature had ever left. Under Blum's leadership the S.F.I.O.'s growth continued, culminating in the Popular Front government of 1936 with Blum as Premier. He and Herriot, as in 1924, led a left wing coalition government, but their roles this time were reversed. Also the international situation was more ominous. Events soon laid bare the dilemmas of a supposedly revolutionary party governing in a non–revolutionary situation on the sufferance of anti–revolutionary parties.[44]

Both in the legislature and elsewhere the great majority of *normaliens* supported the Popular Front in June 1936.[45] But the international situation coupled with the domestic and international economic crisis soon exposed the vulnerability of Blum's coalition government and cast a shadow upon the entire political tradition which the Ecole Normale had come to symbolize. After all, if Radicals and democratic Socialists—led as they were by the Ecole Normale's liberal humanists—could not prevent economic hardship, diplomatic isolation, and finally the disaster of 1940, then perhaps their basic ideas were wrong or out of date. This was the perception at least of a few students at Normale who became Communists or Royalists in this period. Likewise in the legislature there emerged a handful of *normaliens* who were neither Radicals nor Socialists.

Henri Lorin (prom. 1886) and Gaston Deschamps (prom. 1882) entered the *Chambre Bleu Horizon* of 1919 as centrists of the old *Union Républicaine* list in opposition to Radicals and Socialists; in 1924 André François–Poncet (prom. 1907) combatted the *Cartel des Gauches* and won election with the *Bloc National;* and in the 1930s Pierre Duchesne –Fournet (prom. 1901) and Emile Mireaux (prom. 1907) entered the Chamber as members of the *Bloc.* François-Poncet was the most incisive expositor of their political views.[46] He criticized the *Cartel des Gauches* as being demogogic and old fashioned; the Cartel was doctrinaire and hence inflexible and unable to respond to realities. The Cartel's leaders resembled pious theologians who took their texts from Rousseau and Marx. His own party, by contrast, was better equipped to act in the modern world because it was pragmatic and experimental in its method. Although François–Poncet stressed that he was a liberal, it was clear that the society which he supported differed from the one envisioned by his Radical and Socialist opponents. Herriot and other Radicals certainly shared his hostility to the notion of class struggle, but they were far more critical of the existing social hierarchy and of social injustice. François–Poncet believed that social mechanisms which prevailed were effective and justified:

> Class struggle! As if, in France, the bourgeoisie was anything but the most advanced level of the common people [la couche la plus évoluée du peuple]! As if, for a large part, the bourgeois were not sons of workers! As if there was not with us from the bourgeois class to the working class a constant exchange [of place], a continual rise and fall![47]

He proceeded to depict a tyrannous state of equality of misery should the doctrine of class struggle gain acceptance. In fact, he continued, the bourgeois was not "privileged" but only "favored." But in return the bourgeois was called to perform important duties—*noblesse oblige:*

> It has been forgotten that democracy has no other purpose but to assure a wider and more just recruitment of the elite. Little by little we have lost sight of this notion of the elite, which is by far the most important, the only important [concept] for the government of states. We have sacrificed it, little by little, to the concept of number.[48]

The legislature itself constituted an elite and should not, he thought, always do the people's will, for ". . . the parliamentary majority, in contact with realities, has understood that the duty of representatives of the people is not always to obey the people but sometimes to resist them."[49] Although many of the Radicals and Socialists would have agreed with some of these proposals, the cumulative effect, counter to their principles, was to defend the social hierarchy in place. If François–Poncet had not quite stripped "equality" from the Revolutionary and Republican motto, he nevertheless gave it a narrow significance.

> The liberal is a free spirit, without prejudices. . . . He is fundamentally indulgent. Tolerance is in his soul. He detests constraints, violence. He flees excesses, categorical pretensions, references to the absolute.[50]

But what, if not the absolute idea, could provoke a liberal to work for a drastic reordering of his society? In fact men of François–Poncet's party were concerned to make their society function better, not to change it fundamentally.

Both he and Emile Mireaux very soon after the First World War became involved with a publication sponsored by the steel industry (Comité des Forges), the *Société d'Etudes et d'Informations Economiques.* François–Poncet described the enterprise as follows:

> The Company has as its object the collection, analysis, and diffusion of the most important information relative to questions of an economic, social and political order. . . . this work was accomplished by ten or so young men [who had] graduated for the most part from the *grandes écoles,* notably the Ecole Normale Supérieure. They were united by a community of ideas. They derived from the war the same conclusions. They were struck by the backward tendencies of our country, by the lack of cultivation in leading circles, by the ignorance and mutual distrust which prevailed among intellectuals and producers living side by side. They felt strongly the necessity to open the door to a new spirit. . . .[51]

To Radicals and Socialists the war experience led to the *école unique;* to centrists like François–Poncet it suggested better education for the elite and better business methods. The *Société d'Etudes* breathed the general spirit that had been dominant since the end of the nineteenth century at the Ecole Libre des Sciences Politiques. Classical economics was dogma at the Ecole Libre, but there was also a strong Le Playist tradition, which stressed detailed monographic studies of social conditions and a sense of social concern and responsibility on the part of factory owners and managers. Significantly, François–Poncet wrote an admiring (although not uncritical) biography of Robert Pinot, head of the Comité des Forges, who tried to bring such ideas to the leaders of the steel industry.[52]

Both Emile Mireaux and François–Poncet were true to their own ideas that the elite must justify itself by its usefulness to the society. François–Poncet had a brilliant career first as a deputy, then as a diplomat and man of letters. He was elected to the French Academy, served as president of the International Red Cross, and remains the elder statesman and perennial president of the alumni association of the Ecole Normale.

Mireaux very quickly moved from the *Société d'Etudes* to *Le Temps,* which was also controlled by the Comité des Forges, before he entered the Chamber of Deputies in 1935. No less than François–Poncet was he a classical liberal in economics with strong Le Playist modification. In a eulogy to Clément Colson, a professor of political economy at the Ecole Libre for the first four decades of the twentieth century, Mireaux noted with approval that Colson favored state intervention when there was no other possible solution—work accidents and poor relief for instance.[53] But the state should not intervene because of some abstract notion of justice; it should do so only out of a sense of moral obligation. True liberalism did not mean the law of the jungle. It meant a stable and well ordered society suffused by a moral law and a sense of mutual obligation. For this school of thought it was crucial that the managers and owners of capital should have a well developed social conscience and act upon it of their own accord. Only in such a manner could they justify their power and possibly retain it in light of political movements which sought drastic changes in the social order.[54]

Compared with the centrists, of whom there were five in the legislature between the wars, the deviation to the left of the Socialist/Radical consensus was minimal. Paul Nizan (prom. 1924) was the best known of a handful of students who joined the Communist Party in the 1920s and 1930s.[55] Of these students, only Georges Cogniot (prom. 1921) became a Communist deputy before the Second World War. Cogniot had devoured Rousseau and Romain Rolland's *Au dessus de la mêlée* as a *lycée* student during the First World War. Upon his arrival at the rue d'Ulm his political ideas were already well to the left.[56] At Normale the smugness and *arrivisme* which he perceived in many of the students, especially the socialists, turned him toward the Communist Party. After working for the Party for a decade while he taught in the provinces, he was named to Lycée Voltaire in Paris in 1934. In quick succession before the outbreak of the war he became the secretary of Romain Rolland's World Committee against War and Fascism, was elected as a Communist to the Chamber of Deputies, took over the direction of *L'Humanité,* and with Paul Langevin (prom 1894) founded *La Pensée,* the semi–official intellectual journal of the French Communist Party. Furthermore Cogniot remained an important figure in the Party and in the Assembly during the Fourth and Fifth Republics. He has proven to be the exception among *normaliens* who joined the Party in that he has kept the faith despite the Russian purges of the 1930s, the non–Aggression Pact of 1939, Hungary in 1956, and Czechoslovakia in 1968.

For France the nature of the Second World War assured that the list of dead would be shorter than it had been in the First World War, and yet the second struggle with Germany was more cruel morally and psychologically. Everyone confronted the dilemma of whether and in what manner to resist the Germans. The *résistant* was seldom popular, least of all when he provoked German retaliation. Paramount for most people was survival, and the Resistance not only troubled the conscience but, in the short run at least, endangered people it was supposed to liberate. Those who made a clear political choice in this period risked terrible consequences sooner or later, either at the hands of the Germans or at the hands of their neighbors after the war. Every community, group, and individual devised a plan of either action or survival. It was desirable to be employed doing something essential to the national economy and to be as inconspicuous as possible. Some *normaliens* were offered and accepted relatively safe management training positions with Citroën or Renault, companies involved in making vehicles for the Germans. The *caçique* of Normale who declined such a post in a letter to the Director stressed his duty to set an example for others: it was an example of courage and of democracy to refuse special treatment because of his high academic rank.[57]

A lack of evidence and the very nature of the question make it difficult to assess the reaction of *normaliens* as a whole to occupation, Vichy, and the Germans. But in the case of the politicians it is easier to render a judgment. Whereas ordinary citizens might wisely adjust their personal dosage of "resistance" and "collaboration," for once politicians found it difficult to temporize. In the first place the members of the legislature were called upon to vote on 10 July 1940 on the question of whether to surrender full powers to Marshal Pétain. Overwhelmingly, in an atmosphere of panic and fear, the National Assembly voted to do so: 569 yes, 80 no, and 17 abstentions. Herriot, as President of the Assembly, had abstained, but in an opening speech he urged support of the Marshal.[58] Admittedly Herriot quickly cooled toward Pétain and never supported the Vichy regime. Bastid and Delbos were absent, the latter having departed on the *Massilia* for North Africa. (Before a hostile audience Herriot staunchly defended those who had left France on the *Massilia*.) Blum had voted no. Other *normaliens* who were present at that session voted with the majority: the Socialists L'Hévéder and Déat (since 1933 a Neo–Socialist), the Radicals Mistler and Berthod, and two centrists, Mireaux and Duchesne–Fournet. Cogniot had enlisted in the army, for as a Communist deputy he had lost his seat after his party was outlawed following the Non–Aggression Pact.[59]

There were no great surprises in this vote by the *normaliens*. Mistler and Elbel (who died in June before the vote was taken) were on the conservative defeatist wing of the Radical Party. L'Hévéder was in the Faurist pacifist wing of the Socialist Party, in opposition to Blum. Marcel Déat (prom. 1914) seemed destined for a leading role in the Socialist Party when Blum, rather uncharacteristically, decided in 1933 that he and several other "neo–socialists" whose stress upon planning and authority too much resembled the schemes of the fascists, should be excluded from the Party. Although Déat was a member of the Vigilance Committee of Anti–Fascist Intellectuals, by the late 1930s he favored a rapprochement with Germany, and as war approached he adopted an increasingly pacifist line. On 4 May 1939, *L'Oeuvre* published his celebrated article, "Don't Die for Danzig." Soon he gave his full support to Pétain and went on from that point to write books which praised the new Nazi order.[60]

Although the vote of 10 July 1940, *per se,* took on great significance in French politics and in the careers of individual politicians, it should not be construed as a decisive indication of each man's personal mettle or basic political beliefs. It was a difficult choice between evils. Many who had supported Pétain initially soon turned around and worked in the Resistance; some were arrested by the Gestapo or the Milice and sent to prison or kept under guard. The Radicals were generally in the Resistance (Delbos, Anglès, Berthod, Bastid, Borel, and Landry) or imprisoned or kept under house arrest (Delbos, Berthod, and Herriot). Landry presided over the first clandestine meeting of the Radical Party during the war, and Bastid became president of the group of eighty who had opposed Laval's project. The Communist deputy Cogniot was arrested by the Gestapo, but he escaped after several unsuccessful attempts and entered the Resistance.

So far as we know none of the centrists whom we have considered here worked in an active way in the Resistance. Mireaux and François–Poncet became members of Pétain's National Council early in the regime, but this in itself was not the decisive indicator of patriotism that many claimed it to be. Mireaux was Minister of Education only briefly under Pétain in 1940, and then he went to Lyon where he published *Le Temps* until the Germans occupied southern France in 1942. After the war both Mireaux and *Le Temps* received verdicts before the High Court of Justice which cleared them of complicity with the enemy.[61] François–Poncet was deported to Germany and confined there from 1943 to 1945. After the war he resumed his various public activities: Ambassador to the Federal Republic of Germany (1949), President of the International Red Cross, member of the French Academy (replacing Pétain in 1952), President of the French Council of the European Movement, a supporter of the French Committee for the Defense of the Rights of Man (to grant amnesty to the Pétainists), and an administrator of the Société Fermière and *Figaro Littéraire*.[62]

Léon Blum's negative vote in July 1940 was only the first expression of his steadfast opposition to Vichy. He soon became a brilliant symbol in France of the beleaguered democratic tradition and of democratic socialism. Arrested and initially condemned to life imprisonment by Vichy's Council of Political Justice, Blum subsequently revealed his full stature as a political leader and human being at his trial at Riom. By his ringing testimony, a genuine *tour de force*, he stunned his judges and caused the suspension of the entire trial. Then from his cell, through smuggled messages, he encouraged and gave advice to members of the Resistance, Socialists, and statesmen, including Charles De Gaulle. After the war Blum returned to France a national hero after his captivity in Buchenwald and Dachau.[63]

There were both resisters and collaborators in all of the political parties, and thus it seems that factors other than party affiliation played a role in determining what path each politician chose. The mere fact that the *normaliens* were largely Radicals and Socialists was no guarantee that they would turn up in the Resistance rather than at Vichy. A number of *normaliens* had collaborated extensively with the Vichy government or even with the Germans, but Déat was the only parliamentarian to have done so.[64] The long political tradition at Normale which underlay the resistance of alumni such as Pierre Brossolette, Jean Cavaillès, and Marc Bloch was borne out in large measure also in the conduct of the parliamentarians during the Vichy period. After the initial shock it became clear to them that the spirit of 1940 was incompatible with that of 1789. Jean Guéhenno (prom. 1911) has remarked: "[There were] many *khagneux* and *normaliens* in the Resistance. But few polytechnicians, it seems. Why?"[65] If Guéhenno is correct, could it have been in part, and rather ironically, a question of the dominant Kantian tradition at Normale which spoke in moral absolutes versus a more pragmatic Comteian tradition at the Ecole Polytechnique? In any case the post war world quickly made known its preference for Comte.

A score of *normaliens* of the Third Republic served in the legislatures of the Fourth and Fifth. Proportionally they sat in about the same places in the Palais Bourbon as their predecessors had, but of course the whole political situation had changed. Old school and ideological ties which had drawn young *normaliens* into politics no longer had the same value. Almost imperative for political success was a record of service in the Resistance as well as ambition, education, and good connections. On balance this new qualification probably worked to the advantage of the *normaliens,* but those Radicals and Socialists who were elected were no longer part of a strong governing alliance. The Radical Party had suffered a sharp eclipse since it was identified so closely with the discredited Third Republic, and the handful of young Socialists from Normale included no successor to Jaurès or Blum who might have galvanized a new Popular Front. After only a dozen troubled years the Fourth Republic gave way to the Fifth, and it was clear that the old Socialist and Radical preponderance from the rue d'Ulm was a thing of the past. *Normaliens* of the Third Republic became exceedingly sparse in the legislature, and not essentially because they were growing old. Radicals and Socialists, quite simply, found it difficult to win elections.

In the legislature during the Fifth Republic there were no Socialists of the pre–1940 rue d'Ulm. Georges Cogniot, a Communist, remained in the Senate. Aimé Césaire (prom. 1935) followed the course of many intellectuals in leaving the Communist Party in 1956, and he has remained in the Assembly as an independent deputy from Martinique. René Billères (prom. 1931) was the sole Radical. Georges Gorse (prom. 1936), a Socialist after the war, became a Gaullist in the Fifth Republic. Thus the *normaliens* were few in number and ideologically scattered. But perhaps most symbolic of the fact that the dominant political tradition at Normale no longer played a role in the legislature was the career of Georges Pompidou (prom. 1931).

Pompidou's father was an *instituteur,* a socialist, and a reader of Léon Blum's *Le Populaire.*[66] Georges as a child was primed to believe that one day he would be a *normalien* and thus arrive at the summit of his father's profession. He fulfilled his parents' dreams by following the well worn path—scholarships at the local *lycées,* good results at Lycée Louis–le–Grand, and admission finally to the citadel at the rue d'Ulm. Along the way he developed no overt taste for politics, but devoted himself instead to literature and art and did well in his academic work without appearing to have expended any effort. Yet even at Normale he probably contemplated a career outside of the academic world. Like a handful of other *normaliens* who later took up careers in government administration or business, Pompidou while at the rue d'Ulm spent some of his time studying at the Ecole Libre des Sciences Politiques. This center of liberal economic orthodoxy, moderately conservative social philosophy, and functional political science undoubtedly helped to shape his political thought.

In 1944 it was Normale's "old boy network" that snatched Pompidou from the Lycée Henri IV, where he had been teaching literature and "sympathizing" with the *résistants.* Upon the recommendation of René Brouillet (prom. 1930), who was the assistant director of de Gaulle's office in London, the General invited Pompidou to join his staff.[67] Quickly he became a valued aid to de Gaulle. Then when de Gaulle withdrew from politics, the *normalien* served the Rothschild Bank rather than returning to the classroom. This interlude proved to be an excellent (and many would say symbolically appropriate) preparation for his career in the Fifth Republic as Premier under de Gaulle and finally as President in his own right.

Pompidou's posthumous memoirs provide only a superficial glimpse of the man, but probably a fair summary of his political thought.[68] The prose conveys neither the republican fire of a Radical nor the utopian aspiration of a Socialist. Disdainful of such "ideological" parties, he espoused essentially the same moderate ideas that we found in François–Poncet and Mireaux. The nation must become more efficient, create more wealth, increase production and foreign trade, improve living and working conditions, and work toward a prudent and limited redistribution of wealth. Pompidou was no evangelist of Liberty, Equality, and Fraternity. Rather, he understood and accepted the French capitalist–collectivist society which he found. The irony that a *normalien* should become President of the Fifth rather than the Third Republic was only apparent. Pompidou, after all, did not represent the main strand of Normale's political tradition which was rooted in the Revolution of 1789. His political triumph marked the demise rather than the fulfillment of the *république des professeurs.*

Liberals, philosophers, and moralists, the alumni of the rue d'Ulm had contributed much to the establishment and definition of the Third Republic. Not only Normale's politicians, such as Jaurès, Herriot, Blum, and Painlevé, but administrators, writers, and scholars as well captured the public imagination. The politician who had studied at the rue d'Ulm symbolized, as Thibaudet noticed, the new prestige of the teacher, the scholar, and the scientist everywhere in France. But the disaster of 1940 called the entire government elite and their values into question. As a group the *normaliens* could not escape partial responsibility for the recent past. Despite their brilliant record in the Resistance, they did not get the chance to reconstruct the Republic upon new foundations a second time. That task fell largely to men who had learned other lessons at other *grandes écoles.*

7
Conclusion

> La condition du progrès est d'augmenter l'indépendance de chaque génération nouvelle. . . . L'insurrection, la révolte, c'est-à-dire, en langage simple, l'examen et la critique, est un devoir non seulement dans les cas exceptionnels et graves, mais toujours.—Lucien Herr

BETWEEN 1870 and 1940 over four fifths of the 3200 students who attended the Ecole Normale spent the better part of their careers in *lycée* and university classrooms or in offices of educational administration. The authority of the teachers and administrators was undoubtedly enhanced as some graduates became prominent political leaders and public figures. Yet the prestige of the Ecole Normale outside its own sphere of education was fleeting; by the 1950s and 1960s the Ecole had become again essentially what it was a century earlier—an academy for professors, educational administrators, and researchers. The exceptional political rise and fall of the *normaliens* merits an explanation. What circumstances brought fame so quickly to the rue d'Ulm after a frequently troubled past? The state, after all, had never completely trusted the independent, critical, and left-leaning *normaliens.* And what caused the Ecole Normale to slip once again into the background as the Fourth Republic yielded to the Fifth?

Like other *grandes écoles,* the Ecole Normale had been founded to provide the state a loyal and disciplined elite which would accomplish a specific professional task. It trained a small number of highly selected students to fill important positions in a public institution, in this case the Napoleonic University. But the resemblance to other *grandes écoles* was superficial; in essential matters the Ecole Normale was unique.

The professional corps for which Normale prepared did not under normal circumstances exercise effective political power. The educational system did not wield power so much as it did the bidding of the power elite and reflected a class structure in which teachers were marginal and isolated.[1] With others in his profession, the *normalien* competed for academic degrees which led to a social *cul de sac.* Professionally he was most likely to be a captive of his diploma unless he pursued other studies at the law Faculties which could open doors to the *grands corps.* Considering the level of intelligence and the intensity of preparation which were necessary to pass the *concours,* it is striking that so few *normaliens* moved on from responsible positions in education to other higher posts in government. They were blocked in part by their academic degrees, which were seen as valid for the teaching profession and educational administration, but for nothing else.

But in a society such as France entrance into the governing elite depended upon social background as well as education. The upper classes had understood how to defend their status and power through the erection of social barriers in the school system. Education and social class evolved in the nineteenth century as nearly congruent realities.[2] Given the marginal character of education as a profession, therefore, it is hardly surprising that the *normaliens* were socially inferior to students at the other major *grandes écoles.*[3] Their social status, confirmed by their profession, largely determined their place in the pyramid of power and discouraged movement, which their intelligence might otherwise have justified, into higher ruling groups.

Not only social class and profession, but curriculum and intellectual style as well set the *normaliens* apart from graduates of other *grandes écoles.* Whereas the *polytechnicien's* education was practical, technical, and vocational, that of the *normalien* was abstract, general, and academic. The *polytechnicien* mastered a discrete body of knowledge in an atmosphere of discipline and order, often went on to graduate work at the school of Mines or Ponts et Chaussées, and finally assumed a responsible post in the public sector. Frequently, early experience in government agencies was a prelude to a brilliant career in the private sector.[4] By contrast the *normalien's* intellectual development and style prepared him neither for the state's *cursus honorum* nor for that of the developing industrial world. Steeped in classical literature, he seemed to have inherited from the aristocracy that tradition of independence, criticism, and philosophic grasp of the world which often caused the ruling authorities considerable anxiety. Although this inheritance did have socially conservative ramifications, it implied a refusal to defer in important intellectual matters to higher authority or the state. Furthermore, Greek and Latin classics were not incompatible with the liberal political lessons which most *normaliens* took from the Enlightenment and the Revolution. Whereas political dreams at Polytechnique were apt to take a positivist, managerial, and technocratic form, those at Normale tended to be idealistic, democratic, and even egalitarian. But the political idealism which had become a hallmark of the Ecole Normale before the Third Republic was the creation of men excluded from real political power. Other *grandes écoles* and the law faculties assured that there would be a tranquil circulation of their men into the power elite. Before Sedan few *normaliens* penetrated this circle because of their profession, their origins, their education, and their ideas.

Military defeat, the sudden collapse of the Second Empire, and the ensuing political uncertainty presented the *normaliens* with an unexpected opportunity. Precisely those characteristics which had been liabilities earlier proved to be assets in the new situation. Since the Third Republic won the immediate political struggle largely by default, to endure it had to summon popular support and articulate leaders to argue its case. As the public school became the chrysalis of republican citizenship, the scholar from the rue d'Ulm took on the mantle of public philosopher and sage. It was fortuitous, of course, that in addition to filling a political need, public schools also filled an economic one, for the industrial revolution required a more literate and disciplined work force. By definition the *normalien* had always been the state's official expert on educational matters. Now he dominated the educational hierarchy at a time when education at every level was perceived as essential for France's political and economic development.

But the crisis of the political regime provoked an intellectual as well as a structural response. To establish a republic was one thing; to justify its continued existence and to define its characteristics was a long process which engaged scores of intellectuals. France required new ideas as well as new schools to regain her place in Europe, and in the wider intellectual arena as well as in the more limited educational hierarchy, the *normaliens* contributed conspicuously during the Third Republic. In Claude Digeon's important study of the crisis of French thought posed by German culture during the first half of the Third Republic, *normaliens* figure prominently.[5] Fustel de Coulanges and Gabriel Monod had much to say about the extent to which the writing of French history should follow German models. Ernest Lavisse wrote and edited historical manuals whose most salient purpose was to select and embellish a "usable past" for the new regime. Emile Durkheim, who with a circle of *normaliens* founded an entire discipline, argued that the state had the right and obligation to educate its citizens for social solidarity. Other republicans and solidarists based their politics upon a neo–Kantian foundation developed by Jules Lachelier and Emile Boutroux (following the work of Charles Renouvier, who was not a *normalien*).[6] And the political writing of such figures as Jules Simon, Jaurès, Alain, Herriot, and Blum constituted further evidence that the political tradition at the rue d'Ulm was formative in the Republic.

However, the very character of education at the Ecole Normale assured that despite a broad liberal consensus there would be considerable diversity among alumni who were politically active. Jules Lemaître (prom. 1872) was a literary critic of considerable influence not in the usual *normalien* mold—an anti–Semite, an anti–Dreyfusard, and a Maurrassian.[7] Jean Guiraud (prom. 1885), an editor of *La Croix,* led the Catholic opposition to the *école unique.*[8] Louis Doumic (prom. 1879), a member of the French Academy, and Jean Izoulet (prom. 1874), a professor of social philosophy at the Collège de France, where prominent anti–Dreyfusards.[9] Pierre Gaxotte (prom. 1917), a prolific historian and columnist for *Figaro,* and three brilliant men of letters from the *promotion* of 1928—Robert Brasillach, Maurice Bardèche, and Thierry Maulnier—were all audible voices on the right.

There was considerably less ideological space to the left of the Ecole Normale's political consensus. Few joined the Communist Party and remained members, and I have not identified any Trotskyites. Paul Nizan (prom. 1924) was the most important literary figure to join the Party; he left it in 1939 following the Non–Aggression Pact. Similarly the poet and politician Aimé Césaire (prom. 1935) left the Party in 1956 over the Russian suppression of the Hungarian revolt. Jean Paul Sartre (prom. 1924) tried to reconcile existentialism with Marxism but always retained his independence and never became a Party member.[10]

There were numerous other original thinkers critical of bourgeois democracy who remained largely outside party politics. For instance, Romain Rolland (prom. 1886) refused to take sides during the First World War and was almost universally regarded as a dangerous radical.[11] Yet later many *normaliens,* especially Radicals, Socialists, and Communists, joined him on the Committee of Anti–Fascist Action and Vigilance.[12] Simone Weil (prom. 1928) was another figure of great importance difficult to place on a political scale which reads simply from left to right. She was both a passionate religious pilgrim and a champion of the workers; both of these aspects of her brief life cried out against the materialistic, competitive, and bourgeois world which she inhabited.[13] Intellectuals such as these confirmed that the Ecole Normale was hardly a dogmatic church, but rather a forum which provided for a wide range of discourse. Yet although mavericks from the left–of–center consensus did much to enrich the liberal setting at the rue d'Ulm, others who represented this consensus later exercised great influence first in educational administration and subsequently in politics and other fields.

From the early nineteenth century, *agrégés* from the Ecole Normale comprised a professional elite which monopolized the principal government posts pertaining to secondary and higher education. They wielded most power, however, when the state in the 1870s and 1880s considered the expansion and perfection of public education to be critical for its own survival. Jules Ferry, who was not a *normalien,* counted heavily upon *normaliens* to run his various administrations and to carry out his reforms. Albert Dumont (prom. 1861) became Director of Higher education, Charles Zévort (prom. 1836) took over secondary education, Alfred Rambaud (prom. 1867) became Ferry's *chef de cabinet,* and Octave Gréard (prom. 1849) was Vice Rector of Paris from 1879 to 1902. When Dumont died in 1884, Ferry prevailed upon the Minister of Education, Fallières, to select Louis Liard (prom. 1866) as successor; in a thirty–year reign Liard became the architect of the New Sorbonne. But in addition to filling the administrative posts in the state educational bureaucracy, the *normaliens* also dominated editorial boards of new journals of education and pedagogy, such as the *Revue internationale de l'enseignement,* the *Revue de l'enseignement secondaire et de l'enseignement supérieur,* the *Revue pédagogique,* and the *Revue universitaire.* Thus as administrators, educational journalists, and professors at the secondary and higher levels, *normaliens* constituted a visible pressure group whose time had come. How they used their power to direct educational reform is worth reviewing here, although that subject has been thoroughly explored by others.[14]

Educational reform before World War I unfolded in a particular social and political setting: demand for education increased as rural population moved to cities in search of new employment, and both rulers and ruled sensed that it was education even more than income which divided class from class. Thus the legislation of the 1880s which provided "free, obligatory, and laical" education at the elementary level had broad support both among the lower classes who were eager to rise and among enlightened bourgeois republicans who wished to avert the worst manifestations of class struggle. The carefully limited democratization of education was intended to narrow but not eliminate the cultural gap between *bourgeois* and *peuple.* It would promote industrial harmony and progress, social cohesion, and patriotism. Even though it was confined at first to the elementary level, mass education threatened, some thought, to erode the social hierarchy itself. But this was a risk that the ruling class felt compelled to take.

The system which emerged in the 1880s and which the *normaliens* so effectively supported posed no immediate threat to the social structure. The idea that poor boys might rise, which was so pointedly repeated by the Directors of the Ecole Normale, was useful to a government and a ruling class concerned to keep the common man in his place. The brilliant *normalien* of humble background was a misleading stereotype which concealed another reality. Free education as provided by the Ferry laws applied only to the self–enclosed system of the *école primaire.* Normally students attended the *école primaire* until age thirteen and then left school altogether; only a minority went on to an *école primaire supérieure,* which stressed modern studies without Latin, until age seventeen. The certificate at the end of this course was not the equivalent of the baccalaureate, which remained the only degree which admitted students to the universities or Faculties of medicine and law. Only studies at a *lycée* or a *collège* led to the "bac," and these institutions required tuition payments. Furthermore, if the distance from home required the student to board at the *lycée,* he had to pay additional fees. Few working families could afford to send even their eldest son to a *lycée.* The high proportion of professors' sons who were able to attend the Ecole Normale was due in part to the fact that they happened to live near a *lycée.*

As supporters of the Ferry laws, the *normaliens* were politically the moderate progressives of their day. Separate education for the working class provided strictly limited social mobility within a certain sphere and left the liberal professions and higher positions essentially in the hands of the bourgeoisie. Jaurès was a transitional figure from that early republican generation which supported Jules Ferry. He began his political career as an Opportunist republican, but then broke ranks as he discovered that this party's liberalism was in reality a form of social defense for the upper classes.[15] He saw the danger that working people confined to the *école primaire* might become merely efficient machines unless they too were provided a broad liberal education which would awaken the whole person.[16] It was only in the interwar period that a number of *normaliens* began to act upon Jaurès' insight. Before the First World War, however, one cannot escape the conclusion that the *normaliens'* support of the Ferry laws was objectively a conservative act. Although they undoubtedly perceived themselves as progressives, they supported laws which despite liberal aspects reinforced the existing social order.

Gabriel Séailles (prom. 1872) was a good example of the *normalien* whose democratic good will was beyond question but whose basic assumptions barred the way to dramatic social change or revolution. A professor of philosophy at the Sorbonne, a Dreyfusard, and an indefatigable lecturer around the turn of the century at meetings of *instituteurs* and at the *universités populaires,* Séailles taught that education had a moral mission to perform which was superior to that of partisan religion.[17] Its purpose was to bring to light the essential and the human in everyone so that people might recognize what they share. Who could teach the Lutheran to love the Catholic, the Catholic to embrace the Jew? It was not the priest but rather the *instituteur.* Deeply marked by neo–Kantianism, Séailles taught that behind appearances there was a common humanity with certain categorical imperatives, one of which was the universal necessity to work. Work brought dignity, it placed the worker into a relationship with others around him. He thus contributed both to the life of the whole and to himself. He lived not as an individual, but in society. Séailles made frequent reference to "solidarity," which became a key word among liberal republicans around the turn of the century.[18] But solidarity was not to be the result of the imposition of dogma. Under the Republic the free search for truth itself would lead citizens to a realization of their common interests.

> . . . little by little, the new idea becomes clear that society is sufficient unto itself, that it has its own meaning and values, that it offers to the activity of men an ideal which has real worth and which can harmonize the intelligence and the will, whatever may be the religious or metaphysical belief. In fact, the idea becomes clear that society, by whose means alone man truly finds himself, is capable of giving and is obliged to give its members an education whose elements are based upon its own requirements and its own aspiration.[19]

Séailles preached a secular faith which condemned social conflict. He had seen war and revolution first hand in 1870 and was convinced of the futility of armed proletarian revolt. Revolution gave people a false sense of accomplishment; after the Revolution they were apt to rest on their oars. True social change meant getting to the truth about the human condition, working, learning, perfecting oneself and thereby realizing one's own capacities, and relating more consciously to the human situation of the neighbor.

For Séailles, as for Liard and many others influenced by Normale's philosophical tradition, social change was largely an individual moral matter. Although his sympathies were on the left, his philosophy did not permit him to recognize the social basis of public ills. Normale's philosophers of idealism and individualism provided a tenacious tradition which prevented many of the school's Radicals from becoming Socialists. They stopped short of radical reform of social structures which would have significantly aggravated class struggle.

Even a heretic from neo–Kantianism such as Emile Durkheim constructed an alternative social theory which was antirevolutionary. Although he might oppose classical humanism and the Catholic religion on theoretical grounds, he argued that the cults of humanism and religion concealed beneath their forms and symbols genuine social needs which education would of necessity have to accommodate in its own work of socialization. He thought that it was neither possible nor desirable abruptly to eliminate ideas, however wrong, which had achieved the status of social facts. The teacher stood at the very center of the society's attempts to come to terms with what was new in the present and the future and what was essential from the past. No Jacobin who wished to level present structures and replace them with new ones constructed a priori, Durkheim provided a new theoretical underpinning for a rather old political doctrine. Sympathetic toward socialism and a friend of Jaurès, he was also one of a wide circle of Normale's alumni whose progressive social ideas found expression within the conciliatory solidarist framework.[20]

Class antagonisms in any case were never absent from educational debates, although they often took on religious or cultural guises. Just as the Ferry laws provoked an immediate and sustained clerical reaction, attempts to democratize education in France on every level brought to the surface real differences among *normaliens.* Support for the Ferry laws, which provided an educational minimum for the population, was one thing, but support for a democratized secondary system was something else. One step toward the broadening of recruitment of students into the *lycées* was to revise their curriculum. Modern options attracted students from the lower classes in cases where financial problems were not insurmountable. Significantly it was on this point—modern studies versus the classics—that *normaliens* divided most sharply in testimony before the Ribot Commission. Admittedly the point of cleavage was partly a question of generation and partly a question of the *normalien's* professional interest: modernists of the older generation such as Lavisse and Liard were not specialists in the classics, whereas Perrot and Boissier, two of their opponents before the Ribot Commission, were also defending their own professional field. Politics of the Dreyfus Affair and the Combes era further exacerbated differences between *normaliens*, and it is difficult to disentangle political, social, and cultural motives. There is a positive correlation, however, between anti–Dreyfusism, antimodernism, and opposition to the "Nouvelle Sorbonne."[21] In any case before the First World War the issue of whether to extend democracy by way of extensive educational reform was never joined. Questions of peace and war became more urgent.

As the war was ending, however, the issue of access to secondary and higher education squarely confronted educators and the public. In 1918, seven young army officers considered how their country could best recover from the destruction of the previous several years. Five were teachers on the secondary or university level, and the remaining two were *normaliens* of the *promotion* of 1912 who would enter the teaching profession after the war. They proposed a sweeping structural reform of education to strengthen the nation.[22] Their first statement, which they signed "Compagnons de l'Université Nouvelle," called for a new educational system pervaded by a more democratic spirit. It proposed that all children, rich and poor alike, should attend the same kind of primary school, the *école unique*. This term described the most radical facet of their proposal and became a catchword for all of their ideas. There would be no more primary track with its own secondary level, nor a separate and privileged secondary track with its own elementary classes. Toward the end of the common primary school all children would be thoroughly examined to determine which ones were capable of going on to either a classical *lycée* or a technical college. Those who did not qualify by examination to take either course would enter the work force after finishing primary school at age fourteen. The critical innovation in this plan was that the students' abilities rather than their parents' wealth and ambitions would determine their educational paths and professional careers. Under the *école unique* education would cease to be a thinly disguised reflection of social structure but would instead form the basis for a truly democratic society.

This was the kind of program which appealed especially to Radicals: competition, advancement based upon merit and performance, equality under one law, and equal opportunity. Personal wealth would become far less important in the selection process, for education would be free at all levels. The proposal appeared to be in direct line of descent from the ideas of Condorcet, from 1789, and from 1848. Edouard Herriot led the Radical campaign for the proposals and expressed political ideas which had broad support among *normaliens* both in and outside the Parliament:

> We will not have the right to invite the workers to consider themselves members of the common family as long as we have not put our children side by side. . . . If the French people do not have the clairvoyance and the courage to assure regular social advancement by work and knowledge, we will lose any right to protest against revolutionary demands.[23]

Indeed it was the fear of revolutionary demands which persuaded some moderates and conservatives to go along with the *école unique.*

In addition to Léon Blum, Marcel Déat (prom. 1914) was a principal spokesman on educational matters for Socialists in the Parliament.[24] He saw in the *école unique* a way to bring members of the working class into the intellectual cadres which would lead the future revolution. The principle of selection according to merit, once applied to education, would irresistibly spread to other areas of society and result in social upheaval—precisely what conservative critics of the proposals had feared all along.

Outside the parliament although most *normaliens* supported the *école unique,* they did so for a variety of reasons and with various degrees of enthusiasm. Ludovic Zoretti (prom. 1899), a professor of mathematics at the University of Caen and the organizer of a teachers' union for secondary and higher education, published a socialist version of the *Université Nouvelle* in 1918. Zoretti's work actually anticipated that of the Compagnons and resembled it in fundamental aspects. Zoretti was under no illusion that equality was a possibility in a capitalist regime. It was in the name of justice rather than equality that he argued for a common base of studies for all children.[25] Pierre Henri Simon (prom. 1923), a devout Catholic who sought conciliation between Catholics and the Republic, favored democratic educational reform including free education at the secondary level.[26] Jean Guéhenno (prom. 1911) raised the question of culture in connection with the educational debate. He was from a working class family and had been a worker himself, but after he escaped into the bourgeois ranks he always felt that he had deserted his class.[27] He argued nevertheless that although knowledge of the humanities had been the traditional mark of the bourgeois, learning itself was not intrinsically bourgeois in content or results. Although he remained uncertain about the relationship between culture and class, he supported the democratization of education, since he saw no contradiction between the selection of an elite and raising the level of the masses.[28] Guéhenno was exceptional in that he was concerned with the student who was not destined for the elite as well as the one who was.

An indication that the vast campaign for the *école unique* would attract conservative people as well as radical elements was the election of Louis Cazamian (prom. 1896) as president of an enlarged association of Compagnons. In November 1919, Cazamian gave a lecture at the reformist but essentially conservative Ecole des Hautes Etudes Sociales and expressed in vague and idealistic terms the spirit and motivation of the proposed reforms:

> Let France occupy its place in the temple of spiritual grandeur. But let her not be absorbed entirely with that. . . . Without industrial and materialistic frenzy, we desire a vigorous national life. Let us found it upon the mind. Education is at the center, at the origins of all. Intelligence and character will lead the world: both are the domain of the educator. The watchwords of the present are: to know, to understand, to produce, to increase the production of individuals, of the whole.[29]

Presiding at the session was an old reformer of the Ferry era, Alfred Croiset (prom. 1864), Dean and professor of Greek eloquence at the Sorbonne, who was a "modernist" in curricular matters and a veteran of the solidarist movement.[30]

Ultimately differences in doctrine and tactical skirmishes damaged the entente on education between the Radicals and the Socialists. Notoriously factious, the left was not able to unite sufficiently even on a subject where they were in essential agreement, so that by the end of the Third Republic the propositions of the Compagnons had not been realized. Herriot's great triumph in the early thirties, the gradual winning of free tuition in the *lycées* and *collèges,* was a deceptive victory, since tuition was only part of the expense of attending one of these schools. The *lycée* remained substantially the preserve of the Middle and Upper Classes. Furthermore, the Parliament was unable to agree to unite the *écoles primaires supérieures* with the old secondary track or to combine the elementary classes of the *lycées* with the old primary schools. Most of the agenda which the Compagnons had introduced remained for the second post–war generation to take up.

More than ever after the Second World War it seemed urgent that France should achieve an educational system that incorporated the major proposals of the *école unique.* Paul Langevin (prom. 1894), a professor of physics at the Collège de France, headed a Commission in 1944 which began to draw up a detailed proposal for the desired post-war reform. Upon Langevin's death in 1946 another *normalien,* Henri Wallon (prom. 1899), also a professor at the Collège de France, and incidentally the last of a *normalien* dynasty which began with his grandfather, politician Henri (prom. 1831), saw the report to completion. The Langevin–Wallon Plan of 1947 was a new version of the Compagnons' proposals.[31] It affirmed that children should be limited in their education only by their aptitudes, that all kinds of work and education were of equal value, and (as Jaurès had said) that a modern *culture générale* which was the same for all children should preceed specialization. After the plan foundered in the Parliament for lack of votes and money, in 1949 Minister of Education Yvon Delbos (prom. 1907) submitted a more conservative version,[32] but even that failed to become law. Another Radical Minister of Education, René Billères (prom. 1931), submitted a similar comprehensive plan to the Parliament in 1956.[33] It provided for a common elementary school for students from six to eleven years of age, a period of orientation from age eleven to thirteen, and then a more specialized secondary school in which pupils would follow aptitudes determined during the period of orientation. The school leaving age would be raised from fourteen to sixteen, which would have brought French practice in this respect into conformity with most modern states in the West. But the plan got nowhere due in large part to opposition from *agrégés* and other groups whose cultural and pedagogical arguments masked social and professional motives.

As the allies of Jules Ferry in the 1880s, the *normaliens* of that era were in the forefront of educational reform. Later they built the

"Nouvelle Sorbonne" and fought for the *école unique*. But for reasons which were cultural, social, or professional, some stopped short of granting modern studies parity with the old classical curriculum or of uniting the primary and secondary tracks of education into a single integrated system. Ideological diversity further diluted their general impact upon education. And finally, reforming *normaliens* such as Liard, Lavisse, and Lanson, who created the "Nouvelle Sorbonne," contributed in the long run to undermining the hegemony of *normaliens* in the educational establishment. Graduates of the Sorbonne and the provincial universities swiftly increased in number and competed with *normaliens* for advanced degrees, positions, and honors.[34] Within their own profession the *normaliens* declined slowly in importance as increasing numbers of students took degrees at the universities.

How then does one account for the passing of the professors' republic and for the drift of the *normaliens* from center stage to the wings? The answer lies in the changing relationship between the intellectual and social tradition of the Ecole Normale, the place of the *normaliens* in the University, and the political circumstances. The intellectual traditions of the rue d'Ulm were those of the University, which the *normaliens* both created and served. If the *normaliens* best exemplified the rational and critical spirit in the late nineteenth century, it was because they clearly dominated the University. But as the Sorbonne grew in the twentieth century, the *normaliens* lost what had once appeared to be an intellectual monopoly: at the Sorbonne too a critical and philosophic spirit prevailed. Meanwhile at the rue d'Ulm the closed boarding school regime of the nineteenth century (the *internat*) was abandoned, personal freedom to come and go at will was added to intellectual freedom, and inevitably some of the old spirit of solidarity at the school was lost. Pranks and the title *ancien élève de l'Ecole Normale Supérieure* continued to remind *normaliens* that they were a breed apart, but in reality their share of power in the University diminished.

Their influence outside the University was a function of the changing political climate. Before the Dreyfus Affair they were in the vanguard of a movement which synthesized republicanism and nationalism; as Opportunists they were the allies of the new ruling class. But the Dreyfus Affair embarrassed important elements of the ruling majority and simultaneously propelled most the of the *normaliens* into the Dreyfusard camp. On the surface it appeared, nevertheless, that the *normaliens'* power and prestige would only increase, for Dreyfus was vindicated, and after 1910 men of the rue d'Ulm entered the legislature in greater numbers than they had before as Opportunists. However, their electoral triumph as Radicals and Socialists already pointed to their actual estrangement from the real ruling class in France, which invariably placed its trust in the center and the right. The Second World War discredited those politicians of the right and center who had supported Pétain, but it also undermined the credibility of Radicals and Socialists identified with the Third Republic. Thus those parties to which *normaliens* were naturally drawn became far weaker than they had been between the wars.

In any case the political emergence of the *normaliens* was a passing phenomenon. Stepping into a political vacuum, they assisted in France's nervous transition from a republic of notables and dukes to one of businessmen and technocrats. Like the brilliant constellation of men who drew up the American Constitution, they had orchestrated public discourse in such a way as to anchor liberalism and the Republic in the national consciousness. What other institution or group of thinkers was so well prepared to accomplish this? Although the intellectual task may have been achieved by the First World War, the prestige of the men involved kept them in prominent view as active politicians for another generation. Finally, after the Second World War, the spell was broken as France grappled with the problems of economic development and planning. Ideologues and philosophers seemed less important than economic experts, systems analysts, and managers. In short, events had transpired so that the *normaliens* ceased to capture the imagination or to constitute a fairly coherent pressure group with strong ties in the legislature, education, and the republic of letters. They became once again the relatively isolated intellectuals that they were before the Third Republic—outsiders and critics of a regime shaped and managed by others. The social and political mechanisms which had summoned modest *agrégés* for service in a crisis finally restored them to their place.

Leaders of the upper classes, despite their fears, were never really excluded from power during the Third Republic: they continued to dominate government administration even as their political leadership was threatened by the middle class. In 1871 Emile Boutmy founded the Ecole Libre des Sciences Politiques in part to protect the political prerogatives of the traditional ruling groups against threats from below:

> . . . the classes which represent vested positions risk seeing themselves excluded from active citizenship, just as they have for so long

> attempted to exclude most others. A revenge excessive to the point of injustice, but which would leave me rather indifferent if, in affecting men, it did not affect the two vital conditions for any progressive society: the empire of the mind and government by the best. . . . Privilege is gone; democracy will not retreat. Forced to submit to the right of the majority, the classes which themselves claim to be superior can safeguard their political hegemony only by invoking the right of the most able: it is necessary that, behind the crumbling perimeter of their prerogatives and tradition, the democratic wave meet a second rampart made of brilliant and useful merit, of superiority whose prestige is imposing, of ability that cannot sanely be ignored.[35]

The Ecole Libre's students were overwhelmingly from the upper classes, and these graduates practically monopolized the important posts in government administration from the late nineteenth century to the end of the Third Republic.[36] After the Second World War the Ecole Libre (reorganized as the Institut d'Etudes Politiques) prepared students for the newly created and politically powerful Ecole Nationale d'Administration, which also turned out to be a preserve of the upper classes.[37] More than ever, education for political leadership in France was highly centralized: it took place at ENA, Sciences Po, and the Ecole Polytechnique. Those few *normaliens* who continued to make their way into higher echelons of power were obliged to undergo training, acculturation, and rites of passage at Sciences Po or ENA. Thus the circulation of elites in France continues to operate slowly as a resilient social structure endures.

Glossary

agrégation. Competitive examination for the recruitment primarily of *lycée* professors; successful candidates are *agrégés.*

antitalas. *Normalien* slang referring to those who did not attend religious services or who were free-thinkers as opposed to religious in their outlook.

baccalaureate. National examination and degree at the end of secondary *(lycée)* studies; successful candidates may enroll in one of the Faculties of higher education.

Bloc National. A right-of-center political coalition of the years 1919–39.

cacique. *Normalien* slang referring to the member of a *promotion* who was admitted "first", that is who earned the highest score on the entrance examination *(concours).*

cacique général. The *cacique* of the most senior *promotion* at the Ecole Normale, the traditional student leader of the school.

cagne. Slang which refers to special classes held in certain *lycées* which prepare students for the literary section of the Ecole Normale.

cahiers de doléances. Statements of grievances sollicited by the Monarchy in 1788–89 from the three Estates: Clergy, Nobility, and Third Estate.

canular. A prank developed to a fine art by the *normaliens,* whereby the credulity of the subject is cleverly tested.

Cartel des Gauches. A left wing political coalition led by Edouard Herriot and the Radicals in 1924.

Chambre Bleu Horizon. The heavily conservative Chambre of Deputies elected in 1919 consisting of numerous war veterans.

concours général. National competitive scholastic examinations for secondary school students; these examinations played a large role in the distribution of state scholarships.

couches nouvelles. An expression made current early in the Third Republic by the politician Gambetta, who was referring to the middle, lower middle, and working classes which his movement sought to bring into political life.

culture générale. This is approximately the French equivalent of the Anglo-

Saxon "liberal arts" or the German "Bildung," meaning broad studies for the cultivation of mind and spirit as opposed to a narrow curriculum for a specific professional purpose.

diplôme d'études supérieures. A minor degree following the *licence* introduced in 1886 to train students to undertake original research; granted on the authorization of a professor for the completion of a thesis or project, but requiring no examination.

directeur de conscience. An intellectual or spiritual mentor.

dissertation française. An essay in French on a given topic.

doctorate. In our study, the *doctorat d'état,* the highest professional degree conferred by the Faculties; required the writing of both a major and a minor thesis; the professional degree required of full professors at the university level.

Ecole Libre des Sciences Politiques. A private institute of higher education (until it was joined to the University of Paris in 1945), founded in 1872 by Emile Boutmy to train students in contemporary affairs and administration so that they could compete successfully for government administrative posts in the *grands corps.*

Ecole Normale. The name of the subject of this study for most of the period from its founding in 1795 until 1847, when it became the Ecole Normale Supérieure.

écoles normales partielles. Special annexes to certain Royal Colleges of the Restoration period intended to train candidates for the Ecole Normale in Paris who would possess the Catholic and monarchical outlook which the regime sought to foster.

Ecole Polytechnique. *Grande école* founded in 1794 to train engineers for important civil or military posts; always the chief rival institution of the Ecole Normale Supérieure.

écoles préparatoires. Projected teacher training institutes to be attached to the Royal Colleges in 1826–28 to replace the Ecole Normale, which was closed down; in fact only one *école préparatoire* was ever established—at the Royal College of Louis-le-Grand in Paris—and the original Ecole Normale soon reemerged from this institution.

Ecole Pratique des Hautes Etudes. Established by Victor Duruy in 1868, this institution for the disbursement of government funds to support original research in five fields (mathematics, physical science, natural science, history and philology, and economics) made it possible for established and creative scholars to train small groups of students in their fields; the institution itself granted no academic degrees.

école primaire. In the narrow sense this was the public elementary school not attached to a *lycée,* a school whose students would normally enter the work force at age 13 or 14 rather than continuing their education; in a larger sense the term refers to the entire self-enclosed system of education for the masses which had its own certificates, teachers' colleges, and advanced level, but which could not lead to the University. Until reforms which followed the Second World War the world of the *école primaire* and that of the *universitaire* were quite distinct, and indeed the cultural division based upon these traditionally separate structures remains.

école primaire supérieure. The secondary or advanced level of classes of the *école primaire* system.

école unique. A slogan and a movement following the First World War which sought to integrate the two tracks of French education, the *école primaire,* which on the whole served the masses, and the *école secondaire,* which catered to the middle and upper classes.

grands corps. Personnel of the various branches of high government administration, such as the diplomatic corps, the inspectors of finance, or the councillors of state.

grandes écoles. Schools of higher education accessible by rigorous competitive examination and preparing students for particular professions, e.g. Saint-Cyr: the officer corps; the Ecole des Chartes: the direction of archives and libraries; or the Ecole Polytechnique: engineering in civil or military posts.

Grand Master. The highest administrative officer of the Napoleonic University; this figure changes title in 1849 and becomes the Minister of Public Instruction.

internat. A boarding school; a large measure of confinement or restriction of movement is the rule.

internes. Students in an *internat.*

instituteur. Teacher in an *école primaire.*

khagneux. Slang meaning students in a *cagne.*

licence. The first degree granted for studies done at the university level; a degree requiring two years' study in a given field; not, like the doctorate, a research degree.

lycée. The major institution of the *école secondaire,* which alone prepares for the baccalaureate degree and leads to the university; accepts national scholarship holders, is funded by the state instead of by the locality, and offers a wider range of classes than does the *collège.*

maître de conférences. As used in this study, a professor at the Ecole Normale Supérieure; this title was used to refer to men who had professorial credentials to indicate that at Normale they did not, in theory, lecture *ex cathedra,* as they would at the Sorbonne, but instead they ran their classes as discussion groups, seminars, or conferences.

maître d'étude. An instructor or supervisor of studies in a *collège* or *lycée;* at the lowest rank of the *école secondaire*'s professional hierarchy, but essential to the functioning of these boarding schools.

the Massilia. The ship which carried some members of the government from Le Verdon (near Bordeaux) to Casablanca in June 1940; these politicians intended to set up a French government in exile in North Africa and continue resistance to Germany.

ouvriérisme. The belief that workers themselves are best qualified to lead the socialist movement; a challenge to the idea that intellectuals have important roles to play in socialism.

philosophes. French writers and intellectuals of the Enlightenment such as Diderot, Rousseau, and Voltaire.

polytechnicien. Student at the Ecole Polytechnique.

premieure supérieure. Refers to the first year of studies in the *cagne;* also known as *rhétorique supérieure.*

promotion. The class year and also the year of matriculation of a student at the Ecole Normale Supérieure (or other *grande école*).

répétiteur. A teaching assistant, a supervisor of students' study period, or one who assists students in "repeating" and learning their lessons.

république des professeurs. A phrase used by Albert Thibaudet to describe a period following the First World War during which professors played a prominent role in French politics and public life.

résistant. A member of the movement of resistance to the Germans in France during the Second World War.

scientifiques. Used in this book to refer to students of the Division of Sciences of the Ecole Normale Supérieure.

Surveillant Général. The official at the Ecole Normale (for much of the Third Republic, Paul Dupuy) who had charge of the daily extracurricular life of the students; a "Dean of Students".

talas. *Normalien* slang referring to those who did attend religious services or who were religious in outlook.

taupe. Slang which refers to special classes held in certain *lycées* which prepared students for the Division of Sciences of the Ecole Normale, the Ecole Polytechnique, or other scientific *grandes écoles.*

trousseau scholarship. A discretionary grant to assist deserving *normaliens* in the purchase of school uniforms and incidentals.

turne. In *normalien* argot this was a student's study room, usually on the top floor of the school and shared with one or more comrades; often decorated to express the political or cultural style of the occupants.

Union Sacrée. The truce and unity which prevailed between French political parties during the early years of the First World War.

universités populaires. A movement of the 1890s and the first few years of the new century in which Radical or Socialist professors (most typically) lectured and gave informal courses to small groups of workers.

Union Républicaine. A moderate republican political party of the early Third Republic which was outflanked on the left in the twentieth century by the Radical and Socialist parties.

Notes

Introduction

1. Frederick B. Artz, *The Development of Technical Education in France, 1500–1850* (Cambridge, Mass., 1966), pp. 81–109; and René Taton, ed., *Enseignement et diffusion des sciences en France au XVIIIe siècle* (Paris, 1964), pp. 343–62, 386–410, 523–26.

2. No degree was required simply to attend the university, but a student had to have passed the baccalaureate examination following secondary studies before taking examinations for university degrees. More demanding entrance examinations screened applicants for the *grandes écoles,* and the oral part of these examinations has always placed students of the lower classes at a considerable disadvantage.

3. Fundamental works on French education and society since the Revolution are: Antoine Prost, *Histoire de l'enseignement en France, 1800–1967* (Paris, 1968); Félix Ponteil, *Histoire de l'enseignement en France, les grandes étapes, 1789–1964* (Paris, 1966); Joseph N. Moody, *French Education Since Napoleon* (Syracuse, New York, 1978); and Fritz K. Ringer, *Education and Society in Modern Europe* (Bloomington, Indiana, 1979).

4. Maurice Barrès, *Les Déracinés* (Paris, 1898); Julien Benda, *La Trahison des clercs* (Paris, 1927); Hubert Bourgin, *De Jaurès à Léon Blum, L'Ecole Normale et la politique* (Paris, 1938). The *promotion* of each *normalien* mentioned in the text is indicated as follows: Hubert Bourgin (prom. 1895).

5. Pierre Jeannin published an excellent brief history: *Ecole Normale Supérieure: Livre d'Or* (Paris, 1963); for other studies of the school, *see* the bibliography.

7. The centralized University, directed from Paris by its Grand Master, controlled higher and secondary education in large part by monopolizing the granting of valid degrees. Within the overarching University, semi–autonomous Faculties of letters, science, medicine, or law in addition to the *grandes écoles* constituted the essential institutions of higher education; they replaced the independent universities of the Old Regime. *See:* Alphonse Aulard, *Napoléon Ier et le monopole universitaire* (Paris, 1911); Jacques Godechot, *Les Institutions de la France sous la Révolution et l'empire* (Paris, 1941); Louis Liard,

L'Enseignement supérieur en France, 1789–1889, 2 vols. (Paris, 1888–94); and Félix Ponteil, *Histoire de l'enseignement.*

8. The year of a *promotion* was the year that its students began rather than finished their studies. Thus Jean Jaurés (prom. 1878) began his course of study at the rue d'Ulm in the fall of 1878.

9. Dupuy, *Le Centenaire,* pp. 213–14.

10. Shinn, pp. 45, 101–39.

11. The *lycées* and the *collèges* were both schools of secondary education in France, but the *lycées* were supported directly by the central government rather than by more uncertain local levies, offered the entire cycle of secondary studies, were alone permitted to accept holders of government scholarships, and were generally stronger academically than the *collèges: see* Paul Gerbod, *La Vie quotidienne dans les lycées et collèges au XIXe siècle* (Paris, 1968), pp. 12–3.

12. The ongoing studies by Victor Karady of the production of French literary scholarship are particularly illuminating. For the changing professional relationships between *normaliens* and non-*normaliens, see* his articles: "Normaliens et autres enseignants à la Belle Epoque. Note sur l'origine sociale et la réussite dans une profession intellectuelle," *Revue française de sociologie* 13 (1972): 35–58, and "L'expansion universitaire et l'évolution des inégalités devant la carrière d'enseignant au début de la IIIe République," *Revue française de sociologie* 14 (1973): 443–70. Another of Karady's works points out that *normaliens* tended to monopolize those disciplines which carried higher prestige: "Le choix du champ d'étude et la stratification de l'Université dans les disciplines littéraires en France (fin du 19e et début du 20e siècles)," Centre de Sociologie européenne, 1973, typescript.

13. On the changing status of university and secondary professors from regime to regime, *see* in particular: Paul Gerbod, *La Condition universitaire en France au XIXe siècle* (Paris, 1965); for the development of institutions, *see:* Ponteil, *Histoire de l'enseignement;* and on the relationship between education, society, and culture the best work is still Antoine Prost, *L'Enseignement en France, 1800–1967* (Paris, 1968).

14. This was part of a report by Corbières, president of the Royal Council of Public Instruction, as cited in Dupuy, *Le Centenaire,* p. 221.

15. Ibid., p. 236.

16. Paul Dupuy wrote a remarkable history of the buildings of the Ecole Normale which appeared in several issues of the *Bulletin des amis de l'Ecole Normale Supérieure* 18, no. 41 (June 1936): 43–62; no. 42 (December 1937): 13–18; and 19, no. 44 (June 1938): 18–22.

17. Francisque Sarcey, *Souvenirs de jeunesse* (Paris, 1885), p. 45.

18. Prost, p. 81.

19. *See* Gerbod, *La Condition universitaire,* pp. 309–55.

20. One of Fustel's masters judged him as follows: "Great ardor at work, but more ambition than force and measure. Confused mind, not disciplined,

not docile. Despite severe warnings which he has received from the administration, either he has not understood them, or his pride has refused to recognize them, so that this trimester he has recommended studying history, philosophy, and literature from the heights, and to consider such things as he knows nothing about." This report, probably by a school official, is cited by Jeannin, *Ecole Normale,* p. 61. For Fustel's later career as the Director of the Ecole Normale, *see* Chapter Five.

21. On Victor Duruy, consult in particular: Sandra Horvath, "Victor Duruy and French Education," (Dissertation, Catholic University of America, 1971), and Jean Rohr, *Victor Duruy, Ministre de Napoléon III: Essai sur la politique de l'Instruction publique au temps de l'Empire Libéral* (Paris, 1967).

22. This becomes especially clear in Gerbod's *La Condition universitaire,* in which the major actors are predominantly *normaliens.*

23. Prost, p. 83.

24. Ibid., p. 72.

25. Ibid., p. 77.

26. These phrases come from Daniel Halévy, *La Fin des notables,* v. 2: *La République des ducs* (Paris, 1937), and from Alfred Thibaudet, *La République des professeurs* (Paris, 1927).

27. Eugen Weber, *Peasants into Frenchmen: the modernization of rural France, 1870–1914* (Stanford, California, 1976).

1. THE EVOLUTION OF A REPUBLICAN INSTITUTION

1. Examples of these ideas can be found in the thought of LaChalotais, *Turgot, and Voltaire; see* Georges Snyders, *La Pédagogie en France aux XVIIe et XVIIIe siècles* (Paris, 1965), pp. 381 ff. For a general study of education in the Old Regime, consult: Roger Chartier, Marie–Madeleine Compère, and Dominique Julia, *L'Education en France du XVIe siècle au XVIIIe siècle* (Paris, 1976).

2. For a convenient summary of all of the educational projects of the Revolution, *see:* H. C. Barnard, *Education and the French Revolution* (Cambridge, 1969). In addition there is an excellent account of the historical background of the founding of the Ecole Normale in Paul Dupuy, "L'Ecole Normale de l'An III," *Le Centenaire de l'Ecole Normale, 1795–1895* (Paris, 1895), pp. 1–209.

3. On the Ecole Polytechnique, *see:* Jean Pierre Callot, *Histoire de l'Ecole Polytechnique* (Paris, 1958) and Terry Shinn, *Savoir scientifique et pouvoir social: L'Ecole Polytechnique, 1794–1914* (Paris, 1980).

4. Dupuy, *Le Centenaire,* pp. 36–7.

5. Ibid., pp. 48–9.

6. Dupuy has sketched a history of the Ecole from 1810 to 1895 in a "Resumé historique" which follows his work on the "Ecole Normale de l'An III" in *Le Centenaire.* This resumé gives the major development of the cur-

riculum and statutes pertaining to the Ecole. Pierre Jeannin's *Livre d'Or: Ecole Normale Supérieure* (Paris, 1964) is a more general account of the Ecole's history from the beginning to the 1960s which relies far more on literary works by the *normaliens.*

2. THROUGH THE EYE OF A NEEDLE: THE CONCOURS

1. Harvey Goldberg, *The Life of Jean Jaurès* (Madison, Wisconsin, 1962), pp. 12–3.

2. Edouard Herriot, *Jadis,* 2 vols., (Paris, 1948), 1: 39.

3. Interview with M. Cogniot in Paris, August 21, 1971.

4. The rarity of a student's being admitted to the Division of Letters directly from a provincial *lycée* is suggested by Perrot's letter to the Minister of Education in 1890: ". . . I call your attention, sir, to a curious result of the *concours,* which should interest the director of secondary education. Among the students admitted there are two, the third and the fifth in rank, who came to us directly from the classes in rhetoric of Rennes and of Caen; M. Philipot was even the first *admissible* [i.e., he obtained the highest score on the written part of the *concours*]." Archives Nationales, F[17]4220.

5. Raoul Blanchard, *Ma jeunesse sous l'aile de Péguy* (Paris, 1961), p. 133.

6. Paul Dimoff, *La Rue d'Ulm à la belle époque, 1899–1903, mémoires d'un normalien* (Nancy, 1970), p. 4. On the general atmosphere in the *lycée, see* also: Barrès, p. 3, and Paul Gerbod, *La Vie quotidienne.*

7. Jules Isaac, *Expériences de ma vie: Péguy* (Paris, 1960), p. 38.

8. Blanchard, *Ma jeunesse,* pp. 134–5. For a similar schedule in the 1880s at Henri IV, *see* G. Gendarme de Bévotte (prom. 1886), *Souvenirs d'un universitaire* (Paris, 1938), p. 87.

9. Paul Nizan, *La Conspiration* (Paris, 1938), p. 40. Thus Nizan suggests that the cultural bias of the *lycée*'s curriculum had not changed in forty years, for Gendarme de Bévotte records: "They kept us in complete ignorance of the sixteenth century, reputed without doubt to be a period of formation and perhaps also of independence, of dangerous spirit. Montaigne, Rabelais, besides writing in a style judged to be scarcely intelligible to us and of insufficient purity, had in their ideas a skepticism and an irony which were not appropriate for youth. And what to say of the eighteenth century? For three or four years we had been living under a government which claimed to be inspired by the doctrines of the Revolution, and Voltaire and the Encyclopaedists remained outlawed by the University of the Third Republic." Ibid, pp. 50–1.

10. Robert Brasillach, *Notre avant–guerre* (Paris, 1941), p. 7.

11. Numerous memoirs of alumni describe the series of attempts they made to pass the exams, and the pattern of repeated candidacies is evident in the yearly lists of candidates: Archives Nationales, F[17]4216, 4219, 4223.

12. Ibid.

13. On the inquiry for the reform of secondary education of 1902, *see:* Alexandre Ribot, *La Réforme de l'enseignement secondaire* (Paris, 1900); for the reform: Clément Falcucci, *L'Humanisme dans l'enseignement secondaire en France au XIXe siècle* (Toulouse, 1939), pp. 505–45, and Jean–B. Piobetta, *Le Baccalauréat* (Paris, 1937), pp. 206–71; and for the changing relationship between "classical" and "modern" subjects: Prost, pp. 257–61.

14. *See* the report by Célestin Bouglé, "Rapport sur le concours pour l'admission à l'Ecole Normale Supérieure et l'obtention des bourses de licence (Lettres), session de 1928," *Revue universitaire* 38, no. 3, (March 1929): 193–4.

15. Many are available at the Librairie Croville–Morant, 20 rue de la Sorbonne, and the entire collection is at the Bibliothèque nationale.

16. Herriot, *Jadis* 1: 61.

17. In connection with the *concours* of 1890 the Ministry sent to all Rectors a circular letter listing the following items which a prospective candidate had to produce before he was eligible for the written tests:
1. a written request to be inscribed on the list of candidates.
2. a birth certificate stating that the candidate was on January 1 at least eighteen but not more than twenty–four years old.
3. a vaccination certificate.
4. a medical report.
5. a pledge to teach in France for ten years following completion of studies.
6. the consent of the father or guardian if the candidate was a minor.
7. the Mayor's certificate if the candidate had already done his military service (usually one year).
8. curriculum vitae
9. certification of moral aptitude (written by the Rector).
10. for candidates in letters, proof of one year's study in philosophy. For the terms of the *reglement* of 1850, which had set the formalities of the entrance examination and for the text of the 1890 circular letter, *see:* Archives Nationales, F[17]4220.

18. Archives Nationales, F[17]4199.

19. Student dossier from the collection in the Archives Nationales, 61 AJ 209-270, which was unclassified when the author consulted the source at the Ecole Normale.

20. Archives Nationales, F[17]4201.

21. Excerpted reports in this paragraph are taken from student dossiers, Archives Nationales, 61 AJ 209-270.

22. Archives Nationales, F[17]4210.

23. Ibid.

24. Student dossier, Archives Nationales, 61 AJ 209-270.

25. Ibid.

26. Ibid.

27. Archives Nationales, F[17]4265.

28. Student dossier, Archives Nationales, 61 AJ 209-270.

29. *Association Amicale des anciens élèves de l'Ecole Normale Supérieure*, 1897, p. 120. This *annuaire* is an indispensable source for biographical information on *normaliens* through its necrology notices.

30. Ministre de l'Instruction publique et des Beaux-Arts, *Enquête sur l'enseignement secondaire: procès verbaux des dépositions présentés par M. Ribot, Président de la Commission de l'Enseignement* (Paris, 1899), 1: 139–40.

31. Jérôme Carcopino, *Souvenirs de sept ans, 1937–1944* (Paris, 1953), pp. 179–80.

3. SOCIAL ORIGINS AND CAREERS: THE STATISTICAL EVIDENCE

1. Dupuy, *Centenaire*, pp. xliv–xlv.

2. Thibaudet, pp. 121–2.

3. *See* the study by Victory Karady, "Normaliens et autres enseignants," in which he compares the social origins of literary *normaliens* who became teachers with the origins of other secondary teachers studied by Gérard Vincent in "Les Professeurs du second degré au début du XXe siècle," *Le Mouvement social* 56 (April–June, 1966): 47–73. One of Karady's conclusions is that the tendency of over–representation of teachers among the fathers of secondary teachers was exaggerated in the case of the *normaliens*. And in general Karady found that *normaliens* were recruited from higher social strata than were teachers who were not *normaliens*.

4. The data on which the statistics and the general statements in this chapter are based has been gathered from two principal sources: the matriculation registers of the Ecole Normale and the students' individual dossiers, which included all of the documents for application and in some cases records of academic progress. These registers and dossiers, which I consulted at the Ecole Normale, were transferred from the rue d'Ulm to the Archives Nationales (61 AJ 209–270) in 1971. I am grateful to Victor Karady for allowing me to fill gaps in my material by consulting his data on students in the Division of Letters to 1914; he was able to learn the profession of father from local archives in some cases where that information was missing from the school's records.

5. For Polytechnique I have relied on Shinn. My work–in–progress on the Ecole Libre includes an analysis of social origins from archival records at the school; I have worked on a twenty per cent sample of the students who attended from 1886 to 1970. Important published comparative works which consider the *grandes écoles* are: John A.'Armstrong, *The European Administrative Elite* (Princeton, 1973); Alain Girard, *La Réussite sociale en France: ses caractères—ses lois—ses effets* (Paris, 1961); Fritz K. Ringer, *Education and Society in Modern Europe* (Bloomington, Indiana, 1979); and Ezra Suleiman, *Elites in French Society, the Politics of Survival* (Princeton, 1978).

6. In a study of 263 *normaliens* of pre–1870 *promotions* who were still alive in

1900, Richard Seabold found that 27.8 per cent of the literary students and 9.8 per cent of the science students were born in the department of the Seine: "Normalien Alumni in the Faculties and Lycées of France from 1871 to 1910, Promotions 1831 to 1869," UCLA Dissertation, 1970, p. 64.

7. A North–South cultural division of France is suggested by statistics on literacy in the departments in the nineteenth century: Ministère de l'instruction publique et des Beaux Arts, *Statistique de l'Enseignement primaire, II, Statistique comparé de l'enseignement primaire (1829–1877)* (Paris, 1880), pp. cli–clxxxiii. The authors of this report demonstrate a substantial correlation between low literacy and low attendance in primary schools. For the years 1827–1829, 1856–1860, and 1876–1877 the ten lowest departments in both categories were in the South, with only a few exceptions (pp. civ–clviii). But in fact great strides were made in the early Third Republic, and illiteracy was practically eliminated by the beginning of the twentieth century. Although local traditions of literacy or illiteracy undoubtedly left cultural marks, the young people everywhere had been to school, and the traditional North–South cultural division of France did not appear to have influenced the recruitment of *normaliens*. Considering the *normaliens* from the North and the South, excluding Paris, their numbers were roughly comparable to population: North—France 39.9 per cent, Division of Letters 38.0 per cent, Sciences 47.2 per cent; South—France 60.1 per cent, Letters 62.0 per cent, Sciences 52.8 per cent. The exclusion of Paris (in the North) enables us to compare the generally less cultivated "provincial" North and South, but this exclusion may also account in part for the failure of the *normaliens'* origins to repeat the national pattern more precisely. In any case the factor of "literary tradition" is difficult to isolate from other factors such as the numbers of cities of a certain critical size or character.

8. Jean–Richard Bloch,*—and Co.,* trans. Scott–Moncrief (New York, 1929), pp. 347–54.

9. *See* note 3.

10. Education in France, as elsewhere, reflected social status already achieved, but it was also an intermediary between upwardly mobile generations. And educational institutions reflected different cultural levels and preferences, which they passed on to their students. The Ecole Normale itself expressed an incongruity between cultural attainment and social status; the *normaliens* were candidates, because of their cultivation, for higher social status. For a discussion of class, status, and education in general, *see* Ringer, pp. 12–22.

11. Shinn, p. 185; and Ringer, pp. 170, 189, 192. The results of Victor Karady's extensive research on the social origins of students of the Faculties and various *grades écloes* in nineteenth century France are forthcoming.

12. We have grouped thirteen socio–professional categories into three larger categories: Upper, Middle, and Lower class. The criteria for this tripartite division are an assumed degree of economic capital, security, skill, or education. The baccalaureate, or some other mark of culture equivalent to what it

was thought to represent, divided the Upper Class from those below. The secondary professors qualify barely for this class because of their culture despite their presumed lack of capital and low income. The distinction between Middle and Lower class blurs more at the edges. It is particularly difficult to be certain of the cultural and material condition of the farmer. Those who were clearly *propriétaires* who did not work the land themselves were included among the "owners of capital" in the Upper Class.

13. On the Ecole Polytechnique, *see* Shinn, p. 185. For the Ecole Libre, my data on students' social origins comes from records in the school's archives complemented by information from the Etat Civil records at the birthplace of each student. *See* also: Thomas R. Osborne, "Sciences Po and the Concours: the Recruitment of the Bureaucratic Elite in the Early Third Republic," *Third Republic/Troisième République,* no. 2 (Fall 1976): 156–81.

14. Jean Guéhenno, *Changer la vie: mon enfance et ma jeunesse* (Paris, 1961), pp. 127–8.

15. In a suggestive article by Pierre Bourdieu and Monique de Saint–Martin, "Les Catégories de l'entendement professoral," *Actes de la recherche en sciences sociales,* no. 3 (May 1975): 68–93, it is argued that the encouragement or discouragement which teachers subtly dispense by their comments as well as by numerical grading is based upon a perhaps unconscious awareness of each student's social origins and hence his expected real prospects in life.

16. Interview with Monsieur Paul Bastid in Paris, 7 July 1971.

17. Interview with Monsieur Raymond Badiou in Paris, 22 July 1971.

18. Gilberte Brossolette, *Il s'appelait Pierre Brossolette* (Paris, 1976), pp. 18–21.

19. Prost, p. 328. Prost notes that at the end of the nineteenth century the sons of *fonctionnaires* received 59 per cent of the scholarships. This was the approximate percentage of the sons of *fonctionnaires* at the Ecole Normale.

20. Edouard Herriot, *Pourquoi je suis radical–socialiste* (Paris, 1928), p. 12.

21. Seabold, p. 77, found that 22.4 per cent of the *normaliens* in his pre–1870 sample had fathers who were artisans or shopkeepers. This shows that the decline in the representation of these groups at the Ecole Normale began before the Third Republic, for in our study they represent only six and eight per cent by the 1870s.

22. For a discussion of the effects of the Reform upon the Ecole Normale, *see* Chapter Four.

23. Girard, pp. 200–4, found that while the pattern of small families and high age rank was common to all of the *grandes écoles* of his study, it was exaggerated in the case of the *normaliens.* He also noted that higher in the social scale, family size increased and average age rank decreased.

24. Gustave Lanson, "Nos grandes écoles: I, l'Ecole Normale Supérieure," *Revue des Deux-Mondes,* (1926) 1: 516.

25. *Bulletin des amis de l'Ecole Normale Supérieure* 23 (February 1930): 29.

26. John Bush has shown that in the 1890s the Jesuits and other teaching orders in France sent their students to other *grandes écoles,* but not one directly

to the Ecole Normale: "Education and Social Status: The Jesuit Collège in the Early Third Republic," *French Historical Studies* 9 (1975): 125–40.

27. Vice–Rector Liard of the University of Paris conducted a survey of the preparation of candidates for the *concours* in 1896 prior to their final *lycée* and discovered that only an insignificant number had come from Church schools: Archives Natonales, F[17]4224.

28. Blanchard, *Ma Jeunesse,* p. 51.

29. Seabold, p. 107, records that of his pre–1870 sample of *normaliens,* 9.6 per cent of the Parisians and 14.2 per cent of the provincials were republicans before 1870.

30. Ernest Lavisse, "A l'Ecole Normale," *Revue internationale de l'enseignement* 69 (1915): 71.

31. Lanson, p. 516.

32. Seabold's figure of 39.1 per cent who actually retired from *lycée* classroom teaching, p. 177, corresponds roughly with our findings.

33. *See* Pierre Rain, *L'Ecole Libre des Sciences Politiques, 1800–1967,* p. 90.

34. Interview with Monsieur Henri Jourdan (prom. 1921), 10 August 1971, in Noirétable, Loire.

35. *See* pp. 26–27.

36. François–Poncet's career, in part, included: press service at the French Embassy in Berne (1917–1919), economic attaché in the United States in 1919 and in the Ruhr in 1922, member of the Chamber of Deputies from 1924 to 1931, Ambassador to Berlin, 1931 to 1938, Ambassador to Rome, 1938 to 1940, Ambassador to the Federal Republic of Germany, 1949 to 1955, President of the International Red Cross, and member of the French Academy. Massigli was secretary general of the conference of ambassadors in 1920, secretary to the French delegation in Washington in 1921, secretary general at the conference at Laussane, 1922–1923, *maître de requêtes* at the Conseil d'Etat, 1924–1928, *chef de service* at the League of Nations, 1928, member of the French delegation at the Naval Conference in London in 1930 and at the disarmament conference in 1932, Ambassador to Turkey, 1939–1940, Ambassador to London, 1944 (he had joined de Gaulle in 1943), etc.

37. *See* Victor Karady, "L'Expansion universitaire."

4. THE INTELLECTUAL TRADITION: CONTINUITY AND CHANGE

1. Ernest Renan, *Questions contemporaines* (Paris, 1868).

2. Gaston Boissier, "Les Réformes de l'enseignement," *Revue des Deux–Mondes (15 June 1868): 875–876.*

3. Prost, p. 229.

4. On this general subject, *see:* Claude Digeon, *La Crise allemande de la pensée française (1870–1914)* (Paris, 1959). For French scientists' reactions to German competition, *see:* Harry Paul, "The Issue of Decline in Nineteenth Century

French Science," *French Historical Studies* 7 (Spring 1972): 416–50, and *The Sorcerer's Apprentice: The French Scientist's Image of German Science, 1840–1919* (Gainesville, 1972). On French educational reform, *see:* George Weisz, "Le corps professoral de l'enseignement supérieur et l'idéologie de la réforme universitaire en France, 1860–1885," *Revue Française de Sociologie,* 18 (1977): 201–32, and Bernard J. Looks, "National Renaissance and Educational Reform in France, 1863–1914: Normaliens, Political Change, and the Schools," Columbia University Ph.D. Dissertation, 1968.

5. Jules Simon, *La Réforme de l'enseignement secondaire* (Paris, 1874), p. 77.

6. Michel Bréal, *Quelques mots sur l'instruction publique en France* (Paris, 1877).

7. Ibid., pp. 373–74.

8. The student who responded to Bersot was Auguste Burdeau, a decorated veteran of the recent war and nicknamed "the general" by his comrades at the Ecole. After teaching philosophy for a decade he went into national politics (*see* Chapter Six). On Bersot, *see:* Georges Lyon, "Bersot," *Centenaire,* pp. 312–3, and A. Hamon, *Bersot et ses amis* (Paris, 1911).

9. Cited in Jeannin, *Ecole Normale,* p. 82.

10. E.g.: Bersot, *Etudes sur la XVIII*[e] *siècle* (Paris, 1855). On Cousinism in general, *see:* W. M. Simon, "Two Cultures in Nineteenth Century France: Victor Cousin and Auguste Comte," *Journal of the History of Ideas* 26, no. 1 (1965): 45–58.

11. Ferry's own thought, which undoubtedly led to his appointment of a scholar such as Fustel, is examined in: Louis Legrand, *L'influence du positivisme dans l'oeuvre scolaire de Jules Ferry* (Paris, 1961).

12. On Fustel's thought, *see:* Digeon, op. cit., pp. 235–52.

13. Fustel de Coulanges, "Les 'Conférences' et la culture générale," in *L'Ecole Normale Supérieure, d'où elle vient, où elle va* ed. Célestin Bouglé, (Paris, 1934), pp. 46–7, 56–7.

14. Ibid., p. 54.

15. On Fustel's classical bias: Paul Guiraud, "Fustel de Coulanges," *Centenaire,* p. 332. Nevertheless he reinstated the natural sciences at the Ecole Normale against the wishes of the professors at the Sorbonne, the Museum, and the Ecole Normale itself. He did not believe that Normale should ignore such an important field in the century of Darwin. On the development of natural sciences at the Ecole, *see:* Frédéric Houssay, "La Section des sciences naturelles à l'Ecole Normale Supérieure," *Revue internationale de l'enseignement* 21 (1891), no. 1: 364–82.

16. Yet in his correspondence with the Minister of Education Perrot zealously defended the Ecole Normale: Archives Nationales F[17] 4213–225.

17. Charles Andler, *Vie de Lucien Herr* (Paris, 1932), p. 48.

18. Dupuy, *Centenaire,* p. xvi. Perrot was very nearly excluded from the list of candidates for the Ecole by an action of the Minister of Education, Fortoul, who wanted Catholic teachers. Intervention on the part of influential friends as high as the Emperor himself reversed the decision, and the day before the

examinations Perrot received a letter informing him that he was indeed a candidate. In large letters across the top of his *dossier personnel* (Archives Nationales F[17]) there is written the word "protestant". After successful studies at the rue d'Ulm, however, Perrot advanced rapidly in his career. He spent three years at the Ecole d'Athènes (1855–1858), taught briefly in several provincial *lycées,* was appointed to a scientific mission to Asia Minor in 1861–1862, began teaching at Louis-le-Grand in 1863, at the Ecole Normale in 1871, and at the Sorbonne in 1876 at an annual salary of 15,000 francs (more than ten times the salary of a primary school teacher, on the average). But despite his success no doubt his early difficulties because he was a Protestant served to reinforce his democratic instincts.

19. Dupuy, *Centenaire,* p. xlv.

20. *See* pp. 145–6.

21. At the centennial celebration Perrot was unsparing of Lavisse, who was an opponent of Normale's extremely classical curriculum: " . . . Augustin Thierry loved Latin verse, while M. Lavisse has always pursued it with hatred, even since it has died. Is that very generous? Perhaps he owes more than he believes to [Latin] verse and also to Latin discourse, which is not yet buried, but whose existence is very threatened." Dupuy, *Centenaire* p. xxxiv.

22 Ibid., p. 316n.

23. Pierre Nora, "Ernest Lavisse: son rôle dans la formation du sentiment national," *Revue historique* 228 (1962): 73–106.

24. For Lavisse's testimony before the Ribot Commission, *see:* Ministère de l'Instruction publique, *Enquête,* 1: 35–46.

25. On Monod, *see:* Alice Gérard; Benjamin Harrison, "Gabriel Monod and the Professionalization of History in France, 1844–1912," University of Wisconsin Dissertation, 1972; and Martin Siegel, "Gabriel Monod and the Ideological Foundations of the *Revue Historique,*" *Studia Metodologiczne* 9: 3–15.

26. *See* Chapter 5.

27. On Bloch, *see:* Herriot, *Jadis,* 1: 71, and the long notice by Jérôme Carcopino in *Association Amicale,* 1925: 86–109.

28. But similar to Fustel, Vidal saw his discipline as an instrument of French national revival. His nationalism is evident in the following concluding passage of his geography of France: "We firmly believe that our country holds in reserve enough new forces which are entering into play and which permit it to play its part on the infinitely enlarged [international] field, in a more intense competition. We also think that the great changes which we are witnessing will not overcome basically what is essential in our national temperament. The robust rural constitution which the climate and soil give our country is a fact assured by nature and time. It is expressed by the number of property owners unequalled anywhere. In that rests, upon that is supported, a solidity which perhaps is not encountred in any country to the same degree as in ours, a French solidity. Among people of neighboring industrial civilizations we notice that subsistence is drawn more and more from abroad; the

land, with us, remains the nurse of its children. That creates a difference in the affection it inspires." Paul Vidal de la Blache, *La France* (Paris, 1908), p. 351. For Vidal's influence upon French geographical thought, *see:* André Meynier, *Histoire de la pensée géographique en France (1872–1969)* (Paris, 1969).

29. Doris Goldstein, "Official Philosophies in Modern France: the Example of Victor Cousin," *Journal of Social History* 1 (1967–1968): 259–79.

30. Romain Rolland, *Le Cloître de la rue d'Ulm* (Paris, 1952), pp. 138–9.

31. *Ibid.*, p. 124.

32. Herriot, *Jadis*, 1: 73.

33. For a discussion of Lachelier, *see:* Célestin Bouglé, "Spiritualisme et Kantisme en France, Jules Lachelier," *Revue de Paris* (1 May 1934): 198–215.

34. Emile Boutroux, *De la contingence des lois de la nature* (Paris, 1874).

35. On Bergson's thought and influence I have relied upon: *Bergson and the Evolution of Physics*, ed. P. A. Y. Gunter, (Knoxville, Tenn., 1969), and A. E. Pilkington, *Bergson and His Influence, a Reassessment* (Cambridge, 1976).

36. The students involved in a demonstration against him were expelled for two weeks. They were permitted to return only after having written letters of apology according to a set formula. these letters are preserved in the archives of the Ecole Normale. On De la Coulonche, *see* Herriot, *Jadis*, 1: 74, but also Romain Rolland, who acknowleges the generally low opinion of De la Coulonche, which he did not share: *Le Cloître*, pp. 41–42.

37. On Brunetière I have relied chiefly on John Clark, *La Pensée de Ferdinand Bruneitière* (Paris, 1954); but *see* as well: J. Nanteuil, *Ferdinand Brunetière* (Paris, 1933).

38. Bédier's ideas emerge in his correspondence with Paris, preserved at the Bibliothèque nationale, Section des Manuscrits, N.A.F. 24431, ff. 290–317. Also, *see:* Ferdinand Lot, *Joseph Bédier 1864–1938* (Paris, 1939).

39. On Boissier, *see:* Paul Thoulouze, *Gaston Boissier 1823–1908* (Paris, 1923)

40. Herriot, *Jadis* 1: 69.

41. Cited by Thoulouze, p. 154.

42. On Andler there is the biography by his student, Charles Tonnelat, *Charles Andler, sa vie et son oeuvre* (Paris, 1937).

43. Ministère de l'Instruction publique, *Enquête*, 2: 63.

44. On Herr: Andler, *Lucien Herr* and D. Lindenberg and P. .A. Meyer, *Lucien Herr, le socialisme et son destin* (Paris, 1977).

45. Andler, *Lucien Herr*, pp. 46–47. Herr took his case directly to Louis Liard, whom he convinced in a stormy interview. This account by Andler, pp. 48–49, was confirmed in several interviews with Madame Lucien Herr. Meyer is skeptical, however, that Herr intended to use his post, as Daniel Halévy alleged, to convert the university to socialism: Lindenberg and Meyer, p. 59n.

46. Jérome et Jean Tharaud, *Notre cher Péguy*, 2 vols., (Paris, 1926), vol. 1: 90–91.

47. Blanchard, *Ma jeunesse sous* p. 191.

48. Herriot, *Jadis* 1: 63–64.

49. In his testimony before the Ribot Commission, Gaston Boissier stressed that unlike the students in the Faculties, the *normaliens* did not specialize too early—they did not neglect broad humanistic studies as they prepared for the *agrégation:* "From these three years of free and intelligent work, the rapport which the students develop among themselves in the *internat,* as I have already indicated, the ideas and understanding which they share, there is created something special which is called the *normalien* spirit, *esprit normalien.* This spirit is felt not only in their teaching careers; it is found in our contemporary literature, to which the Ecole Normale has furnished distinguished writers. One notices them by a certain skill in composition, a certain way of writing, a manner of considering questions in their broadest sense." Ministère de l'Instruction publique, *Enquète,* 1: 68.

50. *Normaliens* are prominent in the study by Phyllis H. Stock, "New quarrel of Ancients and Moderns: The French University and its Opponents, 1899–1914," Yale University Dissertation, 1965. Eighteen of twenty–seven names in the author's glossary were affiliated with the Ecole Normal as a professor only (Brunetière) or as an alumnus. Roughly two thirds of these men were in the modernist camp.

51. Paul Appell (prom. 1873), Dean of the Science Faculty at the University of Paris, described the preparation of examinations at Normale as follows: ". . . in the first two years we were required to obtain the two diplomas of *licence* in mathematics and *licence* in physical sciences. As students at the Ecole, we had a privilege; so as not to do one year uniquely of mathematics and a second year uniquely of physical sciences, at the end of the first year we passed the half of the mathematics *licence* bearing on infinitesimal calculus and the half of the physical science *licence* dealing with chemistry. At the end of the second year, we passed the two other halves: mathematics, mechanics, and astronomy; and physical science, physics, and minerology. Thus the first two years of the Division of Sciences were consecrated to the *licence;* the third was the year of the *agrégation.* In the Division of Letters, the first year was the year of the *licence,* the second was a year of free studies, which our comrades preferred and which we called jokingly the "year of genius," and the third was the year of the *agrégation.*" *Souvenirs d'un alsacien* (Paris, 1923), pp. 161–2.

52. The following is a report on a practice teaching effort by a *normalien* of the 1890s:

Versailles, April 5, 1898

Monsieur le Proviseur,

I have the honor to send to you according to the custom, a few notes on the teaching done in Rhetoric B from March 21st to April 2nd by M. B____, a student at the Ecole Normale Supérieure. My young replacement, let me say immediately, seems to me to have the makings of an excellent professor.

M. B. will certainly possess authority, an authority which his natural grace will sweeten. The voice is strong and pleasant. The speech is very fluent, always correct, often elegant. The delivery, without ever being listless, is marred by a certain uniformity; but neither spirit nor animation are (sic) lacking in M. B——, and when next year he gives himself entirely to his class, he will be a very engaging young master. . . ." Archives, Ecole Normale Supérieure.

53. Ernest Lavisse, *Questions de l'enseignement national* (Paris, 1885).

54. In his remarks at the centennial celebration Perrot alluded to the issue of the *licence* as follows: ". . . we requested three years ago that this diploma be required of all candidates for admission to the Ecole; our students would profit by having two years instead of one free from the distractions of preparation for the exam. We have not yet succeeded in winning our case; some have opposed us for reasons of the requirements of secondary education, and others because of the interests of higher education." Dupuy: *Centenaire,* p. xxxviii.

55. Archives Nationales, F^{17} 4221.

56. *Enquête* 1: 43–44.

57. Ibid., 1: 140.

58. Georges Perrot, "La Pédagogie à l'Ecole Normale Supérieure," *Revue internationale de l'enseignement,* 44, no. 2 (1902): 516–23.

59. Boissier and Monod testified in support of the classics before the Ribot Commission: Ministère de l'Instruction publique, *Enquête,* 1: 69, 119. Girard, a member of the Academy of Inscriptions and a professor at the Sorbonne, addressed a letter to the same effect to the Minister of Education on 25 March 1902, in the name of the "Association pour l'encouragement des études Grèques en France" (of which Perrot was also a member). Archives Nationales, F^{17} 3946.

60. It is probably safe to conclude that Brunetière was a political victim of Combism, but this is not certain: *see* John Clark, pp. 148–9, 204.

61. Lavisse's address is printed in full in the *Revue internationale de l'enseignement* 43, no. 2 (1904): 481–94.

62. For a discussion of the reform long after the fact, *see* the *Bulletin des amis de l'Ecole Normale Supérieure* 97 (June 1963): 12–28; Raoul Blanchard (prom. 1897) remains convinced (p. 20) of Lavisse's basic ill will toward the Ecole Normale.

63. There was a slight downward shift in *normaliens'* social origins immediately following the reform, but this soon redressed itself. A diplomat and other alumni admitted to me that they were attracted to the Ecole Normale by the prestige of alumni who had become successful politicians.

64. Lavisse took the post of Director on the condition that he could rely on Herr and Dupuy for advice and aid according to Andler, *Lucien Herr,* p. 191.

65. Although Emile Durkheim, the first professor of this course, was widely respected, Pierre Jeannin has discovered that students considered the subject a waste of time: *Ecole Normale,* p. 114.

66. Ibid., p. 116

67. I am grateful to Professor Jean Azéma (prom. 1920) for information about Henri Abraham and for general insights about the Ecole in the 1920s: interview, 22 July 1971.

68. Lavisse soon became aware of the special political utility of the Division of Sciences. In response to those in Parliament who wished to abolish the Ecole completely, Lavisse stressed its contributions to pure science. He noted that the Ecole Normale alone among the *grandes écoles* prepared students for research and pure science; the others such as the Ecole Polytechnique prepared instead for government careers in engineering. Thus Lavisse argued that the Ecole Normale should endure especially to shelter and encourage outstanding students in science. Despite the glorious (and rather aristocratic) tradition of the Division of Letters, it was the Division of Sciences which would shield the Ecole from its detractors. Jeannin, *Ecole Normale,* p. 121.

69. The text of the decree is printed in the *Bulletin des amis de l'Ecole Normale Supérieure* 3, no. 4, (February 1921): 9–12.

70. W. Paul Vogt, "Un durkheimien ambivalent: Célestin Bouglé, 1870–1940," *Revue française de sociologie* 20, no. 1 (January–March 1979): 123–24.

71. Evidence such as the following barbed comment by Jérôme Carcopino suggests that Bouglé's chief contribution to the *normaliens* was his own character: "All of the fine qualities which M. Bouglé possessed to a degree which I envied and on which his popularity was based made it rather difficult for me to restore discipline among the young people that he loved too much to deal severely with them or ever to find them in the wrong." *Souvenirs de sept ans* (Paris, 1953), p. 189. An example of his forbearance occurred in 1928 when he opposed Henri Abraham, who wished that certain political agitators at the rue d'Ulm be expelled. Bouglé insisted upon a lighter punishment and prevailed. Jeannin, *Ecole Normale,* p. 144.

72. Vogt. pp. 123–140.

73. *The French Conception of Culture Générale and its Influences Upon Instruction* (New York, 1938), pp. 15–6.

74. Vogt, pp. 123–40.

6. Society and Politics at the Rue d'Ulm

1. A good collection of *normalien* folklore and humor is: Alain Peyrefitte, *Rue d'Ulm: chroniques de la vie normalienne* (Paris, 1963).

2. A log book containing rules of the Ecole and records of their infraction is extant in the archives of the Ecole Normale. For Pasteur's career as an administrator at Normale, see: Jeannin, *Ecole Normale,* pp. 65–72.

3. Ibid., p. 74

4. Log book, Archives ENS.

5. Ibid.

6. Ibid.

7. Blanchard, *Ma Jeunesse,* p. 183.

8. Ibid., p. 186.

9. There is a lexicon of *normalien* argot in Peyrefitte, pp. 389–405.

10. Dimoff, pp. 25–6.
11. Julien Luchaire, *Confession d'un français moyen* (Marseille, 1943), pp. 65, 187–96.
12. Ibid., p. 193
13. Ibid., p. 195.
14. Ibid., p. 194.
15. Ibid., p. 60.
16. *Journal des débats,* 11 January 1904.
17. For descriptions of Normale's initiation rite for new students, *see:* Peyrefitte, pp. 95–6; R. Rolland, *Cloître* (Paris, 1952), p. 10; Tharaud, 1: 62–3; Madeleine Berry, *Jules Romains, sa vie, son oeuvre* (Paris, 1953), pp. 51–3; and Félicien Challaye, *Péguy socialiste* (Paris, 1954), pp. 40–1.
18. Peyrefitte, pp. 339–40.
19. I am grateful to Professor Jean Azéma for information about the Bourbaki canular. Also for the Bourbaki canulars and the serious professional careers of the group of celebrated mathematicians who signed their collective work Nicolas Bourbaki, consult the recent article by Maurice Avronny, "Quarante ans de Bourbaki," *Le Monde,* 9 April 1980.
20. Brasillach, *Notre avant–guerre* pp. 61–4.
21. Interviews with several *normaliens* yielded identical versions of the story. One alumnus revealed that Jean Paul Sartre was a participant in the prank and that Armand Bérard, later a diplomat at the United Nations, played the part of Lindberg.
22. Peyrefitte, p. 335.
23. Auguste Gérard, *La Vie d'un diplomate sous la Troisième République: mémoires d'Auguste Gérard* (Paris, 1929), p. 21.
24. Gendarme de Bévotte, p. 102.
25. Rolland, *Cloître,* p. 215.
26. Gerbod, *Condition universitaire, passim.*
27. Elie Halévy, *L'Ere des tyrannies: études sur le socialisme et la guerre* (Paris, 1938), p. 216.
28. Tharaud, 1: 91. Tharaud recalled that ". . . the Ecole was rather like a small provincial town whose inhabitants were separated into two camps, the one siding with the *curé* and the other with the *instituteur,* the *talas* and the *antitalas* . . . the latter, however, were much more numerous than the others. . . . Although instruction [at the Ecole] was essentially critical, skepticism was rare among us. . . . Basically this Voltairian school much resembled a neighboring institution of the place Saint–Sulpice. It was a laical seminary." Ibid., 1: 63, 64, 66. Tharaud suggests that although most *normaliens* were anticlerical or non–practicing Catholics, few of them were atheists.
29. Ibid., 1: 66.
30. Challaye, *Péguy socialiste,* p. 38.
31. Ibid., p. 94.
32. Challaye's statement that Herr knew the truth about Dreyfus from the

beginning is corroborated by another of Herr's friends, Léon Blum, *L'Oeuvre de Léon Blum,* 6 vols., (Paris, 1964–72), 4: 522. Citing Jules Isaac, pp. 120–1, Benjamin Harrison, pp. 292–3, notes that Herr may have been drawn into the Dreyfus cause because of information that came to him from Monod via Paul Dupuy. Harrison observes, however, that Herr's close friend and biographer, Charles Andler, does not mention this connection.

33. Joseph Reinach, *Histoire de l'Affaire Dreyfus,* 7 vols., (Paris, 1901–1911), 1: 523.

34. Blum, *Oeuvre,* 4: 517. On Bernard Lazare, *see:* Nelly Wilson, *Bernard Lazare, Antisemitism and the Problem of Jewish Identity in Late Nineteenth–Century France* (Cambridge, 1978).

35. Cited in Reinach, 2: 554–5.

36. *Le Temps,* 6 November 1897.

37. Similarly professor of philosophy Ollé–Laprune had earlier received unanimous support from the *normaliens.* A devout practicing Catholic, Ollé was suspended from his post at Normale for a year in 1880 for having attended a meeting of a dissolved religious congregation. Jean Jaurès was spokesman for the *normaliens* who addressed their letter of support to *Figaro,* 9 November 1880.

38. Monod's passionate concern about political issues is clear in his voluminous correspondence with Joseph Reinach, which extended from 1882 to 1911. The weekly and even daily letters during the Dreyfus period explored every aspect of the case: Archives Nationales, Section des Manuscrits, N.A.F. 24882, ff. 164–412. For a thorough discussion of Monod and the Dreyfus Affair, *see* Harrison.

39. The literature on the Dreyfus Affair continues to grow. However, the fundamental contemporary source remains Reinach. Important modern studies include: Guy Chapman, *The Dreyfus Case* (London, 1955), Douglas Johnson, *France and the Dreyfus Affair* (London, 1966), Pierre Miguel, *Une enigme? L'Affaire Dreyfus* (Paris, 1972), Marcel Thomas, *L'Affaire sans Dreyfus* (Paris, 1961), and Nelly Wilson, who includes an excellent bibliography.

40. 15 February 1898. This letter is also printed in Herr's *Choix d'écrits* (Paris, 1932), 1: 39–50. Some of Herr's allies in the Dreyfus Affair, such as Daniel Halévy and Hubert Bourgin, would later accuse him of using Dreyfus merely as a pretext to attack the army: Alain Silvera, *Daniel Halévy and his Times: A Gentleman Commoner in the Third Republic* (Ithaca, N.Y., 1966), p. 105. Yet it is difficult to understand how anyone who knew Herr well could have made that accusation, whatever the result of the Dreyfusard movement.

41. *La Volonté,* 27 October 1898. Also in *Choix d'écrits,* 1: 65–7.

42. For a poster of the Ligue des Droits de l'Homme bearing Herr's name: Archives Nationales, F^7, 12467. Andler, *Lucien Herr,* p. 117, refers to the political discretion that Herr and others felt they had to demonstrate during the Affair at the Ecole in order not to risk losing their positions.

43. There is an account of these events in Andler, *Lucien Herr,* pp. 143–7.

44. Blanchard, *Ma jeunesse,* p. 210. Under a pseudonym Paul Dupuy wrote two pamphlets which supported Dreyfus: *Le Petit bleu* (Paris, 1898), and *Le Général Roget et Dreyfus* (Paris, 1898).

45. He supported such conservatives at the French Academy as de Broglie, Haussonville, and de Voguë in their opposition to revision of the Dreyfus case. Emmanuel Beau de Lomenie, *Les Respnsabilités des dynasties bourgeoises,* vol. 2: *De Mac Mahon à Poincaré* (Paris, 1947), 304. On 21 February 1899, Gabriel Monod conveyed in a letter to his old friend Gaston Paris his despair over the future of France because of the conduct of professors like Boissier: Bibliothèque nationale, Section des Manuscrits, N.A.F. 24450, ff. 316–7.

46. From a speech made in Besançon at the house of the Carmelite nuns and in the presence of the Archbishop, quoted in Reinach, 3: 546.

47. *See* his article, Ferdinand Brunetière, "Après le procès," *Revue des Deux-–Mondes,* 15 March 1898, pp. 428–46.

48. Perrot to the Minister of Education, 9 May 1899, Archives Nationales, F^{17} 4225^{I}.

49. As reported in *Figaro,* 24 March 1901. The students welcomed the President of the Republic by singing an original "Cantate" composed of two verses and the following refrain: "Honor to your banner./ Venerated Monsieur Loubet,/ May the shepherd, the orchard/ Sing the hymn of peace!" But all of the *normaliens* did not welcome the President with equal enthusiasm, for the text of the cantata, which had been posted, has two slogans penciled in the margins: "A bas l'armée" and "A bas la patrie!" Archives, Ecole Normale Supérieure. Loubet must not have forgotten Paul Dupuy's visit two years before, for there was no compelling reason for him to visit Normale. He took the opportunity to praise the ardent pursuit of truth and justice but to caution the students against violent arguments, pessimism, and cynicism. *Journal des Débats,* 24 March 1901.

50. Bibliothèque Nationale, Section des Manscrits, N.A.F. 24884, f. 76.

51. Blanchard, *Ma jeunesse,* p. 204.

52. Ibid., p. 208. Charles Seignobos (prom. 1874) was a professor of history at the Sorbonne.

53. Interviews: Monsieur Challaye in Paris, 2 December 1964; Monsieur Albert Cans in Versailles, 5 December 1964. Nelly Jussem–Wilson, *Péguy et l'Affaire Dreyfus,* Thesis, University of Paris, Letters, 1958, p. 27, lists sixteen of the twenty–eight members of Péguy's *promotion* as Dreyfusards. Jussem-–Wilson also includes in her list of Dreyfusards several professors: Bédier, Lanson, Gabriel Monod, Ferdinand Brunot, Andler, Boissier, Bloch, and Romain Rolland. In fact one could never call Boissier an active Dreyfusard even though he did withdraw from the League of the French Nation after the death of Henry. Romain Rolland was publicly neutral in the Affair because he saw fanaticism on both sides. *See:* Robert J. Smith, "A Note on Romain Rolland in the Dreyfus Affair," *French Historical Studies* 7, no. 2, (Fall, 1971): 284–7.

54. Ministère de l'Instruction publique, *Enquête*, 1: 109.

55. *Le Figaro*, 20 April 1895.

56. Tharaud, 1: 134.

57. For Jaurès I have relied primarily upon Harvey Goldberg.

58. *See:* Jussem–Wilson.

59. On Péguy's political activity in Orléans, *see:* Archives Nationales, F^{17}13738, and Robert J. Smith, "Le Normalien Péguy, Georges Perrot, et le Ministre de l'Instruction Publique," *Amitié Charles Péguy*, no. 116 (August 1965): 7–17.

60. Ibid.

61. On the circumstances surrounding the opening of the bookshop, *see* the introduction by Péguy's son Marcel in *Péguy: Oeuvres en prose, 1898–1908* Paris, 1959), pp. x–xi.

62. The other three members of Péguy's "utopian study room" at the Ecole Normale were socialists as well. On Albert Mathiez, the historian of the French Revolution, *see:* James Friguglietti, *Albert Mathiez, historien révolutionnaire (1874–1932)* (Paris, 1974). Georges Weulersse's uncle was Georges Renard (prom. 1867), director of the *Revue socialiste;* it was through Weulersse that Péguy contacted Renard and convinced him that he, Péguy, represented a large segment of socialist opinion among students. On Weulersse, *see* the notice in *Association Amicale*, 1951, pp. 30–2. The third of Péguy's friends of the "turne utopie" was Albert Lévy. We have one police report that Lévy was the featured speaker on 20 June 1899, before 800 persons at the Théatre Moncey, 3 Avenue de Clichy, in honor of the defenders of "Justice, Truth, and the Republic:" Archives Nationales $F^7$12464-65. Péguy himself does not appear in the police reports of the Dreyfusard meetings, but he was arrested on 18 July 1898, in front of the Palais de Justice of Versailles, where Zola's trial was being held. Despite the fact that he was charged with "striking police," he was released after an investigation revealed that he came from "a good family," had attended the Ecole Normale, and was not heard to talk politics in his rooming house. Dossier No. 201580 of the Prefecture of Police, Centre Charles Péguy, Orléans.

63. Blum, *Oeuvre*, 4: 548.

64. For the change from the Librairie Bellais to the Société Nouvelle and the ensuing quarrel between Péguy and Herr, *see* Andler, *Lucien Herr*, pp. 151–68. For the other side of the quarrel, *see* Peguy, "Pour Moi," *Oeuvres en prose*, pp. 1263–99.

65. Andler, *Lucien Herr*, p. 160.

66. *See* R. J. Smith, "L'Atmosphère politique à l'Ecole Normale Supérieure (fin du XIXe siècle)," *Revue d'histoire moderne et contemporaine*, 20 (April-June 1973): 248–68.

67. A. Aulard, "La Transformation de l'Ecole Normale," *Revue bleue*, 10 January 1903, p. 53.

68. *Le Temps*, 25 October, 1910. *See* Phyllis H. Stock, "Students versus the

University in Pre–World War Paris," *French Historical Studies* 7, no. 1 (Spring 1971): 104.

69. Agathon (Henri Massis and Alfred de Tarde) is cited by Eugen Weber, *The Nationalist Revival in France, 1905–1914* (Berkeley and Los Angeles, 1968), p. 117. On social recruitment and political tendencies I have relied for the Ecole Polytechnique upon the work of Terry Shinn, and for the Ecole Libre upon interviews with alumni of Normale who also attended that institution in the 1920s and 1930s as well as upon my research in the archives of the Ecole Libre.

70. Cited in Stock, p. 108.

71. Ibid., p. 107.

72. Guéhenno, *Changer la vie,* p. 210.

73. Jeannin, *Ecole Normale,* pp. 127–8.

74. Jean Prévost, *Dix–huitième année* (Paris, 1929), pp. 217–220; interview with Monsieur George Cogniot in Paris, 21 August 1971.

75. *See* Pierre Andreau, "Les Idées politiques de la jeunesse intellectuelle de 1927 à la guerre," *Académie des Sciences Morales et Politiques,* (Paris, 1957), p. 18; Robert Wohl, *The Generation of 1914* (Cambridge, Mass., 1979), pp. 5–41, despite the title, discusses the postwar generation as well.

76. Jean Mistler, *Le Bout du monde* (Paris, 1964), p. 264. Interviews with Monsieur Mistler and other alumni revealed that many *normaliens* had been attracted to the Ecole Normale not by the prospect of a teaching career, but on the contrary, by the knowledge that one did not have to enter teaching: the fame of Normale's politicians and civil servants was ample proof that other careers beckoned.

77. I am preparing a study of the final examinations taken by students at the Ecole Libre for what social and political ideas they reveal. The Ecole Libre staunchly supported classical economic doctrines and warned against the evils of social democracy. The political flavor of the examinations, in fact, was paternalism of a modernizing upper middle class rather than broad popular participation in government. The rhetoric which came from the rue d'Ulm was far more democratic.

78. Jean Prévost, p. 99.

79. Interview with Monsieur Aron in Paris 2 July 1971.

80. Interview with Monsieur Badiou in Paris, 22 July 1971.

81. Interview with Father Ribailler in Paris, 21 July 1971.

82. Brasillach, *Notre avant–guerre,* p. 91.

83. Cited in Jeannin, *Ecole Normale,* p. 132.

84. Ibid., pp. 142–3.

85. Minutes of the Council of Discipline, Archives, Ecole Normale Supérieure. The military test for leftism was not perfect, however, for we are informed by alumni that occasionally a student such as Pierre Boutang (prom. 1935), who held right wing political views, was also irreverent at *bonvoust* (*normalien* vernacular for military drill).

86. On this group *see:* Gabrielle Ferrières, *Jean Cavaillès, philosophe et combattant, 1903–1944, avec une étude de son oeuvre par Gaston Bachelard* (Paris, 1950), pp. 34ff.

87. Peyrefitte, p. 14.

6. THE ALUMNI AND THE REPUBLIC

1. *See* Gerbod, *La Condition universitaire, passim.*

2. Adolphe Robert and Gaston Cougny, *Dictionnaire des parlementaries français* (Paris, 1891).

3. Philip Bertocci, *Jules Simon: Republican Anti–Clericalism and Cultural Politics in France, 1848–1886* (Columbia, Missouri, 1978). For the influence of Victor Cousin on Simon, *see* Doris Goldstein, "Official Philosophies in Modern France: The Example of Victor Cousin," *Journal of Social History,* 1, (1967–68): 259–79.

4. Jules Simon, *Instruction gratuite et obligatoire* (Paris, 1873), pp. 31–2, 39–40.

5. Although Simon was at odds with the Gambettists, he remained loyal to republican traditions. In a short book destined for school children, *Le Livre du petit citoyen* (Paris, 1880), p. 36, he admits that Church marriages should be permitted, but he maintains that civil marriages are necessary, for no one should be compelled to marry in a certain church: "Je crois qu'on pourrait garder les vieilles coutumes sans garder les vieux préjugés."

6. As cited in Auguste Dide, *Jules Barni, sa vie et ses oeuvres* (Paris, 1891), p. 26.

7. "Moeurs républicans," *Société de l'instruction républicaine* (Paris, 1872), as cited by Sanford Elwitt, *The Making of the Third Republic* (Baton Rouge, La., 1975), p. 79. Elwitt sees turn–of–the–century solidarism as essentially a restatement of the social ideas of early republicans like Barni.

8. Barrès, *Les Déracinés.*

9. The story about Kasper the customs official is recounted in Charles Simond, *Histoire d'un enfant du peuple (Auguste Burdeau)* (Paris, 1895), pp. 172–5.

10. Auguste Burdeau, "Notes sur le collectivisme," *Revue politique et parlementaire,* October 1895, 1–30.

11. Auguste Burdeau, *Devoir et patrie, notions de morale et d'éducation civique* (Paris, 1887).

12. From the preface to his *Notions de droit usuel, de droit commercial, et d'économie politique,* as cited by Simond, pp. 176–7.

13. Auguste Burdeau, "Le systéme scolaire de la France et sa réforme urgente," in A. Coste, *Questions sociales contemporaines* (Paris, 1886), pp. 477–93.

14. François Goguel, *La Politique des partis sous la IIIe République,* 3rd ed. (Paris, 1958), pp. 68ff. The three *normaliens* besides Burdeau who were in the Chamber of Deputies as Opportunists in the 1890s were all from solid bourgeois families. Jules Legrand (prom. 1876) was from a family engaged in a small linen and drapery business, first in Paris and then in Biarritz. He wrote articles for *Le Temps* and *La Petite Gironde,* and while in the Chamber (1896–1910) was a member of Charles Dupuy's and Félix Faure's cabinets. Edouard Delpeuch (prom. 1879), the son of a Parisian physician, was the deputy from Tulle from 1890 to 1898, a member of the second Meline cabinet, president of the Association of Gambettists, and a correspondent for *Le Matin* and *Le Petite Gironde.* Etienne Dejean (prom. 1880) came from the rural notability (his father was a *propriétaire* and municipal councillor of Labastide d'Armagnac in the Landes), became a deputy from the Landes in 1893 by defeating the conservative candidate, and remained in the Chamber as a *progressite* until he was defeated in 1898.

15. Although Léon Blum spent only one year at the Ecole Normale, he deserves to be included in this study. From the period of the Dreyfus Affair, he was a central figure among the *normaliens* of Herr's circle. On Blum's education and early career, *see* William Logue, *Léon Blum: The Formative Years, 1872–1914* (DeKalb, Illinois, 1973).

16. *See:* Harvey Goldberg, *The Life of Jean Jaurès* (Madison, Wis., 1962), and Georges Lefranc, *Le Mouvement socialiste sous la Troisième Rèpublicque* (Paris, 1963), *passim.*

17. Jacques Kayser, "Le Radicalisme des radicaux," *Tendances politiques dans la vie française depuis 1789* (Paris, 1960), pp. 70–74; and Peter Larmour, *The French Radical Party in the 1930's* (Stanford, 1964).

18. Emile Chartier, *Eléments d'une doctrine radicale* (Paris, 1925), p. 197.

19. Emile Chartier, *Le Citoyen contre les pouvoirs* (Paris, 1926), p. 87.

20. Ibid., pp. 190–1.

21. Ibid., p. 160.

22. Herriot, *Jadis,* 1: 82–3. Herriot's political references are to Socialists as well as to Radicals and to rational, scientific scholars. In *Pourquoi je suis,* pp. 46–8, Herriot wrote: "M. Paul Dupuy, in the hallway of the house of the rue d'Ulm, revealed [the truth] to me about the memorandum [*bordereau*] . . . . I was on the side of Jaurès, who was not yet impassioned, but who, before a hesitant Chamber [of Deputies], posed . . . the same problem discussed not long before in the peaceful lessons of Gustave Bloch [professor at the Ecole Normale, father of Marc Bloch]: in what manner to reconcile the general laws of a free democracy and the necessary discipline of the army. We were on the side of Anatole France and Séailles, Richet and Havet, and Lucien Herr. I enrolled in that League of the Rights of Man which was founded at the end of February 1898. . . ."

23. Herriot, *Jadis,* 1: 145–6.

24. Herriot, *Pourquoi je suis,* pp. 57–8.

25. On Herriot's role in educational reform between the wars, *see:* John E. Talbott, *The Politics of Educational Reform in France, 1918–1940* (Princeton, 1969). On Herriot's career in Lyon, *see:* Sabine Jessner, "Edouard Herriot in Lyon: Some Aspects of His Role as Mayor," *From the Ancien Regime to the Popular Front: Essays in the History of Modern France in Honor of Shepard B. Clough,* ed. Charles K. Warner (New York, 1969), pp. 145–58. On his political career, *see:* Francis de Tarr, *The French Radical Party from Herriot to Mendès–France* (London, 1961); Sabine Jessner, *Edouard Herriot, Patriarch of the Republic* (New York, 1974); and Michel Soulié, *Le Vie Politique d'Edouard Herriot* (Paris, 1962).

26. In many respects his history of European socialism has not been surpassed: Elie Halévy, *Histoire du socialisme européen* (rédigé d'après des notes de cours par un groupe d'amis et d'élèves d'Elie Halévy) (Paris, 1974).

27. Emile Chartier/Alain, *Correspondance avec Elie et Florence Halévy* (Paris, 1958), p. 328.

28. Ibid., p. 337.

29. Jules Romains, *Le Drapeau noir* (Paris, 1958), pp. 13–14.

30. In Chartier/Alain, *Correspondance,* p. 334.

31. On Jaurès as socialist model for intellectuals, *see:* Georges Lefranc, *Jaurès et le socialisme des intellectuels* (Paris, 1968).

32. *Marxism in Modern France* (New York and London, 1966), pp. 32–3.

33. Lichtheim cites a comment Engels made to Laura Lafargue in 1893: "As to what you say of Jaurès, that fills me with terror. Normalien et ami, sinon protégé, de Malôn—which of the two is worse?" Ibid., p. 30n.

34. Andler sums up his dispute with Jaurès in: Charles Andler, *Le Socialisme impérialiste contemporain. Dossier d'une polémique avec Jean Jaurès (1912–1913)* (Paris, 1918).

35. Harvey Goldberg, *The Life of Jean Jaurès,* pp. 269–73; Charles Seignobos, *L'Evolution de la IIIe République* (Paris, 1921), pp. 211–16.

36. Lefranc, *Jaurès et le socialisme.*

37. Bertus Willem Schaper, *Albert Thomas; trente ans de réformisme social* (Assen, 1959), p. 96.

38. Ibid., p. 116.

39. On Thomas and the B.I.T. *see* the interesting memoir by Pierre Waline (prom. 1919), *Un Patron au Bureau International du Travail (1922–1974)* (Paris, 1976). Waline, who has warm praise for Thomas, was drawn to the agency just after the war by Emile Mireaux.

40. Even Lucien Herr, who before the war had displayed his hostility to the military, cooperated with Thomas and others in the war effort. Mario Roques (prom. 1894), who was Thomas' assistant and later the representative of the B.I.T. in Paris, sought and received Herr's advice on the recruitment of chemists for the war effort. Likewise Herr gave advice to his old friend Ernest Lavisse, who contributed to and edited a series of propaganda publications on the conduct of the war, e.g., Ernest Lavisse and Charles Andler, *Pratique et*

doctrine allemandes de la guerre (Etudes et documents sur la guerre), (Paris 1916). See Herr's letters to Mario Roques in the Roques collection, Bibliothèque de l'Institut.

41. On Blum, in addition to Logue, *Léon Blum, see* Jean Lacouture, *Léon Blum* (Paris, 1977).

42. Joel Colton, *Léon Blum, Humanist in Politics* (New York, 1966), pp. 36–54.

43. Léon Blum, *Pour la vieille maison* (Paris, 1921).

44. *See:* Georges Lefranc, *Histoire du Front Populaire, 1934–1938* (Paris, 1965).

45. Numerous interviews with *normaliens* of the Third Republic confirm this. Likewise in Paul Gerbod, *Les Enseignants et la politique* (Paris, 1976), one is struck by the relatively high proportion of *normaliens* (in particular Radicals and Socialists) compared with non-*normaliens,* who were active in educational or national politics.

46. A close admirer described him as an adherent of the "centrist position, laic and national à la Poincaré:" André François–Poncet, *Au fil des jours, propos d'un libéral* (Paris, 1962), preface by Pierre Brisson, p. 7.

47. André François–Poncet, *Réflexions d'un républicain moderne* (Paris, 1925), p. 105.

48. Ibid., p. 47.

49. Ibid., p. 50.

50. François–Poncet, *Au fil des jours,* p. 120.

51. *Association Amicale,* 1971, p. 34.

52. André François–Poncet, *La Vie et l'oeuvre de Robert Pinot* (Paris, 1927).

53. Emile Mireaux, "Notice sur la vie et les travaux de Clément Colson (1853–1939)," *Institut de France, Académie des Sciences Morales et Politiques* (Paris, 1951) 21: 19–20.

54. For a thorough exposition of Mireaux's political philosophy, *see:* Emile Mireaux, *Philosophie du libéralisme* (Paris, 1949).

55. *See* the autobiographical novel by Paul Nizan, *La Conspiration.*

56. Interview with Monsieur Georges Cogniot in Paris, 21 August 1971.

57. Student dossier, Archives Nationales: 61 AJ 209–270.

58. For a list of those who voted "no" *see* Robert Aron, *Histoirie de Vichy* (Paris, 1954), p. 153n.

59. Interview with Monsieur Cogniot.

60. Marcel Déat, *De l'Ecole d'hier à l'homme de demain* (Paris, 1943), *Le Parti unique* (Paris, 1943), *Révolution française et révolution allemande (1793–1943)* (Paris, 1943), *Pensée allemande et pensée française* (Paris, 1944), and *La Religion, l'Eglise, et la Révolution* (Paris, 1944). On Déat's life, *see;* Jean Jolly, ed., *Dictionnaire des parlementaires français,* 8 vols. (Paris, 1960–1977), and Claude Varennes, *Le Destin de Marcel Déat* (Paris, 1948).

61. *See* François–Poncet's notice on Mireaux: *Association Amicale,* 1971, pp. 38–9.

62. Jolly, *Dictionnaire.*
63. Colton, *Léon Blum,* pp. 385–444.
64. Jérôme Carcopino (prom. 1901) and Emile Mireaux (prom. 1907) each served briefly as Minister of Education under Vichy. Far more wholehearted in their collaboration were Robert Brasillach (prom. 1928), René Gillouin (prom. 1902), and Pierre Pucheu (prom. 1919). *See* especially: Robert O. Paxton, *Vichy France: Old Guard and New Order, 1940–1944* (New York, 1972), *passim.*
65. Jean Guéhenno, *Journal des années noires (1940–44)* (Paris, 1947), p. 313.
66. Merry Bromberger, *Le Destin sécret de Georges Pompidou* (Paris, 1965), pp. 22–3.
67. Several of Pompidou's classmates at Normale have confirmed in interviews that this was how he got the position.
68. Georges Pompidou, *Le Noeud gordien* (Paris, 1974).

7. CONCLUSION

1. Gerbod, *La Condition universitaire,* pp. 625–42; Prost, p. 74ff.
2. *Ibid.,* pp. 10–11 and *passim.*
3. *See* Chapter 3.
4. On the Ecole Polytechnique, *see* Terry Shinn. On the *grandes écoles* as preparation for governmental positions, *see* Ezra N. Suleiman, *Elites in French Society.*
5. Digeon, *Crise allemande.*
6. John A. Scott, *Republican Ideas and the Liberal Tradition in France 1870–1914* (New York, 1951).
7. *See,* for instance, Lemaître, *Lettres à mon ami* (Paris, 1910).
8. In addition to his articles in *La Croix, see:* Jean Guiraud, *La Famille laique* (Besançon, 1905) and *La Séparation et les élections* (Besançon, 1906).
9. Louis Doumic, *Où sont les intellectuels?* (Paris, 1899) and *L'Esprit de secte* (Paris, 1900); Jean Izoulet, *Les quatre problèmes sociaux* (Paris, 1898), *Sans Russie, Pas de France* (Paris, 1920), and *Et pas de France (ni d'Angleterre et d'Amérique) sans Rhénanie* (Paris, 1920).
10. On Sartre, Merleau–Ponty (prom. 1926), and Althusser (prom. 1939), *see:* Mark Poster, *Existential Marxism in Postwar France: From Sartre to Althusser* (Princeton, 1975).
11. On Romain Rolland, *see:* William T. Starr, *A Critical Bibliography of the Published Writings of Romain Rolland* (Evanston, 1950), *Romain Rolland and a World at War* (Evanston, 1956), and *Romain Rolland, One Against All, A Biography* (The Hague, 1971).
12. *Normaliens* who were members of the Comité d'Action anti–Fasciste et de Vigilance included: Albert Bayet (prom. 1898), Marc Bloch (prom. 1904),

Jean Bruhat (prom. 1925), Félicien Challaye (prom. 1894), Georges Cogniot (prom. 1921), Lucien Febvre (prom. 1899), Marcel Granet (prom. 1904), Jean Guéhenno (prom. 1911), Jacques Hadamard (prom. 1884), Albert Kirrmann (prom. 1919), Lucien Lévy-Bruhl (prom. 1876), Louis Longchambon (prom. 1913), Jean Perrin (prom. 1891) and his son Francis Perrin (prom. 1918), Marcel Prenant (prom. 1911), Romain Rolland (prom. 1886), Henri Wallon (prom. 1899), and Ludovic Zoretti (prom. 1899).

13. *See:* Simone Weil, *Attente de Dieu* (Paris, 1950), *La Condition ouvrière* (Paris, 1951), *La Connaissance surnaturelle* (Paris, 1950), *L'Enracinement* (Paris, 1949), *La Pesanteur et la grace* (Paris, 1947), and the biography by Simone Pétrement, *La Vie de Simone Weil,* 2 vols., (Paris, 1973).

14. Prost, and Talbott, *Politics of Educational Reform.*

15. This perception of Opportunism is developed in the excellent study by Sanford Elwitt, *The Making of the Third Republic.*

16. Maurice Dommanget, *Les Grands socialistes et l'éducation: de Platon à Lénine* (Paris, 1970), p. 440.

17. *See:* Gabriel Séailles, *Education ou révolution* (Paris, 1904), a collection of speeches delivered between 1896 and 1902, in which he expresses a clear preference for the former alternative of the title.

18. On the doctrine of solidarity, *see* the two articles by J. E. S. Hayward, "The Official Social Philosophy of the Third Republic: Léon Bourgeois and Solidarism," *International Review of Social History* 6 (1961): 19–48, and "Solidarity: the Social History of an Idea in Nineteenth Century France," Ibid. 4 (1959): 261–84.

19. Séailles, *Education ou révolution,* p. 209.

20. Steven Lukes, *Emile Durkheim: His Life and Work: A Historical and Critical Study* (London, 1973), pp. 350–4 and *passim;* Jean–Claude Filloux, *Durkheim et le socialisme* (Geneva, 1977).

21. This correlation was not perfect, however. Bréal, the reformer of the 1870s, did not in the 1880s wish to see the amount of time devoted to the classics in the *lycées* reduced: Michel Bréal, *Excursions pédagogiques* (Paris, 1882), pp. 332–41. Others like Boissier, Perrot, and Paul Girard, who did not agree about the Affair, shared Bréal's apprehensions about the fate of the classics around the turn of the century. For Boissier, see *Enquête* 1: 65–71; for Perrot, *ibid.*, 1: 133–50; Girard addressed a letter to the Minister of Education on 25 March 1902, supporting the classics in the name of the Association pour l'encouragement des études Grecques en France: Archives Nationales F^{17}3946. Some would scrap Latin in the schools because it no longer served a useful purpose or because it tended to exclude the lower classes. Jules Lemaître opposed the widespread teaching of the classics precisely because he was an elitist. In a famous lecture in 1898 Lemaître argued that it was an anachronism that "the children of the petty bourgeoisie and many children of the people spend eight or ten years learning—very badly—the same things that the Jesuit fathers taught in another time—very well—in a monarchical society to the sons of the noblesse, of the magistrature, and the privileged

classes." Cited in Georges Weill, *Histoire de l'enseignement secondaire en France* (Paris, 1921), p. 196. Lemaître would rest content if there were only a few *lycées* in Paris which would offer the old classical curriculum to sons of the elite.

22. The most thorough study of educational reform between the wars is: Talbott, *Politics of Educational Reform.*

23. As cited in Talbott, ibid., p. 55. Two of Herriot's lieutenants in the Chamber who specialized in educational matters were Yvon Delbos (prom. 1907) and François Albert (prom. 1898). But in addition Herriot could count on a half dozen other Radical deputies from the rue d'Ulm as well as Paul Painlevé (prom. 1883), the Republican Socialist, and Bracke (prom. 1881) and Blum (prom. 1890) of the Socialist Party.

24. On Déat, *see:* Georges Lefranc, *Le Mouvement socialiste,* pp. 288–92; and Charles Varennes, *Le Destin de Marcel Déat* (Paris, 1948).

25. Ludovic Zoretti, *Education: un essai d'organisation démocratique* (Paris, 1918), p. 137.

26. Pierre Henri Simon, *L'Ecole et la nation; aspects de l'éducation nationale* (Paris, 1934); *Les Catholiques, la politique, et l'argent* (Paris, 1936).

27. Jean Guéhenno, *La Foi difficile* (Paris, 1957), p. 21.

28. Talbott, *Politics of Educational Reform,* p. 135.

29. Louis Cazamian, "Les Problèmes de l'université nouvelle," *Revue internationale de l'enseignement* 74 (1920): 125.

30. Alfred Croiset, *L'Education de la démocratie* (Paris, 1903), pp. 37–98.

31. For a summary of this proposal, *see:* Luc Decaunes, *Réformes et projets de réforme de l'enseignement français de la Révolution à nos jours (1789–1960)* (Paris, 1962), pp. 125ff.

32. Ibid., pp. 139ff.

33. Ibid., pp. 185ff.

34. A detailed study comparing educational careers of *normaliens* and non–*normaliens* of the Third Republic before the First World War predicted the relative decline of the *normaliens* which seems to have occurred: Victor Karady, "L'expansion universitaire " 14: 443–70.

35. Emile Boutmy, *Quelques idées sur la création d'une faculté libre d'enseignement supérieur: lettres et programme* (Paris, 1871), pp. 14–5. Similarly the Ecole des Hautes Etudes Commerciales was founded in 1881 in part at least to assure that ". . . the ruling classes do . . . all that is necessary to preserve their relative superiority." This remark is taken from a report which helped to launch the business institute, *Projet de fondation en France d'un 'Institut des hautes études commerciales'* (Lyon: Société National d'Education de Lyon, 1877), as cited in Patrick Garczynski, "Les Origines et la création de l'Ecole des Hautes Etudes Commerciales (1881–1913), Mémoire pour le diplome de l'Ecole des Hautes Etudes en Sciences Sociales," (Paris, 197?), p. 27. Garczynski remarks further (p. 83) that the high tuition charged at E.H.E.C. was intended to assure that the school's clientele would be limited to wealthy merchants and industrialists.

36. Rain, *L'Ecole Libre,* p. 90, gives the following statistics of the school's success in placing its students in four major government departments from the turn of the century to 1934: Conseil d'Etat—113 out of 117; Inspection des Finances—202 out of 211; Cour des Comptes—82 out of 92; and Ministère des Affaires Etrangères—246 out of 280.

37. A recent sociological study of the French "power elite" concludes, as we have, that the *normaliens* had lost under the Fifth Republic the place that they had held: "Let us remark that at present . . . the Ecoles Normales Supérieures themselves [This is a reference to Sèvres, Saint–Cloud, and Fontenay–aux–Roses as well as the more famous and politically important rue d'Ulm.] through which a certain elite passes, are totally absent: that is to say that the *grandes écoles* which are found at the origin of the reproduction of cultural power, do not enter at all into competition, given our definition of the French ruling class, with the scientific and legal *grandes écoles.* We must insist on this point, for we know that the Ecoles Normales Supérieures have long shaped not only the French intellectual elite, but also an essential part of the political personnel under the Third and Fourth Republics. Under the Fifth Republic, their influence seems thus to have diminished rather appreciably, the scientific *grandes écoles,* and above all ENA becoming more vital in producing certain fractions of the French ruling class. The isolation of the great intellectuals is all the more reinforced; they see the levers of power escaping from any control on their part." Pierre Birnbaum, Charles Barucq, Michel Bellaiche, Alain Marie, *La Classe dirigeante française* (Paris, 1978), p. 121. Other recent studies, as well, describe the rigidity of the French class structure: Jane Marceau, *Class and Status in France: Economic Change and Social Immobility, 1945–1975* (Oxford, 1977), and Ezra Suleiman, *Elites in French Society,* and *Politics, Power, and Bureaucracy in France* (Princeton, 1974).

Bibliography

Archives and Manuscript Collections

Ecole Normale Supérieure, Archives.

Rapports quotidiens, 1858–1861, 1872–1875, 1879–1881, 1882–1884, 1884–1888, 1888–1893.

Administrative Correspondence, 1870–1940.

Archives Nationales, Paris.

AP 94 400. Albert Thomas Papers.

40 AQ, 1, 2. Société Nouvelle de Librairie et d'Edition.

61 AJ 209–270. Individual student dossiers, *promotions* 1868–1941, consulted by the author when they were unclassified and kept in the archives at the Ecole Normale Supérieure.

F^{7} 12428–12474, 12487–12518, 12553. General Police on political groups, movements, and situation.

F^{17} 4592–4600, 7486. Bourses d'enseignement supérieur.

F^{17} 7482–3, 7486. Boursiers d'état.

F^{17} 4149–4273. Ecole Normale Supérieure.

F^{17} 12747. Fonctionnaires compromis dans la propagande boulangiste en 1889.

F^{17} 13738. George Perrot to Minister of Education regarding Charles Péguy.

F^{17} 6924–6930. Préparation aux grandes écoles.

Bibliothèque Nationale, Section des Manuscrits, Paris.

N. a. f. series: Collections of letters received from *normaliens* by Ferdinand Brunetière, Louis Havet, Ernest Lavisse, Gaston Paris, Georges de Porto–Riche, Joseph Reinach, and Emile Zola.

Bibliothèque de l'Institut, Paris.

Letters of Mario Roques.

Letters of Lucien Herr.

Official Publications, Dictionaries, Collections

Amat, Roman d'. *Dictionnaire de biographie française.* Paris, 1933.

Charle, Christophe; Nagle, Jean; Perrichet, Marc; Richard, Michel; Woronoff, Denis. *Prosopographie des élites francaises (XVIe–XXe siècles): guide de recherche.* Paris, 1980.

Charton, Edouard Thomas. *Dictionnaire des professions, ou guide pour le choix d'un état.* 3rd ed. Paris, 1880.

Encyclopédie socialiste, syndicale et cooperative de l'internationale ouvrière. 12 vols. Paris, 1912–1921.

Epreuves écrites d'admission à l'Ecole Normale Supérieure. Paris, 1884–1901.

France. Statistique générale. *Résultats statistiques du dénombrement de 1872, 76, 81, 91, 96.* 5 vols. Paris, 1874–99.

———. *Résultats statistiques du dénombrement général de la population effectué le 24 mars 1901.* 5 vols. Paris, 1904–07.

———. *Résultats statistiques du dénombrement général de la population effectué le 5 mars 1911.* 2 vols. Paris, 1913–15.

———. *Résultats statistiques du dénombrement général de la population effectué le 6 mars 1921.* 3 vols. Paris, 1923–28.

France. Ministère de l'Instruction publique et des Beaux–Arts. *Enquête sur l'enseignement secondaire: procès verbaux des dépositions présentés par M. Ribot, Président de la Commission de l'Enseignement.* Paris, 1899.

———. *Statistique de l'enseignement primaire.* 7 vols. Paris, 1880–1904.

———. *Statistique de l'enseignement secondaire en 1876.* Paris, 1878.

———. *Statistique de l'enseignement secondaire en 1887.* Paris, 1889.

———. *Statistique de l'enseignement supérieur.* 4 vols. Paris, 1868–1900.

Jolly, Jean, ed. *Dictionnaire des parlementaires français.* 8 vols. Paris, 1960–1977.

Paris. Ecole Normale Supérieure. *Association Amicale de Secours des anciens élèves de l'Ecole Normale Supérieure.* Annual. Paris, 1877–1981.

———. *Table des notices nécrologiques parues de 1846 à 1974.* Paris, 1974.

Paris. Ecole Normale Supérieure. *Bulletin des amis de l'Ecole Normale Supérieure.* Paris.

Robert, Alphonse, and Cougny, Gaston. *Dictionnaire des parlementaires français.* Paris, 1891.

Books, Articles, and Unpublished Theses

Alroy, Gil Carl. "Radicalism and Modernization: The French Problem." Ph.D. dissertation, Princeton University, 1962.

Andler, Charles. *Le Socialisme impérialiste contemporain. Dossier d'une polémique avec Jean Jaurès (1912–1913).* Paris, 1918.

———. *Vie de Lucien Herr.* Paris, 1932.

Andreu, Pierre. "Les Idées politiques de la jeunesse intellectuelle de 1927 à la guerre," *Académie des Sciences Morales et Politiques.* IIe trimestre. Paris, 1957, pp. 17–33.

Appell, Paul. *Souvenirs d'un Alsacien.* Paris, 1923.

"A propos de l'Ecole normale et de la réorganisation des facultés de province," *Revue internationale de l'enseignement* 53 (1907): 230–40.

Armstrong, John A. *The European Administrative Elite.* Princeton, N. J., 1973.

Aron, Raymond. *Marxism and the Existentialists.* New York, 1969.

———. *The Opium of the Intellectuals.* Translated by Terence Kilmartin. New York, 1962.

———. *La Révolution introuvable. Réflexions sur les événements de mai.* Paris, 1968.

Aron, Robert, *Histoire de Vichy.* Paris, 1954.

Artz, Frederick B. *The Development of Technical Education in France, 1500–1850.* Cambridge, Mass., 1966.

Auclair, Marcelle. *La Vie de Jaurès ou la France devant 1914.* Paris, 1954.

Aucuy, Jean–Marc. *La Jeunesse de Giraudoux.* Paris, 1948.

Aulard, Alphonse. *Napoléon Ier et le monopole universitaire.* Paris, 1911.

———. "La Transformation de l'Ecole Normale," *La Revue bleue,* January 10, 1903.

Avronny, Maurice. "Quarante ans de Bourbaki," *Le Monde,* April 9, 1980.

Ballard, Edward G. "Jules Lachelier's Idealism," *The Review of Metaphysics* 8 (1955): 685–705.

Bardèche, Maurice, and Brasillach, Robert. *Histoire de la guerre d'Espagne.* Paris, 1939.

Barnard, H. C. *Education and the French Revolution.* Cambridge, 1969.

———. *The French Tradition in Education.* Cambridge, 1922.

Barrat, Robert. *Justice pour le Maroc.* Paris, 1953.

Barrès, Maurice. *Les Déracinés.* Paris, 1898.

Bary, Arthur. *Une famille universitaire parisienne au 19e siècle; lettres publiées par Mme. Charles Garnier, née Bary.* Paris, 1911.

Bataillon, Marcel; Berge, André; Walter, François. *Rebâtir l'école.* Paris, 1969.

Bayet, Albert. *La Morale laïque et ses adversaires.* Paris, 1925.

———. *Le Radicalisme.* Paris, 1932.

Beau de Loménie, Emmanuel. *Les Responsabilitiés des dynasties bourgeoises.* 4 vols. Paris, 1943–63.

Beaunier, André. *Les Idées et les hommes.* Paris, 1913.

Bédarida, F. "Elie Halévy et le socialisme anglais," *Revue historique* v. 254, no. 516 (October–December 1975): 371–98.

Belloni, Georges. *Aulard, historien de la Révolution Française.* Paris, 1949.

Benda, Julien. *La Trahison des clercs.* Paris, 1927.

Ben–David, Joseph, and Zloczower, Abraham. "Universities and Academic Systems in Modern Societies," *European Journal of Sociology* 3 (1962): 45–84.

Bérard, Léon. *Un grand universitaire: Paul Crouzet, 1873–1952.* Toulouse, 1956.

Berry, Madeleine. *Jules Romains, sa vie et son oeuvre.* Paris, 1953.

Bersot, Ernest. *Etudes et discours: 1868–1878.* Paris, 1879.

———. *Etudes sur la XVIIIe siècle.* Paris, 1855.

Berthod, Aimé; Fréville, Georges; Landry, Adolphe; Mantoux, Paul; Renard, Georges; Simiand, François. *Le Socialisme à l'oeuvre; ce qu'on a fait—ce qu'on peut faire.* Paris, 1907.

Bertocci, Philip A. *Jules Simon: Republican Anti–Clericalism and Cultural Politics in France, 1848–1886.* Columbia, Missouri, 1978.

Bertrand, Louis. *Une destinée. III. Hippolyte porte–couronnes.* Paris, 1932.

Besnier, Maurice. *L'Oeuvre historique de Gaston Boissier* (Extrait de la *Revue des questions historiques,* 134, pp. 562–84). Paris, 1908.

Billères, René. *Hommage à Emile Boutmy 1835–1906 et Albert Sorel 1842–1906.* Paris. 1956.

Birnbaum, Pierre. *Les Sommets de l'Etat: essai sur l'élite du pouvoir en France.* Paris, 1977.

Birnbaum, Pierre; Barucq, Charles; Ballaiche, Michel; Marie, Alain. *La Classe dirigeante française.* Paris, 1978.

Blanchard, Raoul. *Je découvre l'Université: Douai, Lille, Grenoble.* Paris, 1963.

———. *Ma jeunesse sous l'aile de Péguy.* Paris, 1961.

Bloch, Jean–Richard. — *and Co.* Translated by Scott Moncrief. New York, 1929.

Bloch, Marc. *L'Etrange défaite.* Paris, 1957.

Blum, Léon. *L'Oeuvre de Léon Blum.* 6 vols. Paris, 1954–1972.

———. *Pour la vieille maison.* Paris, 1921.

———. *Souvenirs sur l'Affaire.* Paris, 1935.

Boissier, Gaston. "Les Réformes de l'enseignement," *Revue des deux-mondes,* June 15, 1868, pp. 875–87.

Borel, Marguerite. [Marbo, Camille]. *A travers deux siècles, souvenirs et rencontres (1883–1967). Paris, 1967.*

Bottomore, Thomas B. *Classes in Modern Society.* London, 1965.

———. *Elites and Society.* London, 1964.

———. "Higher Civil Servants in France," *Transactions of the Second World Congress of Sociology,* vol. 2. London, 1954, pp. 143–152.

Bouglé, Célestin. *De la sociologie à l'action sociale; pacifisme, féminisme, coopération.* Paris, 1923.

———. *La Démocratie devant la science.* Paris, 1904.

———, ed. *L'Ecole Normale Supérieure, d'où elle vient—où elle va.* Paris, 1934.

———. *The French Conception of Culture Générale and its Influences upon Instruction.* New York, 1938.

———. *Les Maîtres de la philosophie universitaire en France.* Paris, 1938.

———. *Pour la démocratie française. Conférences populaires.* Preface by Gabriel Séailles. Paris, 1900.

———. "Rapport sur le concours pour l'admission à l'Ecole Normale

Supérieure et l'obtention des bourses de licence (Lettres), session de 1928," *Revue universitaire* 38, no. 3 (March 1929): 193–211.
———. *Socialismes français du "socialisme utopique" à la "démocratie industrielle."* Paris, 1932.
———. "Spiritualisme et Kantisme en France, Jules Lachelier," *Revue de Paris,* May 1, 1934, pp. 198–215.
———. *Soldarisme et libéralisme, réflexions sur le mouvement politique et l'éducation morale.* Paris, n.d.
———. *Syndicalisme et démocratie; impressions et réflexions.* Paris, 1908.
Bourbon–Busset, Jacques de. *La Nature est un talisman; journal.* Paris, 1966.
Bourdieu, Pierre, and Saint–Martin, Monique de. "Les Catégories de l'entendement professoral," *Actes de la recherche en sciences sociales,* no. 3 (May 1975), 68–93.
Bourdieu, Pierre, and Passeron, Jean. *Les Etudiants et leurs études.* Cahiers du Centre de Sociologie Européenne, no. 1. Paris, 1964.
———. *Les Héritiers: les étudiants et la culture.* Paris, 1964.
———. *La Réproduction.* Paris, 1970.
Bourgeois, Emile. "Un centenaire: Fustel de Coulanges," *La Revue bleue,* March 15, 1930.
Bourget, Paul. *L'Etape.* 2 vols. Paris, 1902.
Bourgin, Hubert. *Cinquante ans d'expérience démocratique.* Paris, 1925.
———. *De Jaurès à Léon Blum, l'Ecole Normale et la polique.* Paris, 1938.
———. *L'Ecole nationale.* Paris, 1942.
———. *Parti contre la Patrie.* Paris, 1924.
———. *Pourquoi la France fait la guerre.* Montes–sur–Seine, 1914.
———. *Socialisme, anarchisme, communisme.* Paris, 1936.
———. *Le Socialisme universitaire.* Paris, 1942.
Boutmy, Emile. *Quelques idées sur la création d'une faculté libre d'enseignement supérieur: lettres et programme.* Paris, 1871.
Boutroux, Emile. *De la contingence des lois de la nature.* Paris, 1874.
———. *Un demi–siècle de civilisation française.* Paris, 1916.
Brasillach, Robert. *Journal d'un homme occupé.* Paris, 1955.
———. *Lettre à un soldat de la classe 60.* Paris, 1946.
———. *Notre avant–guerre.* Paris, 1941.
Bréal, Michel. *Excursions pédagogiques.* Paris, 1882.
———. *Quelques mots sur l'instruction publique en France.* Paris, 1877.
Broadbent, P. N., and Flower, J. E. "The Intellectual and his Role in France between the Wars," *Journal of European Studies* 8 (1978): 246–57.
Bromberger, Merry. *Le Destin sécret de Georges Pompidou.* Paris, 1965.
Brossolette, Gilberte. *Il s'appelait Pierre Brossolette.* Paris, 1976.
Brunetière, Ferdinand. "Après le procès," *Revue des deux-mondes* 146 (1898): pp. 428–446.
Burdeau, Auguste. *Devoir et patrie, notions de morale et d'éducation civique.* Paris, 1887.
———. *Une famille républicaine: les trois Carnot.* Paris, 1888.

———. *L'Instruction morale à l'école. Devoir et Patrie.* Paris, 1883.

———. "Notes sur le collectivisme," *Revue politique et parlementaire,* October 1895, pp. 1–30.

Bush, John W. "Education and Social Status: The Jesuit *Collège* in the Early Third Republic," *French Historical Studies* 9, no. 1 (Spring, 1975): 125–140.

Callot, Jean Pierre. *Histoire de l'Ecole polytechnique: ses légendes, ses traditions, sa gloire.* Paris, 1958.

Canivez, Andrè. *Jules Lagneau: professeur de philosophie; essai sur la condition du professeur de philosophie jusqu'à la fin du XIXe siècle.* Paris, 1965.

Capelle, Jean. *L'Ecole de demain reste à faire.* Paris, 1966.

Carcopino, Jérôme. *Souvenirs de sept ans.* Paris, 1953.

Caute, David. *Communism and the French intellectuals, 1914–1960.* London, 1964.

Cazamian, Louis. "Les Problèmes de l'université nouvelle," *Revue internationale de l'enseignement* 74 (1920): 123–34.

Challaye, Félicien. *Jaurès.* Paris, 1936.

———. *Péguy socialiste.* Paris, 1954.

———. *La Philosophie du pacifisme.* Auberville–sur–Mer, 1958.

Chapman, Guy. *The Dreyfus Case.* London, 1955.

Chardonnet, Jean. *L'Université en question.* Paris, 1968.

Charlot, Jean and Monica. "Un Rassemblement d'intellectuels: La Ligue des droits de l'homme," *Revue française de science politique* 9 (1959): 995–1028.

Chartier, Emile [Alain]. *Le Citoyen contre les pouvoirs.* Paris, 1926.

———. *Correspondance avec Elie et Florence Halévy.* Paris, 1958.

———. *Eléments d'une doctrine radicale.* Paris, 1925.

Chartier, Roger; Compère, Marie–Madeleine; and Julia, Dominique. *L'Education en France du XVIe siècle au XVIIIe siècle.* Paris, 1976.

Chase, Myrna, *Elie Halévy: An Intellectual Biography.* New York, 1980.

Chaumeix, André. *Le Lycée Henri IV.* Paris, 1936.

Chevalier, Jacques. *Les Evénements d'Espagne.* Paris, 1937.

———. *France: Pétain m'a dit, les préceptes du maréchal, appel aux jeunes.* Paris, 1941.

Claretie, Léo. "Centenaire de l'Ecole Normale Supérieure," *Illustration,* April 20, 1895.

———. "Le Grand canulard des normaliens," *Illustration,* November 18, 1893.

Clark, John. *La Pensée de Ferdinand Brunetière.* Paris, 1954.

Clarke, Terry N. *Prophets and Patrons: The French University and the Emergence of the Social Sciences.* Cambridge, Mass., 1973.

Clavel, Maurice. *Combat de Franc–Tireur pour une libération.* Paris, 1968.

Cohen, Robert Carl. *Giraudoux: Three Faces of Destiny.* Chicago, 1968.

Cohen, William B. *Rulers of Empire: The French Colonial Service in Africa.* Stanford, California, 1971.

Colton, Joel. *Léon Blum: Humanist in Politics.* New York, 1966.

Coste, Adolphe. *Les Questions sociales contemporaines. (Avec la collaboration pour la partie relative à l'enseignement de MM. Auguste Burdeau . . .).* Paris, 1886.
Croiset, Alfred. *L'Education de la démocratie.* Paris, 1903.
Crozier, Michel. *The Bureaucratic Phenomenon.* Chicago, 1964.
———. *La Société bloquée.* Paris, 1970.
Crouzet, Paul. *L'Enseignement: est–il, responsable de la défaite?* Paris, 1943.
———. *Le Régionalisme et le redressement français.* Paris, 1943.
———. *La Vraie révolution nationale dans l'instruction publique.* Paris, 1941.
Darbel, Alain, and Schnapper, Dominique. *Les Agents du systeme administratif.* Paris, 1969.
Déat, Marcel. *Le Front populaire au tournant.* Paris, 1937.
———. *Le Parti unique.* Paris, 1942.
———. *Perspectives socialistes.* Paris, 1930.
Decaunes, Luc. *Réformes et projets de réforme de l'enseignement français de la Révolution à nos jours (1789–1960).* Paris, 1962.
Delefortrie–Soubeyroux, Nicole. *Les Dirigeants de l'industrie française.* Paris, 1961.
DeTarr, Francis. *The French Radical Party from Herriot to Mendès–France.* New York, 1961.
Dide, Auguste. *Jules Barni, sa vie et ses oeuvres.* Paris, 1891.
Digeon, Claude. *La Crise allemande de la pensée française (1870–1914).* Paris, 1959.
Dimoff, Paul. *La Rue d'Ulm à la belle époque, 1899–1903, mémoires d'un normalien supérieur.* Nancy, 1970.
Dommanget, Maurice. *Les Grands socialistes et l'éducation: de Platon à Lenine.* Paris, 1970.
Doumic, Louis. *L'Esprit de secte.* Paris, 1900.
———. *Où sont les intellectuels?* Paris, 1899.
Dunbar, Harry B. *The Impact of the Ecole Normale Supérieure on Selected French Men of Letters, 1875–1902. Ph.D. dissertation, New York University, 1961.*
Dupuy, Paul. *L'Ecole Normale de l'An III.* Paris, 1882.
———., ed. *Le Centenaire de l'Ecole Normale, 1795–1895.* Paris, 1895.
———. [Paul–Marie]. *Le Général Roget et Dreyfus.* Paris, 1898.
———. *Lucien Herr, 1863–1926.* Paris, 1927.
———. [Paul–Marie]. *Le Petit bleu.* Paris, 1898.
Durkheim, Emile. *L'Evolution pédagogique en France.* Paris, 1938.
Elwitt, Sanford. *The Making of the Third Republic.* Baton Rouge, La., 1975.
Eros, John. "The Positivist Generation of French Republicanism," *Sociological Review* 3 (1955): 255–77.
Faguet, Emile. *L'Anticléricalisme..* Paris, 1905.
———. *Le Culte de l'incompétence.* Paris, 1910.
———. *Le Libéralisme.* Paris, 1902.
———. *Problèmes politiques du temps présent.* Paris, 1914.
Falcucci, Clément. *L'Humanisme dans l'enseignement secondaire en France au XIXe siècle.* Toulouse, 1939.

Ferrières, Gabrielle. *Jean Cavaillès, philosophe et combattant, 1903–1944, avec une étude de son oeuvre par Gaston Bachelard.* Paris, 1950.
Fiechter, Jean–Jacques. *Le Socialisme français: de l'Affaire Dreyfus à la Grande Guerre.* Geneva, 1965.
Filloux, Jean Claude. *Durkheim et le socialisme.* Geneva, 1977.
Flacelière, Robert. *Normale en péril.* Paris, 1971.
Fleg, Edmond. *Why I am a Jew.* Translated by Victor Gollancz. London, 1943.
Focillon, Henri. *Témoignage pour la France.* New York, 1945.
Fraisse, Simone. "Lucien Herr, journaliste (1890–1905)," *Le Mouvement social.* no. 92 (July–September 1975), 93–102.
François–Poncet, André. *Au fil des jours; propos d'un libéral.* Paris, 1962.
———. *La Politique générale du Parti républicain, démocratique, et social.* Paris, 1924.
———. *Réflexions d'un républicain moderne.* Paris, 1925.
———. *La Vie et l'oeuvre de Robert Pinot.* Paris, 1927.
Frédéricq, Paul. *The Study of History in Germany and France.* Baltimore, 1890.
Friedmann, Georges. *La Crise du progrès.* Paris, 1936.
———. *Humanisme du travail et humanités: pour l'unité de l'enseignement.* Paris, 1950.
———. *La Puissance et la sagesse.* Paris, 1970.
Friguglietti, James. *Albert Mathiez, historien révolutionnaire (1874–1932).* Paris, 1974.
Frijhoff, Willem, and Julia, Dominique. *Ecole et société dans la France d'ancien régime.* Paris, 1975.
Fustel de Coulanges, Numa. *La cité antique.* Paris, 1864.
Garczynski, Patrick. "Les Origines et la création de l'Ecole des Hautes Etudes Commerciales (1881–1913)." Mémoire pour le diplôme de l'Ecole des Hautes Etudes en Sciences Sociales. Paris, 197?.
Gasquet. Amédée. *Auguste Burdeau.* Paris, 1895.
Gastinel, Georges. "Célestin Bouglé (1870–1940)," *Revue universitaire* v. 49 (January–February 1940): 1–4.
Gautier, Jules. "L'Ecole Normale (1795–1895)," *Revue internationale de l'enseignement* 30, no. 1 (1895): 19–38.
Gendarme de Bévotte, Georges. *Souvenirs d'un universitaire.* Paris, 1938.
Gérard, Alice. "Histoire et politique. La *Revue historique* face à l'histoire contemporaine (1885–1898)," *Revue historique,* no. 518 (April–June 1976: 353–406.
Gérard, Auguste. *La Vie d'un diplomate sous la troisième république; mémoires d'Auguste Gérard.* Paris, 1929.
Gerbod, Paul. *La Condition universitaire en France au XIXe siècle.* Paris, 1965.
———. *Les Enseignants et la politique.* Paris, 1976.
———. *La Vie quotidienne dans les lycées et collèges au XIXe siècle.* Paris, 1968.
Germain, Gabriel. *Le Regard intérieur.* Paris, 1968.
Gernet, Louis. *Le Communisme et la liberté de pensée.* Algeria, 1943.
Gillouin, René *J'étais l'ami du maréchal Pétain.* Paris, 1966.

———. *Problèmes français, problèmes humains.* Geneva, 1944.

Girard, Alain. *La Réussite sociale en France: ses caractères—ses lois—ses effets.* Institut National d'Etudes Démographiques, Travaux et Documents, Cahier 38. Paris, 1961.

Giraudoux, Jean. *Armistice à Bordeaux.* Neuchâtel, 1945.

———. *Ecrit dans l'ombre.* Monaco, 1944.

———. *Juliette au pays des hommes.* Paris, 1924.

———. *Pleins pouvoirs.* Paris, 1939.

Glachant, Victor. "Pasteur disciplinaire: un incident à l'Ecole normale supérieure (novembre 1864)," *Revue universitaire* v. 47, no. 2: 97–104.

Goblot, Edmond. *La Barrière et le niveau, étude sociologique sur la bourgeoisie française moderne.* Paris, 1925.

Godechot, Jacques. *Les Institutions de la France sous la Révolution et l'empire.* Paris, 1951.

Goguel, François. *La Politique des partis sous la IIIe République. 3rd ed. Paris, 1958.*

Goldberg, Harvey. *The Life of Jean Jaurès.* Madison, Wis., 1962.

Goldstein, Doris. "Official Philosophies in Modern France: The Example of Victor Cousin," *Journal of Social History* 1 (1967–1968): 259–79.

Gosse, Lucienne. *Chronique d'une vie française, 1883–1943.* Paris, 1963.

Greenberg, Louis M. "Bergson and Durkheim as Sons and Assimilators: The Early Years," *French Historical Studies* 9, no. 4 (Fall 1976): 619–34.

Guéhenno, Jean. *Ce que je crois.* Paris, 1964.

———. *Changer la vie: mon enfance et ma jeunesse.* Paris, 1961.

———. *La Foi difficile.* Paris, 1957.

———. *Journal des années noires (1940–44).* Paris, 1947.

———. *Journal d'un homme de 40 ans.* Paris, 1934.

———. *L'Université dans la Résistance et dans la France nouvelle.* Paris, 1945.

Guillemin, Henri. *Charles Péguy.* Paris, 1981.

Guindey, Guillaume [Bernard Baudry]. *Euro–America.* Paris, 1962.

Guiraud, Jean. *La Famille laïque.* Besançon, 1905.

———. *Pourquoi je suis catholique.* Paris, 1928.

———. *La Séparation et les élections.* Besançon, 1906.

Gunter, P. A. Y., ed. *Bergson and the Evolution of Physics.* Knoxville, Tenn., 1969.

Gusdorf, Georges. *Autobiographie.* (La Table Ronde, no. 138) Paris, 1959.

Halévy, Daniel. *La Fin des notables.* Paris, 1931.

———. *La République des ducs.* Paris, 1937.

———. *Péguy et les "Cahiers de la quinzaine."* Paris, 1941.

Halévy, Elie. *L'Ere des tyrannies: études sur le socialisme et la guerre.* Paris, 1938.

———. *Histoire du socialisme européen* (rédigé d'après des notes de cours par un groupe d'amis et d'élèves d'Elie Halévy). Paris, 1974.

Harrigan, Patrick. *Lycéens et collégiens sous le second empire: étude statistique.* Paris, 1980.

Harrison, Benjamin. "Gabriel Monod and the Professionalization of History in France 1844–1912." Ph.D. dissertation, University of Wisconsin, 1972.

Hayward, J. E. S. "The Official Social Philosophy of the Third Republic: Léon Bourgeois and Solidarism," *International Review of Social History* 6 (1961): 19–48.

———. "Solidarity: The Social History of an Idea in Nineteenth Century France," *International Review of Social History* 4 (1959): 261–84.

Hazard, Paul. *Ce que nous devons défendre.* Paris, 1939.

Hémon, Félix. *Bersot et ses amis.* Paris, 1911.

Hermant, Abel. *Monsieur Rabosson.* Paris, 1884.

Herr, Lucien. *Choix d'écrits.* 2 vols. Paris, 1932.

Herrick, Jane. *The Historical Thought of Fustel de Coulanges.* Washington, D. C., 1954.

Herriot, Edouard. *Episodes 1940–44.* Paris, 1950.

———."L'Esprit de Normale," *Le Temps,* May 20, 1935.

———. *Jadis.* 2 vols. Paris, 1948, 1952.

———. *Nos grandes écoles: Normale.* Paris, 1932.

———. *Pourquoi je suis radical–socialiste.* Paris, 1928.

Hesse, Germaine André. *Painlevé, grand savant, grand citoyen.* Paris, 1933.

Horvath, Sandra. "Victor Duruy and French Education, 1863–1869." Ph.D. dissertation, Catholic University of America, 1971.

Houssay, Frédéric. "La Section des sciences naturelles à l'Ecole Normale Supérieure," *Revue internationale de l'enseignement* 21, no. 1: 364–82.

Hughes, H. Stuart. *Consciousness and Society: The Reconstruction of European Social Thought, 1890–1930.* New York, 1958.

———.

———. *The Obstructed Path: French Social Thought in the Years of Desperation, 1930–1960.* New York. 1964.

Isaac, Jules. *Expériences de ma vie: Péguy.* Paris, 1959.

Izoulet, Jean. *Et pas de France (ni d'Angleterre et d'Amérique) sans Rhénanie.* Paris, 1920.

———. *Les Quatre problèmes sociaux.* Paris, 1898.

———. *Sans Russie, pas de France.* Paris, 1920.

Jaurès, Jean. *Histoire socialiste de la Révolution française.* 8 vols. Paris, 1922.

———. *Pages choisies.* Paris, 1928.

Jeannin, Pierre. *Ecole Normale Supérieure: Livre d'or.* Paris, 1963.

———. "Une lettre d'Augustin Périer sur la suppression de l'Ecole Normale," *Revue d'histoire moderne et contemporaine* 15 (1968): 466–70.

Jessner, Sabine. "Edouard Herriot in Lyon: Some Aspects of His Role as Mayor." Edited by Charles K. Warner, *From the Ancien régime to the Popular Front: Essays in the History of Modern France in Honor of Shepard B. Clough.* New York, 1969.

———. *Edouard Herriot, Patriarch of the Republic.* New York, 1974.

Johnson, Douglas. *France and the Dreyfus Affair.* London, 1966.

Jussem–Wilson, Nelly. "Péguy et l'Affaire Dreyfus," Unpublished thesis, University of Paris, 1958.

Karady, Victor. "Le Choix du champ d'étude et la stratification de l'Université dans les disciplines littéraires en France (fin du 19e et début du 20e siècles)." Typescript, Centre de Sociologie Européenne, Paris, 1973.

———. "L'Expansion universitaire et l'évolution des inégalités devant la carrière d'enseignant au début de la IIIe République," *Revue française de sociologie* 14 (1973): 443–470.

———. "Normaliens et autres enseignants à la Belle Epoque. Note sur l'origine sociale et la réussite dans une profession intellectuelle," *Revue française de sociologie* 13 (1972): 35–58.

Kayser, Jacques. *Les Grandes batailles du radicalisme, des origines aux portes du pouvoir, 1820–1901.* Paris, 1962.

———. "Le Radicalisme des radicaux," *Tendances politiques dans la vie française depuis 1789.* Paris, 1960.

Kessler, Marie-Christine. *Le Conseil d'état.* Paris, 1968.

Keylor, William R. *Academy and Community: The Foundation of the French Historical Profession.* Cambridge, Mass., 1975.

LaCapra, Dominick. *Emile Durkheim.* Ithaca, N.Y., 1972.

Lacour, Léopold Marie Gabriel. *Humanisme intégral. Le duel des sexes—la cité future.* Paris, 1897.

———. *Une lonque vie; histoire d'un homme.* 2 vols. Paris, 1938, 1958.

Lacouture, Jean. *Léon Blum.* Paris, 1977.

Lagneau, Jules. *Ecrits de Jules Lagneau et souvenirs.* Paris, n.d.

Lalumière, Pierre. *L'Inspection des finances. Paris, 1959.*

Lanson, Gustave. "Nos grandes écoles: I, l'Ecole Normale Supérieure," *Revue des deux-mondes 31 (1926): 512–41.*

———. "La Réorganisation de l'école normale," *Revue de Paris* 10 (December 1, 1903): 522–24.

Larmour, Peter. *The French Radical Party in the 1930s.* Stanford, 1964.

Laurin, Jean–Marc. "Essai sur la productivité intellectuelle des départements français," *Revue de psychologie des peuples,* no. 3 (1959): *277–94.*

Lavisse, Ernest. "A l'Ecole Normale," *Revue internationale de l'enseignement 69 (1915): 70–2.*

———. *L'Education de la démocratie; leçons professées à l'Ecole des hautes études sociales.* Paris, 1903.

———. *L'Allemagne et la guerre de 1914–15, d'aprés les travaux de MM. Durkheim, Denis, E. Lavisse, Andler, et A. Weiss publiés par le Comité des études et documents sur la guerre sous la présidence de Ernest Lavisse.* Paris, 1915.

———. *Questions de l'enseignement national.* Paris, 1885.

———. *Souvenirs.* Paris, 1912.

———. "Université de Paris. Ecole Normale Supérieure. Séance du mercredi 20 novembre 1904. (Discours de M. Lavisse et réponse de M. Chaumié)," *Revue internationale de l'enseignement* 48 no. 2 1904); 481–94.

Lavisse, Ernest, and Andler, Charles. *Pratique et doctrine allemandes de la guerre.* (Etudes et documents sur la guerre). Paris, 1915.

Lécuyer, Bernard. "De la rue d'Ulm à l'Année sociologique. Les camarades de l'Ecole," *Le Monde,* May 3–4, 1970.

Lefranc, Georges. *Contribution à l'histoire du socialisme en France dans les dernières années du XIXe siècle: Léon Blum, Lucien Herr, et Lavrov.* Paris, 1960.

———. *Histoire du front populaire, 1934–1938.* Paris, 1965.

———. *Jaurès et le socialisme des intellectuels.* Paris, 1968.

———. *Le Mouvement socialiste sous la Troisième République (1870–1940).* Paris, 1963.

Legrand, Louis. *L'Influence du positivisme dans l'oeuvre scolaire de Jules Ferry.* Paris, 1961.

Lemaître, Jules. *Lettres à mon ami.* Paris, 1909.

Léon, Paul. *Du Palais–Royal au Palais–Bourbon.* Paris, n.d.

Liard, Louis. *L'Enseignement supérieur en France (1789–1893).* 2 vols. Paris, 1884, 1894.

Lichtheim, George. *Marxism in Modern France.* New York, 1966.

Lindenberg, Daniel, and Meyer, P. A. *Lucien Herr, le socialisme et son destin.* Paris, 1977.

Lindenberg, Daniel. *Le Marxisme introuvable.* Paris, 1975.

Logue, William. *Léon Blum: The Formative Years, 1872–1914.* DeKalb, Illinois, 1973.

Looks, Bernard J. "National Renaissance and Educational Reform in France, 1863–1914: *Normaliens,* Political Change, and the Schools." Ph. D. dissertation, Columbia University, 1968.

Lot, Ferdinand. *Joseph Bédier 1864–1938.* Paris, 1939.

Loubet del Bayle, Jean Louis. *Les Non–conformistes des années 30: une tentative de renouvellement de la pensée politique française.* Paris, 1969.

Luchaire, Julien. *Confession d'un français moyen.* Marseille, 1943.

Lukes, Steven. *Emile Durkheim: His Life and Work: A Historical and Critical Study.* London, 1973.

MacRae, Duncan, Jr. *Parliament, Parties, and Society in France, 1946–1958.* New York, 1967.

Malègue, Joseph. *Augustin, ou le Maître est là.* Paris, 1935.

Mann, Hans Dieter. *Lucien Febvre: la pensée vivante d'un historien.* Paris, 1971.

Marceau, Jane. *Class and Status in France: Economic Change and Social Immobility, 1945–1975.* Oxford, 1977.

Massis, Henri. *L'Esprit de la nouvelle Sorbonne. La crise de la culture classique. La crise du français.* Paris, 1911.

———. *Evocations, souvenirs, 1905–1911.* Paris, 1931.

Massis, Henri, and Tarde, Alfred de [Agathon]. *Les Jeunes gens d'aujourd'hui; le goût de l'action, la foi patriotique—une renaissance catholique, le réalisme politique.* Paris, 1913.

Meisel, James H. *The Myth of the Ruling Class: Gaetano Mosca and the "Elite".* Ann Arbor, Michigan, 1958.

Meynier, André. *Histoire de la pensée géographique en France (1872–1969).* Paris, 1969.

Mézières, Alfred. "L'Ecole Normale Supérieure en 1848," *Revue des deux--mondes* 64 (September 1, 1894): 73–93.

Miguel, Pierre. *Une énigme? L'Affaire Dreyfus.* Paris, 1972.

Mireaux, Emile. "Notice sur la vie et les travaux de Clément Colson (1853–1939)," *Institut de France, Académie des Sciences Morales et Politiques* 21 (1951).

———. *Philosophie du libéralisme.* Paris, 1949.

Mistler, Jean. *Le Bout du monde.* Paris, 1964.

Monod, Gabriel. "La Pédagogie historique à l'Ecole Normale Supérieure en 1888," *Revue internationale de l'enseignement* 54 (1907): 199–207.

Moody, Joseph N. *French Education since Napoleon.* Syracuse, New York, 1978.

Nancey, A. "Souvenirs de l'Ecole Normale: M. Jean Jaurès normalien," *Le Figaro,* April 20, 1895.

Nanteuil, Jacques. *Ferdinand Brunetière.* Paris, 1933.

Nizan, Paul. *La Conspiration.* Paris, 1938.

Noland, Aaron. *The Founding of the French Socialist Party, 1893–1905.* Cambridge, Mass., 1956.

Nora, Pierre. "Ernest Lavisse: son role dans la formation du sentiment national," *Revue historique* 227 (July–September 1962): 73–106.

Nordmann, Jean–Thomas. *Histoire des radicaux.* Paris, 1974.

Nye, Mary Jo. "Science and Socialism: The Case of Jean Perrin in the Third Republic," *French Historical Studies* 9, no. 1 (Spring 1975), 141–69.

Ocagne, Mortimer d'. *Les Grandes écoles de France.* Paris, 1873.

Osborne, Thomas R. "Sciences Po and the Concours: the Recruitment of the Bureaucratic Elite in the Early Third Republic," *Third Republic/Troisième République,* no. 2 (Fall 1976), 156–81.

Painlevé, Paul. *Paroles et écrits.* Paris, 1936.

Parodi, Dominique. *Traditionalisme et démocratie.* Paris, 1909.

Paul, Harry. "The Issue of Decline in Nineteenth–Century French Science," *French Historical Studies* 7, no. 3 (Spring 1972): 416–50.

———. *The Sorcerer's Apprentice: The French Scientist's Image of German Science, 1840–1919.* University of Florida Social Science Monographs, no. 44. Gainesville, Florida, 1972.

Paxton, Robert O. *Vichy France: Old Guard and New Order, 1940–1944.* New York, 1972.

Péguy, Charles. *Péguy: oeuvres en prose: 1898–1908.* Edited by Marcel Péguy. Paris, 1959.

———. *Péguy: oeuvres en prose: 1909–1914.* Edited by Marcel Péguy. Paris, 1961.

Perrin, Jean. *Pour la libération.* New York, 1942.

Perrot, Georges. "La Pédagogie à l'Ecole Normale Supérieure," *Revue internationale de l'enseignement* 44, no. 2 (1902): 516–23.

———. *Rapport adressé à M. le Ministre de l'Instruction publique.* Paris, 1902.

Pétrement, Simone. *La Vie de Simone Weil.* 2 vols. Paris, 1973.

Peyre, Henri. "Paul Hazard (1878–1944)," *The French Review* 17, no. 6 (May 1944): 309–19.

Peyrefitte, Alain. *Rue d'Ulm: chroniques de la vie normalienne.* Paris, 1963.
Picard, Emile. *La Vie et l'oeuvre de Jules Tannery.* Paris, 1926.
Piobetta, Jean B. *Le Baccalauréat.* Paris, 1937.
Plinkington, A. E. *Bergson and His Influence, A Reassessment.* Cambridge, 1976.
Polin, Raymond. *Ethique et politique.* Paris, 1968.
Pompidou, Georges. *Le Noeud gordien.* Paris, 1974.
Ponteil, Félix. *Histoire de l'enseignement en France, les grandes étapes, 1789–1964.* Paris, 1966.
Poster, Mark. *Existential Marxism in Postwar France: From Sartre to Althusser.* Princeton, 1975.
Prenant, Marcel. *Biology and Marxism.* Translated by C. Desmond Greaves. New York, 1938.
Prévost, Jean. *Dix–huitième année.* Paris, 1929.
Prost, Antoine. *Histoire de l'enseignement en France, 1800–1967.* Paris, 1968.
Pucheu, Pierre. *Ma vie.* Paris, 1948.
Rageot, Gaston. *L'Homme standard.* Paris: 1928.
Rain, Pierre. *L'Ecole Libre des Sciences Politiques, 1871–1945.* Paris, 1963.
Rauh, Frédéric. *Expérience morale.* Paris, 1903.
Ravon, G. "Qu'est–ce que les lettres françaises doivent à l'Esprit normalien?" *Le Figaro littéraire,* December 17, 24, 31, 1938.
Rebérioux, Madeleine. "Histoire, historiens et dreyfusisme," *Revue historique,* no. 518 (April–June 1976), 407–32.
Reignup, J. *L'Esprit de Normale.* Paris, 1935.
Reinach, Joseph. *Histoire de l'Affaire Dreyfus.* 7 vols. Paris, 1901–1911.
Renan, Ernest. *Questions contemporaines.* Paris, 1868.
Rey, Etienne. *Refus de comprendre.* Paris, 1943.
———. *La Renaissance de l'orgueil français.* Paris, 1912.
Ribot, Alexandre. *La Réforme de l'enseignement secondaire.* Paris, 1900.
Richard, Gaston. *La Vie et l'oeuvre de Raoul Allier.* Paris, 1948.
Ringer, Fritz K. *Education and Society in Modern Europe.* Bloomington, Indiana, 1979.
Robert, Fernand. *Un mandarin prend la parole.* Paris, 1970.
Robichez, *Jacques. Romain Rolland.* Paris, 1961.
Rohr, Jean. *Victor Duruy, Ministre de Napoléon III: essai sur la politique de l'instruction publique au temps de l'Empire libéral.* Paris, 1967.
Rolland, Romain. *Le Cloître de la rue d'Ulm.* Paris, 1952.
———. *Jean–Christophe.* Translated by Gilbert Cannan. New York, 1910.
———. *Péguy.* 2 vols. Paris, 1944.
Rolland, Romain, and Gillet, Louis. *Correspondance entre Louis Gillet et Romain Rolland.* Paris, 1949.
Romains, Jules. *Le Drapeau noir.* Vol. 14 of *Les Hommes de bonne volonté.* Paris, 1936.
Romilly, Jacqueline de. *Nous autres professeurs.* Paris, 1969.
Rustow, Dankwart A. "The Study of Elites: Who's Who, When, and How," *World Politics* 18, no. 4 (July 1966): 690–717.

Rutkoff, Peter M. "The Ligue des Patriotes: The Nature of the Radical Right and the Dreyfus Affair," *French Historical Studies* 8, no. 4 (Fall 1974): 585–603.

Ruyssen, Theodore. *Itinéraire spirituel (histoire d'une conscience).* Paris, 1960.

Sagnac, Philippe. *La Formation de la société française moderne.* 2 vols. Paris, 1945–1946.

Saint Martin, Monique de. *Les Fonctions sociales de l'enseignement scientifique.* Cahiers du Centre de Sociologie Européenne, no. 8. Paris 1971.

Sarcey, Francisque. *Souvenirs de jeunesse.* Paris, 1885.

———. "Souvenirs de l'Ecole Normale," *Le Figaro,* November 18, 1882.

Sarton, George. "Paul, Jules, and Marie Tannery," *Isis* 38 (1947): 33–50.

Sartre, Jean Paul. *Les Mots.* Paris, 1963.

Schaper, Bertus Willem. *Albert Thomas; trente ans de réformisme social.* Assen, 1959.

Scott, John A. *Republican Ideas and Liberal Tradition in France, 1870–1914.* New York, 1951.

Seabold, Richard. "Normalien alumni in the *Facultés* and *Lycées* of France from 1871 to 1910, *Promotions* 1831–1869." Ph.D. dissertation, University of California at Los Angeles, 1970.

Séailles, Gabriel. *Education ou révolution.* Paris, 1904.

———. *La Philosophie de Jules Lachelier.* Paris, 1935.

Seignobos, Charles. *L'Evolution de la IIIe République.* Paris, 1921.

Shinn, Terry. *Savoir scientifique et pouvoir social: L'Ecole Polytechnique, 1794–1914.* Paris, 1980.

Siegel, Martin. "Gabriel Monod and the Ideological Foundations of the *Revue Historique,*" *Studia Metodologiczne* 9: 3–15.

———. "Science and the Historical Imagination: Patterns of French Historiographical Thought, 1866–1914," Ph.D. dissertation, Columbia University, 1965.

Silvera, Alain. *Daniel Halévy and His Times: A Gentleman Commoner in the Third Republic.* Ithaca, New York, 1966.

Simon, Jules. *Instruction gratuite et obligatoire.* Paris, 1873.

———. *Le Livre du petit citoyen.* Paris, 1880.

———. *Les Normaliens peints par eux–mêmes.* Paris, 1895.

———. *La Réforme de l'enseignement secondaire.* Paris, 1874.

Simon, Pierre Henri. *Les Catholiques, la politique, et l'argent.* Paris, 1936.

———. *Ce que je crois.* Paris, 1966.

———. *L'Ecole et la nation; aspects de l'éducation nationale.* Paris, 1934.

———. *La France à la recherche d'une conscience.* Paris, 1944.

Simon, W. M. "The 'Two Cultures' in Nineteenth Century France: Victor Cousin and Auguste Comte," *Journal of the History of Ideas* 26, no. 1 (1965): 45–58.

Simond, Charles. *Histoire d'un enfant du peuple (Auguste Burdeau).* Paris, 1895.

Siwek–Pouydesseau, Jeanne. *Le Corps prefectoral sous la troisième et la quatrième république.* Paris, 1969.

———. *Le Personnel de direction des ministères.* Paris, 1969.

Smith, Robert J. "L'Atmosphère politique à l'Ecole Normale Supérieure (fin du XIXe siècle)," *Revue d'histoire moderne et contemporaine* 20 (April–June 1973): 248–68.

———. "Le Normalien Péguy, Georges Perrot, et le Ministre de l'Instruction Publique." *Amitié Charles Péguy,* no. 116 (August 1965), 7–17.

———. "A Note on Romain Rolland in the Dreyfus Affair," *French Historical Studies* 7, no. 2 (Fall 1971): 284–7.

Snvders, Georges. *Ecole, classe, et lutte des classes: une relecture critique de Baudelot–Establet, Bourdieu-Passeron, et Illich.* Paris, 1976.

———. *La Pédagogie en France au XVIIe et XVIIIe siècles.* Paris, 1965.

Soulié, Michel. *La Vie politique d'Edouard Herriot.* Paris, 1962.

Starr, William Thomas. *A critical Bibliography of the Published Writings of Romain Rolland.* Evanston, Illinois, 1950.

———. *Romain Rolland and the World at War.* Evanston, Illinois, 1956.

———. *Romain Rolland, One Against All, a Biography.* The Hague, 1971.

Stock, Phyllis H. "New Quarrel of Ancients and Moderns: The French University and its Opponents, 1899–1914." Ph.D. dissertation, Yale University, 1965.

———. "Students versus the University in Pre-War Paris," *French Historical Studies* 7, no. 1 (Spring 1971): 93–110.

Suleiman, Ezra. *Elites in French Society, The Politics of Survival.* Princeton, 1978.

———. "The French Bureaucracy and its Students: Toward the Desanctification of the State," *World Politics* 23, no. 1 (October 1970): 121–70.

———. *Politics, Power, and Bureaucracy in France.* Princeton, 1974.

Talbott, John E. *The Politics of Educational Reform in France, 1918–1940.* Princeton, 1969.

Tannery, Jules. "Les Agrégations d'ordre scientifique et les universitiés," *Revue internationale de l'enseignement* 23, no. 1 (April 15, 1892): 364–71.

———. "L'Enseignement pédagogique à l'Ecole Normale Supérieure," *Revue internationale de l'enseignement* 43, (1902): 305–14.

———. "Les licences et les agrégations d'ordre scientifique," *Revue internationale de l'enseignement* 20, no. 2 (December 15, 1891): 473–98.

Taton, René. *Enseignement et diffusion des sciences en France au XVIIIe siècle.* Paris, 1964.

Tharaud, Jérôme and Jean. *Notre cher Péguy.* 2 vols. Paris, 1926.

Thibaudet, Alfred. *La République des professeurs.* Paris, 1927.

Thomas, Jean. *Sainte–Beuve et l'Ecole Normale, 1834–1867.* Paris, 1936.

Thomas, Marcel. *L'Affaire sans Dreyfus.* Paris, 1961.

Tonnelat, Ernest. *Charles Andler, sa vie et son oeuvre.* Paris, 1937.

Touchard, Jean. *La Gauche en France depuis 1900.* Paris, 1977.

Thoulouze, Paul. *Gaston Boissier 1823–1908.* Paris, 1923.

Tucker, William R. *The Fascist Ego: A Political Biography of Robert Brasillach.* Berkeley, California, 1975.

Valter, J. "Une Suspension à l'Ecole Normale," *Le Figaro,* November 9, 1880.
Varennes, Charles. *Le Destin de Marcel Déat.* Paris, 1948.
Vidal de la Blache, Paul. *La France.* Paris, 1908.
Villiers, Marjorie. *Charles Péguy: A Study in Integrity.* New York, 1965.
Vincent, Gérard. "Les professeurs du second degré au début du XXe siècle," *Le Mouvement social,* no. 56 (April–June, 1966), 47–73.
———. *Les Professeurs du second degré: contribution à l'étude du corps enseignant.* Paris, 1967.
Vogt, W. Paul. "Un Durkheimien ambivalent: Célestin Bouglé, 1870–1940," *Revue française de sociologie* 20, no. 1 (January–March 1979): 123–40.
Waline, Pierre. *Un patron au Bureau International du Travail (1922–1947).* Paris, 1976.
Wallon, Henri. *Matérialisme dialectique et psychologie.* Paris, 1946.
Weber, Eugen. *The Nationalist Revival in France: 1905–1914.* Berkeley, California, 1959.
———. *Peasants into Frenchmen: the modernization of rural France, 1870–1914.* Stanford, California, 1976.
Weil, Simone. *Attente de Dieu.* Paris, 1950.
———. *La Condition ouvrière.* Paris, 1951.
———. *La Connaissance surnaturelle.* Paris, 1950.
———. *L'Enracinement.* Paris, 1949.
———. *La Pesanteur et la grace.* Paris, 1947.
Weill, Georges, *Histoire de l'enseignement secondaire en France, 1802–1920.* Paris, 1921.
———. *Histoire de l'idée laïque en France au XIXe siècle.* Paris, 1929.
———. *Histoire du mouvement social en France, 1852–1924.* 3rd. ed. Paris, 1924.
Weiss, Jean Jacques. "L'Education classique," *Revue des deux-mondes* 43 (September 15, 1873): 392–418.
———. *Notes et impressions.* Paris, 1902.
Weisz, George. "Le Corps professoral de l'enseignement supérieur et l'idéologie de la réforme universitaire en France, 1860–1885," *Revue française de sociologie* 18 (1977): 201–32.
Wilbois, Joseph. *La Nouvelle éducation française.* Paris, 1922.
Wilkinson, Rupert, ed. *Governing Elites: Studies in Training and Selection.* New York, 1969.
Wilson, Nelly. *Bernard Lazare, Antisemitism and the Problem of Jewish Identity in Late Nineteenth–Century France.* Cambridge, 1978.
Wohl, Robert. *The Generation of 1914.* Cambridge, Mass., 1979.
Zamansky, Marc. *Mort ou résurrection de l'Université?* Paris, 1969.
Zoretti, Ludovic. *Education. Un essai d'organisation démocratique.* Paris, 1918.
———. *La Réforme de l'enseignement.* Paris, 1937.
Zwerling, Craig. "Scientific Education at the Ecole Normale Supérieure." Ph.D. dissertation, Harvard University.

Interviews

I am grateful to the following people who granted interviews. Alumni of *promotions* of the Third Republic (with four exceptions), they generously answered my questions concerning life and politics at the Ecole Normale and the careers of its graduates: Louis Althusser (prom. 1939), Raymond Aron (prom. 1924), Raymond Arasse (prom. 1933), Jean Azéma (prom. 1920), Raymond Badiou (prom. 1924), Jean Baillou (prom. 1924), Paul Bastid (prom. 1910), Michel Bruguière (prom. 1959), Albert Cans (prom. 1896), Félicien Challaye (prom. 1894), Georges Cogniot (prom. 1921), Jean Cottier (prom. 1932), René Fredet (prom. 1925), Georges Friedmann (prom. 1923), André Guérin (prom. 1919), Guillaume Guindey (prom. 1927), Michel Herr (prom. 1938), Henri Jourdan (prom. 1921), Raymond Labelle (prom. 1933), René Massigli (prom. 1907), Robert Meyer (prom. 1939), Louis Michaut (prom. 1916), Jean Mistler (prom. 1919), André Monteil (prom. 1937), Pierre Moussa (prom. 1940), Charles Parain (prom. 1913), Francis Perrin (prom. 1918), Maurice Ponte (prom. 1920), "a diplomat", Clémence Ramnoux (prom. 1927), Jean Ribaillier (prom. 1927), Jean Claude Richard (prom. 1946), Michel Soulié (prom. 1937), Jacques Viot (prom. 1943), Jean Wahl (prom. 1907), Etinne Weill–Raynal (prom. 1906).

I am also grateful to those alumni of Normale who so carefully answered my letters and sent copies of their articles or books.

Index